# DATE DUE

| | | | |
|---|---|---|---|
| | | | |
| | | | |
| | | | |
| | | | |
| | | | |
| | | | |
| | | | |
| | | | |
| | | | |
| | | | |
| | | | |
| | | | |
| | | | |
| | | | |
| | | | |
| | | | |
| | | | |
| | | | |

DEMCO 38-296

# POPULAR RELIGION
# IN AMERICA

# Popular Religion in America

## THE EVANGELICAL VOICE

## Erling Jorstad

CONTRIBUTIONS TO THE STUDY OF RELIGION,
NUMBER 57
Henry Warner Bowden,
*Series Editor*

GREENWOOD PRESS
Westport, Connecticut • London

**Library of Congress Cataloging-in-Publication Data**

Jorstad, Erling, 1930–
    Popular religion in America : the evangelical voice / Erling
Jorstad.
        p.   cm. — (Contributions to the study of religion, ISSN
0196–7053 ; no. 57)
    Includes bibliographical references and index.
    ISBN 0–313–27969–1 (alk. paper)
    1. Evangelicalism—United States—History—20th century.
2. United States—Religion—1960–   3. United States—Religious life
and customs.   4. Christianity and culture—History—20th century.
I. Title.   II. Series.
BR1642.U5J684   1993
277.3′0825—dc20        92–35919

British Library Cataloguing in Publication Data is available.

Library of Congress Catalog Card Number: 92–35919
ISBN: 0–313–27969–1
ISSN: 0196–7053

First published in 1993

Greenwood Press, 88 Post Road West, Westport, CT 06881
An imprint of Greenwood Publishing Group, Inc.

Printed in the United States of America

The paper used in this book complies with the
Permanent Paper Standard issued by the National
Information Standards Organization (Z39.48-1984).

10 9 8 7 6 5 4 3 2 1

## Copyright Acknowledgments

To Jessica and Krista

# Contents

# Tables

# Acknowledgments

It is a pleasure to recognize again that a book is not the product of a single individual's endeavor; it is a many-personed product. Whatever merits it may have rise from those contributions; the defects in interpretation and documentation are mine.

Thanks to Dean Jon Moline, Academic Vice President at St. Olaf College for support from the Dean's Small Grant Fund; to the Institute for the Study of American Evangelicalism at the Billy Graham Center in Illinois for similar support, as well as that from the Midwest Faculty Seminar Program at the University of Chicago. The reference staff at the Graduate Theological Union in Berkeley, California, was of considerable help during my research time there.

So many people made helpful suggestions I run the risk by making a list here of omitting some. Thanks always again to colleagues Susan Hill Lindley, Michael Leming, and H. Stewart Hendrickson, as well as the colleagues in the Department of History at St. Olaf. My son Eric, daughter-in-law Becky, daughter Laura, brothers Curtis and Oscar, and sister Elsie offered again their great support. The reference and circulation staffs at Rolvaag Memorial Library again offered superb professional and cheerful assistance at every phase of the work. They have created an atmosphere congenial to the best of scholarship, with special thanks to Kirk Moll, Connie Gunderson, Kris Huber, and Betsy Boyum Busa. And for one more time, many thanks to Emily and Jim White for encouragement, evaluation, and friendship far and above. My indebtedness to my good spouse Ruth is truly ineffable; this book would not have been completed without her loving support; the old adage of "best friend" and "strongest critic" holds here.

Some day the two to whom this book is dedicated will understand what dedications are all about, granddaughters Jessica and Krista.

# POPULAR RELIGION
# IN AMERICA

# Introduction

Those who track or participate in the course of religion in the United States come to recognize the recurrence of certain modes of thought and behavior. Among those that stand out vividly within the North American setting are the modes of irony, paradox, and contradiction. Although not unique to the American scene, they take on a certain compelling veracity by being located within the nation frequently known as having "the soul of a church." For example, believing this land was created to make straight the way of the Lord, many people of faith ironically have committed great sins against their own people and innocents abroad. To win the world to their ancient and unchanging truths, the faithful paradoxically employ the most up-to-the-minute technology, which inevitably reshapes their message. Finally, faith seekers continue to stay mired in the contradictory expressions of committed discipleship and yet of continuing racism, prejudice, sexism, and ecological despoilment.

Rather than despair over such a situation, trackers choose to accept such modes as givens, as expressions of the human condition but not as controlling determinants of their searches. They affirm that, in their tracking, they find authentic paths, trails, avenues, and even some highways leading them to greater understanding of the terrain. At times these roads even overlap, crisscross, bisect, or disrupt each other. Viewed from a distance, however, they form patterns and configurations. The knowledgeable tracker will detect both those features that are familiar and those that are new; both those that come most clearly into view when viewed through the lens of irony, paradox, and contradiction and those that are better understood by the use of other instruments of study.

These lenses help frame the perspective for pursuing evangelical popular religion (these terms are defined later). The central paradox may be stated as this: Committed as evangelicals are to the full authority of the Bible, they take with the greatest seriousness admonitions such as that of the apostle Paul writing to the Philippians to reflect on the excellence of those things that are true, noble, right, pure, lovely, and admirable (Phil. 4:8). An evangelical critic of popular culture, Ken Myers, comments that this admonition means commitment to those things that are *"objectively* true and noble and right."[1] Of equal centrality to evangelicals' commitment is the need to obey what they know as the "Great Commission," that is, to convert every resident of this planet to be a Christian. As evangelicals they are called to evangelize.[2]

The great paradox of such God-given mandates is that, to express them in everyday life, this community of faith has utilized in the past and continues to utilize a great deal of popular religion for their implementation. The difficulty with this appears when it is realized that popular religion often embraces and reflects thought processes, forms, styles, and genres of culture that are deeply embedded in secular sources and that often do not stand out as lovely, admirable, true, or noble.

Herein lies the paradox. Evangelical Christianity bases its truth claims on the existence of knowable, permanent, absolute, unchanging, eternal God-given teachings and salvific actions that make their faith unique among world religions. These ingredients are the noble things for which to strive in life. Yet their expression in everyday life is possible only by their practitioners' participation in secular means and modes of expression.

Such a situation is hardly new to our age, those years explored in this study spanning the 1970s and 1980s. Popular religious expression is as old as recorded history itself, in all ages and on all continents. Its specific forms reflect in everyday fashion the traditions, societal norms, and hopes for the future of the people. It has been and continues to be paradoxically both general and specific: general in that it reflects nothing less than the aspirations of the human condition and specific in that it has been and continues to be made manifest in earthen vessels, the ingredients of society that make social life possible.

Searchers for the roads connecting such movements have been content to categorize such ingredients into configurations such as "elite" versus "popular" or "high," "middle," and "low" taste cultures, reflecting clearly that popular expressions in, say, the fine arts are understood as reflecting lower aesthetic merit. Some expressions such as symphony music or classical drama or formal theology are "higher" or more refined or more intellectually sophisticated than other forms that are seen to rest on a middle or lower level of cultural appreciation.[3] Other observers make comparable distinctions among religious seekers, as existing in the "Great Tradition" of classical music, seminary-informed learning, liturgies performed in great cathedrals, and liturgical formality or in the "Little Tradition" of everyday expressions of faith in the lives of ordinary people, expressed in simple, popular idioms.

Such classification schemes might well have been useful categories to use here to understand our subject, evangelical popular religion, had not the worlds of both formal scholarship and high tech mass media consumption undergone profound transformations in the past quarter century. Whereas earlier roads for trackers to follow had led to predictable destinations of high and low, or great and small groupings, today we no longer espouse such tidy categorization. One critic notes, "As every postmodernist knows, there is no more 'inside' and 'outside,' no more clear boundary between high and low, mainstream and alternative culture."[4]

## GROWTH FACTORS

Such being the case, we look here at the forces that have created this surge of popular culture throughout the United States. As historians we ask: As popular religion as one form of popular culture has been in existence for millennia, why has it come to flourish so strongly in these days?

### High Technology

In this book we examine four specific causes for this phenomenon, each of which is described only briefly in this introduction as prolegomena to extended discussion. First would be an ingredient rarely influential before post–World War II America, but thereafter turning into a force of immense influence, that of high technology. By its ever-improving expertise, it has made available in a volume never before known enormous amounts of cultural artifacts, these at affordable prices, being infinitely reduplicatable, of acceptably good quality, and made alluring through motivational advertising. In the arts, for example, artifacts that once defined high religion (such as expressed by Michelangelo, Bach, or Milton) no longer define any such category for today's Great Tradition, given as it is largely to nonrepresentational, abstract forms and styles.

Contemporary manifestations of popular religious expression, by and large, are shaped by their creators' desire to portray spiritual insight through conscious utilization of today's popular culture. What high technology has done is to make available to millions of people for the first time in history the visual and audio expressions of popular religion that constitute the primary source of expression by American evangelicals. These expressions, so abundantly available, create a new subculture well defined by Wayne Elzey:

Popular religion insists that even though the world often works at cross purposes and seems organized in contradictory ways, reality is finally neither unpredictable nor confusing. The images and constructs upon which popular religion relies are not those of the scholar and scientist who probe for invisible causes and intangible connections. Instead popular religion works by reminding believers that meaning resides in the logical affinities one dimension of sensible experience has with another.[5]

The way in which high technology facilitates the legitimation of popular religion is found in the need to evangelize the world. Elzey continues, "Popular religion appropriates the latest advances in technology and the recent fads and shifting tastes in popular secular culture as proof that things are as they always have been."[6] Thus, in postmodernist terms, those things noble and true, permanent and lovely, are just as likely to be expressed in mundane forms and models as in earlier high culture. Most evangelicals discover authentic religious experience in the ordinary and everyday unfolding of life, in finding *a spiritual version of everything the world produces*," in searching for "a biblical warrant, a reference point in the biblical revelation."[7] Tex Semple adds that this ambiguity, at the core of popular religion, should not be praised affectively as the " 'authentic' grass-roots populist religion of those who live simple, less estranged folkways."[8]

In a word, well used by Martin E. Marty, "irony" as a unifying concept helps put this apparent contradiction between the eternal and the mundane in perspective. "Hindsight reveals that no outcomes ever quite match intentions, that all events make some sort of mockery of the promise and fitness of things."[9]

### Heritage

This embrace of high technology, understood through the lenses of ambiguity and irony, paradox and contradiction, comes as no surprise after we make a backward glance at evangelical history, the second of the four major shapers of evangelical popular religion. Although that particular expression of faith has a very strong "now" dimension with its contemporary flair, its historical roots reach back far into this nation's history, where the seedbed for today's popular acceptance was laid.

Briefly, to draw on the recent interpretation of historian Nathan Hatch, within evangelicalism "the democratization of Christianity, then, has less to do with the specifics of polity and governance and more with the incarnation of the church into popular culture."[10] Evangelicalism's unique characteristic, "a profoundly democratic spirit," emerged in at least three areas, the first being a denial of the traditional separation between learned clergy as a distinctive "order of men" and the attendant refusal by the people to defer to the latter's theological expertise. Second is the tendency of ordinary citizens to accept their most profound religious impulses as these occur, without giving them the same rational analysis sure to be bestowed on those impulses by learned religionists. Third is the embrace of popular religion, because evangelicals believed they had been given by God the opportunity to create a "new age" of socioreligious goodwill, free from traditional authorities such as those in the Great Tradition.[11]

All this occurred during the eighteenth and nineteenth centuries. Hatch goes on in another work to show that, from about 1930 to the present, evangelical thinking has continued to reflect the same general dynamics, in the belief that "religious knowledge is not an arcane science to be mediated by an educated elite"; in the choice by their formal scholars to write and speak more to popular evangelical audiences than to pursue "serious scholarship"; in the evangelical tendency to judge the significance of contemporary public issues by their popular reception; and, finally, in the acceptance of the everyday values of the audiences, those known as the "popular mores" of ordinary citizens coloring the agendas established by their leaders to evangelize the world.[12]

That heritage over the decades, however, has helped produce some sharp internal criticism from evangelicals. Hatch himself deplores the anti-intellectualism inherent in such populist tendencies, as evangelicals nurtured the simple verities of the gospel but "abandoned the universities, the arts, and other realism of 'high culture.' " Other leading evangelicals such as Carl F. H. Henry and Francis Schaeffer made much the same case. Writers in a more popular mode, such as Chuck Westerman of *The Door* and Ken Myers, also deplore similar tendencies.[13] Mass media critic Quentin J. Schultze has suggested this tendency has made "traditional Protestantism combined with the mass media" into "a pervasive pop religion, 'the most characteristic form of religious expression in the United States.' "[14]

Yet odd as it may seem to some outsiders, in a superb example of irony at work, such criticisms can arguably be considered a sign more of strength than of possible weakness within this community. As James H. Moorhead suggests, such fragmentation improved the hold evangelicals have established. "By allowing the faith to permutate in dozens of ways the process of democratization [and the attendant internal criticism] has assured that *virtually every group can find some version of the gospel to which it can adhere.*"[15]

## Parachurch Preference

That fragmentation constitutes the third major force helping to strengthen the evangelical voice in the last quarter of this century, that is, the "parachurch" expression within the movement. By contrast to mainline Protestants, who spent considerable time and energy during these same years trying to define and protect their distinctive denominational identities as, say, Presbyterians or Episcopalians, evangelicals with their active populism could concentrate on the teachings and outreach of the local congregation, thus avoiding the acrimony of ecclesial dispute.[16]

Denominational loyalty to a long-established tradition complete with careful boundaries and familial loyalties of long standing rarely entered into evangelical church participation. They gave comparatively little time to such identity crises and more to supporting, say, interdenominational evangelical groups such as Youth for Christ or World Vision or Campus Crusade for Christ.[17]

Two specialists in evangelical religion have added to our understanding of this phenomenon. James Davison Hunter has pointed to the more democratic quality of evangelical life, allowing for a wider involvement of laity, thus creating institutional vitality outside the formal denominations. George M. Marsden comments on evangelical "general disregard for the institutional church," with participants instead finding the less exclusive "free" or "independent" church expansion in postwar America more to their liking.[18]

This opportunity meshed frequently with the general tendency of postwar American society to remain mobile, fluid, often uprooted. Evangelicals could identify more directly with the large number of electronic religious leaders (often known as "televangelists") who flourished in those years. Eschewing denominational loyalties such as a viewer would find in Roman Catholic or Lutheran programming, media preachers offered a nondenominational, generalized message that avoided the complexities and animosities created by intramainline body loyalties. Participants could move or switch more easily from one independent evangelical congregation to another, believing that the central focus was always on winning the world for Christ while avoiding the divisive trappings of denominational identity. Churchgoers could often find the same teachings on most topics in most evangelical churches, regardless of their geographical location.[19]

## Mass Media

Fourth, and finally, evangelical popular religion grew rapidly because its laity and leaders alike, in contrast to their mainline counterparts, learned how to understand and utilize the mass media for evangelizing. They not only mastered the technical side of mass communication but also came to understand how media such as television and radio could bring the movement coherence, energy, and funding. Of major importance was the threat perceived by evangelicals to traditional moral authority and teachings, especially to the nuclear family. Evangelical use of media provided "an umbrella under which the remnant of God's people could come together" to preserve their traditional values.[20] The evangelical mass media with its glamor and glitz surrounding media celebrity personalities created, in Larry K. Eskridge's careful analysis, a nearly total "Christian" version of the larger society with its own music, art, radio, books, magazines, advice to parents, dieters, spouses, singles, sports fans, and the like—indeed the full gamut of popular religious subjects that constitute the body of this study.[21] Mass media could thus be used to evangelize, to attack the enemies of the faith, to entertain, to instruct. When these four ingredients are joined—high technology, heritage, parachurch preference, and mass media—they go far to explain why evangelicalism grew so rapidly in postwar America.

One other explanation for that growth lies in the respected interpretation by Dean Kelley in his book *Why Conservative Churches Are Growing* (1972), which documents the expansion. Kelley insists that the conservatives grew because, by contrast to the mainliners, they offered "meaning"—absolute, unambiguous answers to life's greatest mysteries. They offered orthodox theology, moral rectitude, and committed discipleship. Kelley argues that millions of Americans responded to that appeal by supporting the evangelicals.

By whatever interpretation one chooses to approach the evangelical voice, it stands as a dominant force throughout the last twenty-five years. Yet the causes for its appearance alone are not the subject of this book; we need in this introduction to define just who the evangelicals are, what in fact constitutes their popular religion, and how we will in subsequent chapters pursue the understanding of these themes. We will look at the tools and instruments, the sources of information, and the insider vocabulary in tracking down this way of understanding popular religion.

## DEFINITIONS AND PROCEDURES

At the risk of starting with a negative, it should be said here that some highly knowledgeable evangelical scholars such as Donald W. Dayton and Robert Wuthnow believe that because the traditional definitions and current practices within this broad community are so diffuse, contradictory, and confused, it is of no particular value to locate and define "evangelicals" and "evangelicalism" at all. That term, it is argued, is no longer helpful in searching to understand the general phenomenon. Many others see these believers simply by who and what they are not: mainline, liberal, modernist, ecumenical, and the like. But, they say, too much diversity exists under the all-purpose, umbrella term "evangelical" to make it very helpful.[22]

By way of definition, the term "evangelicalism" has over the centuries meant many different things to a wide variety of religious bodies. Lutherans first claimed the term from their German origins, *evangelische*, translatable as the "gospel" or "the good news."[23] Later in nineteenth-century American history, its authority as an identifying element came to be associated with the practice at revivals of being "born again," defined by Samuel S. Hill as

the direct experience of a person in a notable single event or a specifiable period when that person shifts his or her life focus from any other center to Jesus Christ. It is as if that person had undergone a personal microchronic passage from B.C. to A.D. Whenever used, it bespeaks an earnest, outspoken and transformed Christian and refers to churches that preach that message.[24]

As the movement continued its rapid growth into the twentieth century, it emerged on the theological continuum of major Protestant groupings to embrace at least four central ingredients, again as defined by Hill. First, it upheld the Bible as its "sole reference point"; second, it endorsed "direct and intimate access to the Lord"; third, evangelicalism defined Christian morality as being individualistic and personal (as opposed to being communal); and fourth, it sponsored spontaneous, informal styles of worship for church services.[25]

All these blended together to create a unique evangelistic characteristic, that of assurance. Evangelicalists came to know they had been saved for eternity because of their conversion experience, their reading of biblical teachings, and their direct experience of God's presence. Dennis E. Owen comments, "It appears almost as an evangelical personality style or perhaps a state of being—warm, confident, immediately and openly religious, intensely yet comfortably intimate with a somewhat domesticated deity, but also quite unquestioning and rather unteachable."[26]

Such defining traits emerged as standing considerably distant from the more liturgical, sacramental churches of the Protestant main line and Roman Catholicism. The participants continued into the late twentieth century to hold fast to their individualistic priorities, a feature that makes difficult any tightly worded definition of characteristics common to all evangelicalists. In recent years, several experts have produced a variety of classification typologies or schema, each attempting to find pattern and coherence among American religious seekers, including the subjects of this book. Among the most thorough and influential of these have been Arthur Carl Piepkorn and

J. Gordon Melton.[27] For evangelicalists as such, classifications such as by Robert Webber, Donald G. Bloesch, and James W. Skillen have been favorably received.[28]

This author accepts a classification scheme that locates the movement as flourishing among four historical groupings, often sharply critical of one another, yet at root being parts of the same family. Historian Timothy L. Smith suggests that evangelicalism is better understood as a "movement" than as an organization; it is best understood as "horizontal" rather than "vertical" with its vast network of communications; it unites people both by what it affirms and by what it rejects from those it sees as adversaries within the Christian community; and it responds "readily to grass roots sentiment in the shaping and reshaping of objectives and standards."[29] Another measurable means of definition is to list those denominations that belong to the National Association of Evangelicals; this is done in the Appendix.[30]

I also follow the schema made by historian George M. Marsden, which contains three essential ingredients. Evangelicalism, first, demonstrates a unity emerging from its distinctive theological ideas and doctrines. Second, it has identity as something of a family of loosely connected traditions and denominations. Third, it cohered as a unity (as already suggested) when, in the last half of the twentieth century, it became a definable coalition of several groups who centered around the ministry of revivalist preacher Billy Graham, magazines such as *Christianity Today*, and colleges such as Wheaton of Illinois. These, more than many others in the same world of ministry, came to be identified by the specialists as "evangelicals."[31]

Observing those boundaries, I suggest that by the time of its greatest popularity within American life evangelicalism was serving as an umbrella spread over these four bodies of believers: evangelicals, fundamentalists, Pentecostalists, and charismatics. "Evangelicalism" is used by adherents, observers, and critics in two ways. First is its use as the overall umbrella term given to the entire movement, as definably different from "main line" or "liberal." Second, "evangelicalism" is one of four rather specific groupings under the inclusive classification of "evangelicalism." This group is seen as cohering around several traits, the first being a very high regard for biblical authority, showing strong trust in the accuracy of the text "but not necessarily a commitment to read the Bible literally at every possible point." Evangelicals espouse an experientially informed faith, focusing on being born again. Most exhibit a willingness to cooperate with other believers, including mainline Christians in selected areas of ministry.[32]

Fundamentalists, the second grouping, are more oriented toward discovering and practicing strict loyalty to the teachings of the inerrant Bible, including separation from cooperation with any non–like-minded believers. In recent years some fundamentalists have moved into a more "open" posture toward such cooperation and the pursuit of more scholarly qualities as opposed to the old-line "closed" fundamentalists.

A helpful summary of fundamentalist traits is that by James Davison Hunter. He finds the fundamentalist camp to be definable, first, by being caught up in protecting theological orthodoxy against modernist revisions; second, by seeking to restore a course of sacred history in this world, which modernism had derailed; third, by identifying strongly with American military policy in the post–World War II era; and fourth, by using the Bible as a weapon to reject what it perceives as theological error. In all areas fundamentalists are well known for their combative, often pugnacious style of confrontation against those they define as adversaries.[33]

Pentecostalists and charismatics, the third and fourth groupings, while sharing many of the theological convictions of the former two communities, focus on expressing the dimensions of religious life as inspired by what they teach as the indwelling power of the third part of the Trinity, the Holy Spirit. Accepting the conversion experience as normative, these two groups go beyond that event, in the words of David B. Barrett, to

hold the distinctive teaching that all Christians should seek a post-conversion religious experience called baptism in the Holy Spirit, and that a Spirit-baptized believer may receive one or more of the supernatural gifts known in the early church: instantaneous sanctification, the ability to prophesy, to practice divine healing through prayer, to speak in tongues (glossolalia), or to interpret tongues; singing in tongues, singing in the Spirit; praying with upraised hands; dreams, visions, discernment of spirits, words of wisdom, words of knowledge, emphasis on miracles, power encounters, exorcisms (casting out demons), resuscitations, deliverances, signs and wonders.[34]

From the first public signs of such experiences early in the twentieth century, those accepting this conversion left their former churches and created new denominations devoted to pursuing these opportunities; the best known have come to be the Assemblies of God, the Pentecostal Holiness Church, the International Church of the Four Square Gospel, and related denominations. People who experience such conversions join one of these groups for continued growth.

In the fourth group, the charismatics claim the same experience of baptism in the Holy Spirit as do the Pentecostals but choose to maintain membership in their parent churches rather than to leave to join a Pentecostal body. Their numbers include believers from most Protestant bodies as well as from Roman Catholicism and Eastern Orthodox bodies.

Significant and often immense differences over doctrine, modes of expression, liturgy, and related matters exist among these four groups. Certain fundamentalists often make sharp, even bitter attacks against nonadherents. They and most evangelicals stand apart from that phase of Pentecostal ministry that emphasizes the expression of spiritual gifts such as healing and speaking in tongues. A careful student, Elaine Lawless, noted that "very clear distinctions are made between modern charismatics (pentecostal with a lower case 'p' and Pentecostalism). . . .Charismatics generally emphasize the quiet, intellectual nature of their evening meetings, held perforce in homes rather than in the church proper. The Holy Spirit is gently wooed through quiet individual prayer and testimony; connotations of Pentecostalism's loud, raucous meetings are vociferously denied and discouraged." By contrast much of Pentecostalism is an expression of "religious frenzy, established and maintained as a mechanism for group identity and boundary maintenance."[35]

It is within this kaleidoscopic, four-sided family that evangelical popular religion has made its auspicious appearance. The nature of so many-headed a movement points to the need to view it through the lens of irony and paradox. Its unity amid complexity leads its trackers to draw from a wide variety of sources of information, instruments of research, and tools of analysis to keep the many lanes, paths, roads, and avenues together in some kind of manageable perspective.

Already several early studies of the topics explored in this book are available. In the early 1980s two pathfinding works appeared. In 1982 Richard Quebedeaux's *By What Authority: The Rise of Personality Cults in American Christianity* used largely scholarly tools and concepts. Two years later, Carol Flake brought out *Redemptorama: Culture, Politics, and the New Evangelicalism*.[36] Both authors reported as active participant-observers of their subject and of contemporary religious culture in general. In more recent times Kenneth A. Myers brought out *All God's Children and Blue Suede Shoes: Christians and Popular Culture* (1989); and from academe have come Quentin J. Schultze, ed., *American Evangelicals and the Mass Media*, and Roy M. Anker et al., eds., *Dancing in the Dark: Youth, Popular Culture, and the Electronic Media*. More recently Michael Scott Horton's *Made in America: The Shaping of Modern American Evangelicalism* has appeared. A searching probe by James Davison Hunter, *Culture Wars: The Struggle to Define America*, also contains much recently mined material on this general subject.[37]

Widespread interest continues. New books that discuss some of this book's issues are now coming into the market. Not all of these could be utilized in the completion of this manuscript.

That situation reflects a larger matter regarding the contemporary religious scene that its trackers must face. In the last two decades, with an ever-increasing velocity, formal scholarship focusing on religious issues has produced an enormous amount of materials for consideration. What was once considered the "canon" for American religious history, for instance, through works such as those by Robert T. Handy and Sydney A. Ahlstrom, now stand as documents of an earlier age, while new historians find new instruments and theories for new issues.[38] Today, methodologies and schools of interpretation such as postmodernism, structuralism, deconstruction, and semiotics inform much of the new research. New models, paradigms, theories, and genres (to name a few) offer new opportunities for the ongoing process of explaining our past and our present.

Undoubtedly, the field of evangelical popular religion is made even more complicated than certain others to delineate because the field of religion, when defined as a humanistic study, encompasses most areas of human thought and behavior. It has been investigated and informed (to cite a familiar metaphor), from "A to Z," from Art to Zoology, from Aesthetics to Zen. Hence, in the scholar's zeal to invent or discover a workable theory or thesis around which to construct an investigation, no single instrument is viable. Religion encompasses too many areas of existence to be subsumed under one all-purpose theory of interpretation.[39]

But that does not mean, by way of logical inference, that we are unable to use any contemporary tools of scholarship to our benefit. It does not mean that all possible instruments or theories are of equal value or equal nonvalue. In this work, as the themes are presented, I identify those publicly known methodological and definable theories and world-views that can help to enrich our understanding of this particular subject, tools that were not available in their present form to earlier trackers along these same trails.

Briefly, by way of this preview, we will consider the extent to which popular religion becomes accepted as a part of the larger popular culture of American society. We will explore at some length the conflicts between the several critics of evangelical popular religion and its promoters and advocates. This discussion will provide a major insight into our overall understanding. It will demonstrate that the proponents see popular religion not so much as the product of such dependent variables as class, race, gender, formal education, or geographical locale but as speaking the truth God has given them to proclaim. That belief takes popular religion away from being a human product and into the domain of what its adherents are convinced is God-given truth. Hence, regardless of its alleged superficiality or affinity for secular models, popular religion has a legitimate high priority in the believer's mandate for living out the faith.

We will emphasize strongly the fact that evangelical popular religion came into its great popularity in large part because it had available the resources of high technology for mass media evangelization. How that communication reshaped the consciousness and sensibilities of its recipients is still a mystery, but unquestionably our sensibilities are different from those of the pretelevi-sion world; in this study we raise the question of how that can be explained.

Further, the great bulk of this new scholarship from the academy rarely considers what are usually considered the issues and questions in the field of religious studies. Only in recent years has the evangelical community started to address such issues as theory-making in the fields of communications, popular culture, music, literature, and related areas.[40] In such a situation, some trackers may come to despair of finding any connecting trails simply because the road maps all this new scholarship offers are so diffuse. Other trackers may see all this as an opportunity for new understanding.

That discussion leads to two final methodological matters: the criteria I used to select materials for consideration as evangelical popular religion and the rationale for structuring and presenting the materials as done here. I draw criteria from a variety of norms: from the artifacts and themes that clearly attracted the greatest attention from leaders and laity alike in the evangelical world; from items that were the most widely viewed, purchased, attended, and supported in ways that we can measure quantitatively; from interviews, field research, conferences, and related interchange with specialists in this general field; and, finally, from this author's own criteria. My eclecticism may not be the most satisfying methodology, but for the time being it will do.[41] Regrettably, several potentially helpful participants in popular religion and its critics from whom I requested information or critiques failed to respond.

This introduction concludes with some personal comments. Although my own commitment is to an ecumenical mainline religious expression, I admire much of popular religion and have tried to avoid "the liberal error of regarding evangelicals in the manner of an explorer 'peering through the foliage at a stone wielding prehistoric tribe.' "[42] Finally, writing about the recent past raises the valid issue of whether the issues explored here are the essence of the issues discussed. I can only respond that because religion springs from such powerful human needs and its social expression is always in such a volatile condition, no one can estimate or predict its fate in future years. Only the centuries will take its final measure. Meanwhile, a start should be made, and this book is such an effort.

To summarize my thesis: Evangelical popular religion flourished as it did in its myriad forms in the 1970s and 1980s because it was able to draw from its heritage, to channel its transdenominational proclivities into channels of outreach to others, and to make use of the most advanced contributions of high technology to create through the mass media a faith that would succeed or fail on the basis of three criteria: whether it would help win the world for Christ, whether it would help recharge the sources of daily renewal within the believer, and whether it would provide the whole armor to withstand through doctrine, ethics, and discipleship a confused and sinful world.

## NOTES

1. Kenneth A. Myers, *All God's Children and Blue Suede Shoes: Christians and Popular Culture* (Westchester, Ill.: Crossway, 1989), p. 98; see the comments by Harold O. J. Brown, "The Refiner's Fire," *Christianity Today*, July 6, 1973, p. 1036.

2. "Evangelism" is well defined; see S. S. Hill, "Born Again," in Daniel G. Reid et al., eds., *Dictionary of Christianity in America* (Downers Grove, Ill.: InterVarsity, 1990), p. 177; see the multiauthored forum, "Who's Really Doing Evangelism," in *Christianity Today*, December 16, 1991, pp. 34–36; Chris Wright, "Preaching to the Converted: Conversion Language and the Constitution of the TV Evangelical Community," *The Sociological Review*, 37, 3 (1989): 733–60.

3. Vera L. Zolberg, *Constructing a Sociology of the Arts* (New York: Cambridge University Press, 1990); on the influence of postmodernism, see Jeffrey Louis Decker, "Postmodernity, or, The Worlding of America," *American Quarterly*, 44, 1 (March 1992): 146–54; Herbert J. Gans, *Popular Culture and High Culture: An Analysis and Evaluation of Taste* (New York: Basic Books, 1974); Allene Stuart Phy, ed., *The Bible and Popular Culture in America* (Philadelphia: Fortress Press, 1985), pp. 1–23; Russell B. Nye, *The Unembarrassed Muse: The Popular Arts in America* (New York: Dial, 1970), pp. 3–4; a helpful summary is Dan Streible, "Review Essay: Recent Television Scholarship and 'Democratic' Evaluation," *Journal of American Culture*, 14, 4 (Winter 1991): 85–93.

4. Elayne Rapping, "Books and the Arts," *The Nation*, August 27–September 3, 1988, p. 206; Scott Lasch and John Urrey, *The End of Organized Capitalism* (Madison: University of Wisconsin Press, 1987), pp. 1–16, 285–313; Peter W. Williams, *Popular Religion in America: Symbolic Change and the Modernization Process in Historical Perspective* (Urbana: University of Illinois Press, Illini Books Edition, 1990); Charles H. Lippy, ed., *Twentieth-Century Shapers of American Popular Religion* (Westport, Conn.: Greenwood Press, 1989); Robert J. Screiber, "Constructing Local Theologies," *Popular Religion and Official Religion* (Mary Knoll, N.Y.: Orbis, 1985); Tex Semple, "Popular Religion and Folk Theology," *U.S. Lifestyles and Mainline Churches: A Key to Reaching People in the 90s* (Louisville: Westminster/John Knox, 1991), pp. 83–95; news story, *National Christian Reporter*, March 6, 1992, p. 4.

5. Wayne Elzey, "Popular Culture," in Charles H. Lippy and Peter W. Williams, eds., *Encyclopedia of the American Religious Experience*, vol. 3 (New York: Scribners, 1988), p. 1740; also see Elzey, "Liminality and Symbiosis in American Protestantism," *Journal of the American Academy of Religion*, 3, 1 (1982): 148–63; Andrew M. Greeley, *God in Popular Culture* (Chicago: Thomas More Press, 1988); George Lipsitz, "The Politics and Pedagogy of Popular Culture in Contemporary Textbooks," *Journal of American History*, 78, 4 (March 1992): 1395–1400.

6. Elzey, "Popular Culture," p. 1740.

7. James Long, "Commentary," *Christianity Today*, November 12, 1982, p. 89, emphasis mine.

8. Semple, "Popular Religion and Folk Theology," p. 88.

9. Martin E. Marty, *Modern American Religion: The Irony of It All* (Chicago: University of Chicago Press, 1986), pp. 318–19.

10. Nathan O. Hatch, *The Democratization of American Christianity* (New Haven, Conn.: Yale University Press, 1989), p. 9.

11. Ibid., pp. 10–16.

12. Nathan O. Hatch, "Evangelicalism as a Democratic Movement," in George M. Marsden, ed., *Evangelicalism and Modern America* (Grand Rapids, Mich.: Eerdmans,

1984), pp. 80–81; Hatch, "Evangelicalism as a Democratic Movement," *The Reformed Journal*, October 1984, pp. 10–16; Quentin J. Schultze, *Televangelism and American Culture: The Business of Popular Religion* (Grand Rapids, Mich.: Baker, 1991), pp. 196–97; Nancy Tatom Ammerman, *Bible Believers: Fundamentalism in the Modern World* (New Brunswick, N.J.: Rutgers University Press, 1987), pp. 114–16.

13. Chuck Westerman, "A Confusion of Aims," *The Door* [formerly *The Wittenburg Door*], November/December 1989, pp. 3–4; Hatch, "Evangelicalism," in Marsden, ed., pp. 81–82.

14. News story citing Schultze in *Christian Century*, November 30, 1990, p. 1086.

15. See the review of Hatch in James H. Moorhead, "Book Review Digest," *Theology Today*, 47, 1 (1990): 90, emphasis mine.

16. Erling Jorstad, *Holding Fast/Pressing On: Religion in America in the 1980s* (Westport, Conn.: Greenwood Press, 1990), pp. 19–39.

17. Jerry White, *The Church and the Parachurch: An Uneasy Marriage* (Portland, Ore.: Multnomah, 1983), pp. 23–112; Richard G. Hutcheson, Jr., *Mainline Churches and the Evangelicals: A Challenging Crisis?* (Atlanta: John Knox, 1980), pp. 62–79.

18. James Davison Hunter, "American Protestantism: Sorting Out the Present: Looking toward the Future," *This World*, 17 (Spring 1987): 53–76; George M. Marsden, "Unity and Diversity in the Evangelical Resurgence," in David W. Lotz, ed., *Altered Landscapes: Christianity in America, 1935–1985* (Grand Rapids, Mich.: Eerdmans, 1985), pp. 61–76; a helpful theological explanation of evangelical ecclesiology is Donald A. Carson, "Evangelicals, Ecumenism, and the Church," in Kenneth S. Kantzer and Carl F. H. Henry, eds., *Evangelical Affirmations* (Grand Rapids, Mich.: Zondervan, 1990), pp. 347–85; Ron Wilson, "Parachurch: Becoming a Part of the Body," *Christianity Today*, September 9, 1980, pp. 18–20; Hutcheson, *Mainline Churches*, pp. 62–79.

19. Marsden, "Unity and Diversity," p. 75; see Stewart M. Hoover, "Television Myth and Ritual: The Role of Substantive Meaning and Spatiality," in James W. Carey, ed., *Media, Myth, Narrative* (Newbury Park, Calif.: Sage, 1988), pp. 168–71.

20. Robert Wuthnow, "The Social Significance of Religious Television," *Review of Religious Research*, 29, 2 (December 1987): 134–35.

21. Larry Eskridge, "Evangelical Broadcasting: Its Meaning for Evangelicals," in M. L. Bradbury and James Gilbert, eds., *Transforming Faith: The Sacred and Secular in Modern American History* (Westport, Conn.: Greenwood Press, 1989), pp. 127–39.

22. Donald W. Dayton, "Some Doubts about the Usefulness of the Category 'Evangelical,'" in Donald W. Dayton and Robert K. Johnston, eds., *The Variety of American Evangelicalism* (Knoxville: University of Tennessee Press, 1991), pp. 245–51; Robert Wuthnow, "The World of Fundamentalism," *Christian Century*, April 22, 1992, pp. 426–27.

23. Mark Ellingson, *The Evangelical Movement: Growth, Impact, Controversy, Dialog* (Minneapolis: Augsburg, 1988), pp. 116–22, and the many references in his index to "Gospel."

24. Hill, "Born Again," p. 177.

25. Samuel S. Hill, "Religion," in Charles Reagan Wilson and William Ferris, eds., *Encyclopedia of Southern Culture* (Chapel Hill: University of North Carolina Press, 1989), p. 1272.

26. Dennis E. Owen, "Protestantism," in Charles Reagan Wilson and William Ferris, eds., *Encyclopedia of Southern Culture* (Chapel Hill: University of North Carolina Press, 1989), pp. 1302–3; Gary B. Ferngren, "The Evangelical-Fundamentalist Tradition," in Ronald L. Numbers and Darrell W. Amundsen, eds., *Caring and Curing: Health and Medicine in the Western Religious Tradition* (New York: Macmillan, 1986), pp. 486–513.

27. J. Gordon Melton, *The Encyclopedia of American Religions*, 3d ed. (Detroit: Gale, 1989); Arthur Carl Piepkorn, *Profiles in Belief: The Religious Bodies of the United States and Canada*, 7 vols. (New York: Harper and Row, 1979).

28. Robert Webber, *Common Roots* (Grand Rapids, Mich.: Zondervan, 1978); Donald G. Bloesch, *The Future of Evangelical Christianity: A Call for Unity amid Diversity* (Garden City, N.Y.: Doubleday, 1983); James W. Skillen, *The Scattered Voice: Christians at Odds in the Public Square* (Grand Rapids, Mich.: Zondervan, 1990).

29. Timothy L. Smith, "The Evangelical Kaleidoscope and the Call to Christian Unity," *Christian Scholar's Review*, 14, 2 (1986): 115–43, especially p. 129.

30. See Appendix.

31. George M. Marsden, rephrased in Edith L. Blumhofer and Joel A. Carpenter, *Twentieth-Century Evangelicalism: A Guide to the Sources* (New York: Garland, 1990), pp. 1–6.

32. Dennis E. Owen, Kenneth D. Wald, and Samuel S. Hill, "Authoritarian or Authority-Minded? The Cognitive Commitments of Fundamentalists and the Christian Right," *Religion and American Culture: A Journal of Interpretation*, 1, 1 (Winter 1991): 91–92.

33. News story, *St. Paul Pioneer Press*, December 13, 1988, p. 3B; James Davison Hunter, "Fundamentalism in Its Global Contours," in Norman J. Cohen, ed., *The Fundamentalist Phenomenon: A View from Within: A Response from Without* (Grand Rapids, Mich.: Eerdmans, 1990), pp. 56–72; Wuthnow, "World," pp. 426–29.

34. David B. Barrett, "The Twentieth-Century Pentecostal/Charismatic Renewal in the Holy Spirit with Its Goal of World Evangelization," *International Bulletin of Missionary Research*, 12, 3 (1988): 124; Grant Wacker, "The Pentecostal Tradition," in Ronald L. Numbers and Darrell W. Amundsen, eds., *Caring and Curing: Health and Medicine in the Western Religious Tradition* (New York: Macmillan, 1986), pp. 514–32.

35. Elaine J. Lawless, *God's Peculiar People: Women's Voices and Folk Tradition in a Pentecostal Church* (Lexington: University of Kentucky Press, 1988), p. 43.

36. Richard Quebedeaux, *By What Authority: The Rise of Personality Cults in American Christianity* (San Francisco: Harper and Row, 1982); Carol Flake, *Redemptorama: Culture, Politics, and the New Evangelicalism* (Garden City, N.Y.: Doubleday, 1984).

37. For Myers, see n.1; Michael Scott Horton, *Made in America: The Shaping of Modern American Evangelicalism* (Grand Rapids, Mich.: Baker, 1991); James Davison Hunter, *Culture Wars: The Struggle to Define America* (New York: Basic Books, 1991); Quentin J. Schultze, ed., *American Evangelicals and the Mass Media* (Grand Rapids, Mich.: Zondervan, 1990); Roy M. Anker et al., eds., *Dancing in the Dark: Youth, Popular Culture, and the Electronic Media* (Grand Rapids, Mich.: Eerdmans, 1991); also R. Laurence Moore, "American Religion in Popular Culture," *Religious Studies Review*, 17, 3 (July 1992): 190–95.

38. Lotz, *Altered Landscapes*; Philip R. Vandermeer and Robert P. Swierenga, eds., *Belief and Behavior: Essays in the New Religious History* (New Brunswick, N.J.: Rutgers University Press, 1991).

39. Eric J. Sharpe, "Study of Religion: Methodology and Issues," in Mircea Eliade, ed., *The Encyclopedia of Religion*, vol. 14 (New York: Macmillan, 1987), pp. 83–88.

40. For example, see John Fiske, *Understanding Popular Culture* (Boston: Unwin Hyman, 1989); George Lipsitz, *Time Passages: Collective Memory and American Popular Culture* (Minneapolis: University of Minnesota Press, 1989); Henry A. Giroux et al., eds., *Popular Culture: Schooling and Everyday Life* (Westport, Conn.: Bergin and Garvey, 1989).

41. See the many entries on these and related subjects in the four-volume work, Eric

Barnouw, ed., *International Encyclopedia of Communications* (New York: Oxford University Press, 1989).

42.  See Catharine R. Stimson's review of Flake, *Redemptorama*, in *The Nation*, November 17, 1984, p. 512; see also Mark Hulsether, "Evangelical Popular Religion as a Source for North American Liberation Theology? Insights from Postmodern Popular Culture Theory," *American Studies*, 33, 1 (Spring 1992): 63–81.

# Part I

# THE SETTING

Where to start the discussion of such a subject and to locate its inner dynamics must be decided before the subject itself is explored. Acknowledging that the sources of any movement can be traced back endlessly into the historical past, we start here in the 1960s. A good reason for so late a chronological start is that an excellent study of this subject from the years 1925 to 1975 is already available, in David Harrington Watt's doctoral dissertation, at Harvard University, later a book.[1] Although its structural and subject matter reflect differences with this book, Watt's volume constructively furnishes the kind of introduction a historian fervently hopes exists when deciding at what point in the river of time her or his own toe should be dipped.

The major issue, of how the story unfolds, occupies chapter 1. Obviously, the subject matter of the entire work can be arranged and evaluated in ways other than those used by this writer. This brief introduction to Part I is included here to suggest the dynamics of "the evangelical voice" that are at work. Clearly, the form and shape if not much of the content of that voice have undergone a profound change during these decades. That change points us as does all religious history to the existence of the necessary tension in the need of believers to find some kind of balance between permanence and change. As the record shows, the change within popular evangelicalism between about 1970 and 1990 is profound and pervasive. Yet, in paradoxical form, religious faith survives because it seeks to hold on to that which is permanent, absolute, eternal, unchanging, and partaking of the divine. Still, during these years enormous changes occurred within social institutions, values, and technology in adaptation to a world in which the one thing permanent, as the old adage has it, was change.

The extent to which compromise has been made, necessary or otherwise to this age-old dilemma in religious life, is a matter for each tracker and each participant to evaluate for herself or himself. Given that, some defensible conclusions as to the major directions the participants took during these years can be made; it is on behalf of that enterprise that the text starts where it does and Part I covers the ground that it does.

## NOTE

1. David Harrington Watt, *A Transforming Faith: Explorations of Twentieth-Century American Evangelicalism* (New Brunswick, N.J.: Rutgers University Press, 1991). I am aware of the implications of the work of Dean Kelley for my thesis. See his *Why Conservative Churches Are Growing*, rev. ed. (New York: Harper and Row, 1977). I am completing an extended monograph on this for publication elsewhere.

# 1

# The Shaping of the Evangelical Subculture: 1960–1990

The time frame spanning the decades of the 1960s, 1970s, and 1980s embraces the growth of revitalized evangelical popular religion from early puberty to full maturity. The tracker using the lens of irony and paradox could locate the rapidly increasing number of patterns of new life crisscrossing, reformulating, and redesigning the map of American religious life. Clearly, within this budding subculture, the growth in size and in scope of its outreach and the increasing technological sophistication in its communications programs stand out as major accomplishments.

Even as it achieved greater visibility and energy, however, the new evangelicalism became ensnarled within itself, renewing old battles and starting new ones inside its own ranks. The four major groupings often found themselves in sharp competition with one another for new members and new revenue and also in older internal theological disputation. Evangelicals would in this era discover anew how difficult the task would be to hold fast to the great truths of the past in a society that demanded and rewarded change and innovation. The several paths taken by the four groupings are tracked in this chapter as the basic map of the terrain in which the specific expressions of the new popular religion would become visible, the expressions that occupy the balance of this book. This chapter offers both measurable and anecdotal evidence that evangelicalism was in the process of redefining itself.

Among the most visible and influential expressions of evangelical resurgence was its creation of a subculture that would nourish its popular religion. Emerging out of its unique historical heritage of populist priorities and democratic organization, this subculture would carry out a central mission in its response to the Great Commission. It would absorb the centuries-old teachings in theology and ethics of its Protestant heritage and then blend them together through the power of the new mass media to create a movement of great energy and appeal. The subculture was, to mix metaphors here, much like the large works of modern sculpture found today in public places; one could see the single piece but also detect different shadings and expressions of that unity from the many angles available for its viewing. So with evangelical popular religion; its mission to win the world for Christ reflected other dimensions of its nature: the rekindling of the believer's own faith, the struggle to turn back the powers of secularization, and the determination to preserve something close to a "Christian Civilization" for America and for the spiritual kingdom around the globe.[1]

For all its newly found energy and revitalized public image in these years, this subculture found its chief source of strength to be the heritage of its past. One of its most recent historians, David Harrington Watt, in his history covering the years 1925–1975 suggests that the later twentieth-century expression was not merely a dormant force waiting for a new spark of energy. Its history in this century rather was one of sustained steady growth.[2] Its Pentecostal, evangelical, and fundamentalist ancestries had been active during the earlier decades of the twentieth century, choosing for the most part to maintain their respective identities, to preserve the faith, and to stand apart from cooperation or affiliation with mainline churches. During the first forty years of this century the evangelical mission thus took on a strongly negative cast based on its criticism of that mainstream and existed in cultural isolation as it sought to preserve its identity in a land of many competing faiths.

Without question, the enormous changes in American and global society created by the impact of World War II brought about new opportunity for evangelical expansion. For one thing, that war and the staggering price paid in human life and physical destruction ended whatever hopes church people had held out for capitalist, politically liberal values to engulf the world, making it safe for democracy. The devastation of the Holocaust and the implications of the detonation of the atomic bomb stood as overwhelming reminders of the antihuman powers of human sin. Humankind would soon realize, as the Cold War unfolded, as the old colonial empires collapsed, and as the new arms race began, that it could not recover whatever optimism and confidence it had espoused earlier for progress toward a just and peaceful future.[3]

The postwar years, generally lasting as a definable era until about 1960, thus offered new opportunities for appealing religious enterprises to be given serious consideration by the general populace. And so the public discourse of leaders and observers centered on identifying the appearance of a resurgence, of even a revival, of religious concern across the land. Revivalist preachers of the traditional school such as the young Billy Graham received wide support as well as sharp criticism for traditionalist theology and ethics; attendance and membership in churches, mainline and evangelical, increased greatly; new church edifices were constructed; more interest on campuses was shown in religion courses; and books of the positive thinking and historical religious romance genres continued to head the bestseller lists.

Through the early postwar years in America, evangelical leaders attempted a widely varying series of ministries and programs: one would revitalize the faith to combat the spread of communism, another would reclaim their heritage as America's mainstream religious tradition, and a third would seek to preserve a society of explicit Christian morality at home. Their parachurch organizations such as Youth for Christ, Campus Crusade for Christ, Inter-Varsity, and similar groups sought to extend their programs into the life of American youth and young adults in a fresh, energetic manner.[4] The first extended national attention to the ministry of Billy Graham emerged during the 1950s, suggesting to those outside the fold what the new postwar evangelicalism might be all about.[5]

## THE 1960s

That new form, however, would emerge not only by way of updating old-time evangelicalism and Pentecostalism. It would burst onto the national scene also as a reaction, largely against what has been called "The Great Awakening" of the 1960s.[6] During that decade at least four major social transformations swept through the country, each calling into question deeply ingrained American institutions. These four were the black civil rights movement, the women's movement, the ecology-environment movement, and the peace movement (the latter specifically against American military involvement in Vietnam).

By the decade's end, after escalating violence in the ghettos and on the campuses, the awakening came to an unceremonious conclusion; the assassinations of President John Kennedy, Senator Robert Kennedy, and Rev. Martin Luther King, Jr., as well as pitched battles between police and minority groups, which bordered on warfare in several inner-city areas and on college campuses, served as the most dramatic examples of the excesses that the destructive energies of the decade could reach. So too did the demonstrations for ending the war in Vietnam, which included the burning of draft cards and the unrelated but meteoric rise to popularity of rock music with its invitation to tune in, turn on, and drop out by joining the escalating drug culture. During all the turmoil those revered social institutions of government, the churches, the military, the business world, and the schools seemed singularly unprepared to stop the apparent slide toward massive social change bordering on anarchy.

Out of such a world, sketched here in broad-stroke brevity, the new evangelical subculture started to appear in the patterns that later would create its unique configuration. Its roots reached down into at least four revitalized movements, all of which came into clear view during that decade. First would be the theological renaissance known as the "Neo," later the "New" Evangelical movement. A significant number of younger evangelical scholars had become dissatisfied with the lack of sustained, informed theological inquiry within the older evangelical-fundamentalist aegis. Starting with the founding in 1947 of Fuller Theological Seminary in California, a number of academicians and pastors attempted to bring the older tradition more into the mainstream of academic life by upgrading academic standards at their own seminaries, expecting their new teachers to study at the famous seminaries of the East Coast and Chicago, and exploring where evangelicals might be able to cooperate or at least be in dialogue with mainstream leaders over areas of potential common benefit, to somehow make the world of formal academic theology more relevant and lively for a larger audience.[7]

The appearance of the academic new evangelicals was, if nothing else, a clear sign of increasing dissatisfaction with much of prewar evangelicalism and a belief that formal theological study had much to contribute to the redress of the many crises of public morality facing Americans. Some measure of success had by the decade's end already been achieved with the continued growth in circulation and influence of the journal *Christianity Today*, located in Wheaton, Illinois. Within a short time after its first appearance in 1956 it was clear to critics and friends that here was no old-style fundamentalist fulmination, but a magazine with theological acumen and a broad range of interests.[8]

As well, evangelicals continued to support a small but energetic new attempt at improving internal cooperation, the National Association of Evangelicals (NAE), founded in 1942. Serving as an alternative to the mainstream Federal (in 1950, reformulated as the National) Council of Churches and the fundamentalist American Council of Christian Churches, the NAE offered its services as a voluntary association in which Pentecostals, evangelicals, and other like-minded conservatives could cooperate.[9] Its budget and staff were modest in size, but its appearance suggested potential for further growth.

A second major source of new life appeared unexpectedly in what came to be known as the "Charismatic Renewal Movement." Almost all of those who chose to become Pentecostalist had accordingly joined and remained within the denominational world of such bodies as Assemblies of God, Four Square Gospel, or Pentecostal Holiness, to worship and work with like-minded believers, all of whom had received the "second baptism," or baptism in the Holy Spirit, in which they received one or more of the New Testament spiritual gifts, such as discernment of spirits, healing, speaking in tongues (glossolalia), or interpretation of tongues. That experience had given the Pentecostalists their unique identity within the larger evangelical family.[10]

However, on Whitsunday in 1960, a high-ranking Episcopalian rector, the Rev. Dennis Bennett of St. Mark's, Van Nuys, California, announced to his congregation that for several weeks he and some members had been participating in these Pentecostalist expressions and were ready now to share them with others. They made the crucial decision that their second baptism would not necessarily have to lead them to leave their parent church and join a Pentecostalist body; rather they could participate in this new experience and keep their current church membership.

The governing board of that parish, however, thought otherwise. Members refused to allow Pentecostal worship and teachings into the life of the congregation. They called on Bennett to resign. His bishop transferred him to a small parish in Seattle, where Bennett could remain an Episcopalian priest, as he wanted to be. The movement continued to spread, attracting Lutherans and later members of most major mainline denominations. In each case the new converts chose to remain within their parent church; yet often they were told by ranking officials that they would have to leave for introducing what were acknowledged to be expressions of worship and understanding that stood outside the standards of the respective denomination. For several years the issues were vigorously, often acrimoniously, debated throughout mainline Protestantism, leading some congregations to expel the new charismatics or grudgingly to accept them as long as disruption in the parish was avoided. Within the larger framework, the appearance of the charismatic movement with its more conservative theology and traditional social morality created what would become one of the four major families within the emerging evangelical movement.[11]

A third major root of that movement was more difficult to identify by way of organizational structure, but became a powerful force nonetheless. It would become the primary catalyst for embracing the new popular religion, namely, the revitalization of youths and young adults in the evangelical world. With some trained leadership coming from parachurch groups such as Campus Crusade for Christ, led by Bill Bright, and InterVarsity Christian Fellowship and the Christian World Liberation Front, younger American adults and teens started to express their religious convictions, surprisingly traditional in content, in a variety of ways, none of which were especially conventional. In a phenomenon later known as the "Jesus People" movement, during the 1960s, in southern California and elsewhere, youthful seekers, often a part of the drug subculture, sought escape from its control by joining in religious communal living and sharing centers. There they would study the Bible, decide to make a commitment for conversion, absorb that into their desire to be rid of their drug dependence, and then go out to share their experiences with others.

This movement clearly reflected the absorption by its participants of much of the counterculture, flower-power, hippie explosion of the mid-1960s. Accenting independence, spontaneity, affectivity, and a variety of clothing and hair styles and enthusiastic about the new rock music, the youth demonstrated to their more conservative elders that the old-time religion still had some life left in it, as long as some of the cultural forms of expression could follow in the way so popular among the larger counterculture.[12]

Fourth among the new forces to shape evangelical popular religion was the movement (described by historian Grant Wacker) to bring nothing less than a "Christian Civilization" (Wacker's caps) to America. Not so much a movement as those described above, it was more "a coherent world view, a way of seeing reality" based on the existence of God-revealed theological and moral absolutes.[13] Watching with increasing alarm the increase in public immorality and certain federal governmental policies, evangelicals called on fellow believers to come together to resist the growing power of secularization, understood by them to be the steadily diminishing and perhaps eventually disappearing influence of consensus religious teachings and practices in public life.

Focusing at the beginning on court decisions forbidding public prayers and Bible reading in the schools and later including the growing rate of cohabitation among unmarried couples, the escalating divorce rate, the spread of secular feminist ideals, the increase in single-parent families, the coming out of lesbian and gay advocates, the secular and often antireligious tone of the mass media, public education that required sex education and the teaching of evolutionism, and similar developments, the Christian Civilization world-view wanted to restore to the United States, God's special domain, the rule of law informed and legitimated by traditional conservative doctrine and ethics. The spokespersons agreed America must maintain its traditional separation of church and state but should not deny to religious influences their historical domain of influence. Americans, they insisted, should tolerate a variety of religious expressions, but that must not include a rampant pluralism that aimed at overturning orthodox Christianity and replacing it with atheism.[14]

Against such forces evangelicals would find in popular religion the renewing energy and forms of expression that allowed them to stand up for their convictions. Paradoxically, as Dennis E. Owen notices, in these years, "Southern evangelicalism again stands at the center of action, emerging as the most modern and energetic American religion. . . . Proponents of Christian civilization have reappeared, creating new voluntary societies aiming to save America for Christendom and the world." To do this the evangelicals, Owen concludes, "have discovered that their religious style with its emphasis on ministerial action and congregational consumption translates easily to television, making possible the dawn of evangelical media empires."[15]

These four forces, the new theological leadership, the charismatic movement, the youth explosion, and Christian civilization came out of the turmoil of the 1960s. In the next decade both leaders and participants in the larger evangelical family would find means and ways to bring forward the new subculture making itself known through popular religion.

## THE 1970s

In a vivid expression of irony and paradox, American life during the 1970s became both more religious and more secular. Clear, verifiable data demonstrate a large increase in the indices used to measure religious growth. Yet by equally documentable standards, much of American secular life continued to increase its influence without reference to traditional religious norms, raising the possibility that America was overturning or at least drastically reshaping its traditional heritage of faith. This apparent anomaly can be understood in large part by recognizing that during the 1970s religion in America became major mass media news. During these years the term "media event" came into widespread usage; religion, especially evangelical popular religion, became a media event.

The total created a dilemma for trackers and others as to how much of the media news reflected more than trendy, superficial religious activity. If the 1970s boom, as evinced by *Newsweek* magazine's making 1976 "The Year of the Evangelical," were authentic, then why did crime, public violence, pornography, infidelity, and related malbehaviors continue and even increase in volume? If the boom, or revival, were only a media event, then how could one explain the solid growth in areas of religious commitment such as the growth of evangelical colleges and Bible schools, increased financial giving, and enlarged voluntary commitment on the local level to church programs?[16]

Certainly, the media event within evangelicalism that captured the most widespread public attention was the appearance of the Jesus people. Openly drawing much of their flamboyance, irreverence, informality, and experiential insight from the 1960s psychedelic drug culture, they brought something new to the religious scene. As the next twenty years would show, their contribution marked the beginning of national attention to this form of popular religion.

The description by Robert Ellwood of its beginnings is worth quoting:

Then, suddenly, it happened. Where for a few summers there had been a moral-political movement of people who dressed in white shirts and ties there was now a whole new pop culture. It exploded in San Francisco, in Greenwich Village, on campuses across the country. A new kind of person, almost it seemed a new species, walked the streets. With the swagger of corsair voyagers from Xanadu abruptly disembarked in our drab cities, they flaunted their vivid red, purple and green paisley shirts, their sandals and buckskins, their hair and headbands, their tinted glasses, even their bizarre gold-painted eyelashes. They dwelt in gypsy-gay flats furnished mostly with huge posters of foliating startling surreal dreamlike scenes and clothes of India with bright jewels. Incense hung in the air; from stereos came the sound of the dulcet or the hard rhythms of rock music.[17]

The Jesus people, made up mostly of white youths between ages 14 and 24, identified directly with the contemporary psychedelic culture but created several unique forms of expression. Many lived very informally in communes seeking through group interaction to resist hang-ups on drugs or other substance addictions. They valued personal experience over any kind of theological sophistication, even though what doctrine they espoused seemed fundamentalist and anticipating the imminent second coming of Christ. They witnessed on street corners, they invaded regular evangelical churches to testify, and they held mass baptisms at various beaches along the Pacific Ocean, all the while attracting considerable media attention.[18]

As it unfolded, the Jesus movement found its greatest appeal and impact in its unique music, "Jesus rock." Music was at the center of its outreach, its most important instrument. Drawing from the models of the burgeoning rock music culture of the larger society, Jesus movement musicians and fans established a genre in words, rhythm, and scope and in the unique public concerts that became their chief vehicle of recruitment and of testimony to the world.[19]

What was being created here was what Carol Flake calls "Christian pop culture," a new entity on the religious landscape. It chose to go beyond the older evangelical culture described by Martin E. Marty as "sometimes stodgy and unnecessarily crabby"; the youth opted for an experience that had flair, dash, experimentation, spontaneity—qualities not widely known within evangelical ministries. With their style the Jesus movement people would become the first to broaden for themselves and later for others the definition or boundary line of how seekers could follow the "One Way" of evangelical teaching.

None of this was overlooked by the national mass media. The print and electronic commentators noted that the movement provided attractive alternatives to those already disillusioned with the church life of their elders. The media noted with fascination how the participants could choose to emulate secular rock music models, whose music was often blatantly nonreligious, and yet hold on to their new-found conversion faith. Jesus people could have the fun of the long hair, outrageous clothes, and free and easy social interaction belonging to the larger counterculture but still maintain their religious commitment. The media gave all this extended attention. Long articles appeared in *Life* (1971), *Look* (1971), *Time* (1971), and *Life* (1972). The three national television networks carried information programs on the movement.

Within the larger youth culture of the country, many who were not runaways or into drugs or psychedelia were drawn powerfully to the images portrayed by the media. As early as 1972, for instance in Dallas, some 80,000 young people from the United States and seventy-five foreign countries participated in a mass rally, "Explo," sponsored by Campus Crusade for Christ. *Life* commented, "But long hair, pot and Jesus freaks were not the hallmarks of the Dallas scene."

Campus Crusade was launching a decade-long evangelistic crusade to win the world for Christ by 1980. To do so it was holding training sessions across the city in which the youth listened at length to religious rock music and heard encouragement from Billy Graham, Dallas Cowboy quarterback Roger Staubach, and Florida Governor Reuben Askew. Graham was delighted with Explo's unstuffy, right-on mood. "We've sort of made an end run around the church," he commented. Many of the key ingredients in the rapidly emerging evangelical popular religion were evident in Dallas, specifically, its parachurch connections, its awareness of nonevangelical celebrities from the world of entertainment, its enthusiasm for sports heroes, its absorption with high technology media, and its goal of evangelization.[20]

Further evidence of continuing new energy came from the expansion of both the Pentecostal and the charismatic movements. The beginnings of what Dean Kelley found to be the take-off period occurred at about this time, the early 1970s, with denominations such as the Assemblies of God growing by several percentage points annually. The charismatic renewal had spread first slowly but then with great force, throughout Roman Catholicism in the late 1960s and early 1970s, adding to its growing general acceptance by Christians outside its ranks. Like the Jesus people, Pentecostalists and charismatics chose to express their worship in more informal, relaxed forms, eschewing the more liturgical expressions of mainline bodies. Charismatics remaining within their own parent bodies identified closely with evangelical teachings on the authority of the Bible, the necessity for a born-again experience, and the need to answer the call to win the world for Christ.

Beyond that, as one of its historians, Richard Quebedeaux, concludes, these two movements became legitimized during the 1970s in a key area. Where once many outsiders had considered the expression of speaking in tongues to be at least "evidence of a subnormal psychological state," now certain mental health experts found it to be no such thing. It was in religious terms more of a language for private and corporate prayer. Further, by the late 1970s the mainline churches had, often grudgingly, come to accept their charismatic fellow parish members as responsible, sincere seekers. The latter, in turn, found they could in good conscience stay with their parent church while finding association with evangelicals outside their realm to be enriching and complementary to their own faith.[21]

Among classical Pentecostalists the television ministry of Oral Roberts stood at the top of the most-watched list of religious programs. Much of the appeal for new viewers resided in the ministry of faith healing, a tradition heretofore not well known outside Pentecostalist circles, but one of powerful visual and emotional appeal. In the 1970s also the Assemblies of God found an increasingly wide interest in its ministries in all parts of the country. Its rapid growth in membership started to take clear visibility in the same decade, favorable as these times were to rapid evangelical expansion.

Of special emphasis in these circles was the strong emphasis on traditional capitalist values of individual initiative, self-reliance, and material success seen by believers as gifts from God for living righteous lives. While mainline bodies found themselves caught up in struggles over denominational identity or national public policy, the Pentecostalists pursued the goals of doctrinal orthodoxy, moral rectitude, and committed discipleship, the ingredients identified by Dean Kelley. They pursued these goals all the while through both traditional and newly inspired high technology means such as door-to-door evangelism, prayer, meetings, small-group Bible study, and television, radio, and printed materials, among other ingredients in popular religion.[22]

Among fundamentalists similar opportunities for new, expanding life became evident. The trend toward building large auditoriums featuring high-voltage preachers and aggressive neighborhood evangelism proved to be highly attractive in specific locales. A marked increase appeared in the number of small, independent seminaries for training future ministers. These schools proudly, even derisively, rejected mainline scholarship and current teachings in the standard areas of seminary curriculum: scripture, doctrine, ethics, missions, and related fields. Also in education, fundamentalists added largely to the number of religious day schools, especially for the first eight grades of their children's training. Some schools undoubtedly were started to avoid having to send white children to integrated public schools; others, to avoid the growing influence of secular education and permissive behavior in those schools. Everywhere observers noted the "media explosion" among fundamentalists, as the statistics indicate.[23]

## THE 1980s

By 1980, for instance, expenditures for religious television, dominated almost totally by evangelicals, had grown to $600 million annually, a rise from $50 million ten years earlier. In February 1980, Oral Roberts took in some $60 million, Pat Robertson some $58 million, Jim Bakker $51 million, and Jerry Falwell some $50 million.[24] Among viewers the polls showed that evangelicals were clearly the heaviest users; 63 percent of them, compared to 32 percent of the larger nationwide society, stated that they had watched a religious television program in the past week.[25]

In private religious schools a 47 percent increase occurred among Protestants, a 95 percent increase in pupils enrolled and a 116 percent increase in the number of teachers. By 1978 among conservative Protestant day schools more than 1 million pupils were in regular attendance.[26]

The statistics for overall membership in a specific congregation across the nation indicated the same pattern reported annually in the statistical section of *The Yearbook of American and Canadian Churches*. The largest conservative bodies continued their growth, including Southern Baptists, Mormons, Assemblies of God, Seventh-Day Adventists, and Church of the Nazarene.[27]

So also with religious books. A *Publishers Weekly* story showed that, on the average, about three people in eight in 1980 purchased a religious book, compared with one person in eight ten years earlier. In keeping with the spread of popular religion, a content analysis showed "a significant level of concern with psychological and family-oriented issues" among evangelical publishers.[28] In one year, 1976, the Christian book market underwent a 19.3 percent increase in gross sales over the previous year. Although not reported in the widely accepted bestseller list of the *New York Times*, evangelical titles actually outsold most of the latter's highly rated titles, the most popular in the 1970s being Billy Graham's *Angels*, Marabel Morgan's *The Total Woman*, and Hal Lindsey's *The Late, Great Planet Earth*.[29]

Throughout all this growth, the involvement of the evangelical African-American community closely paralleled that of the white participants. Although statistical studies here are inconclusive, it appears that among those African Americans identifying with the evangelical tradition of having had a born-again experience, some 52 percent said they were born-again, compared to 32 percent of white respondents. The largest denominations, such as the National Baptist Convention, USA, Incorporated; National Baptist Convention of America; African Methodist Episcopal Church; African Methodist Episcopal Zion Church; and the National Primitive Baptist Convention all in their own manner expressed strong evangelical convictions in theology, evangelism, and widespread popular participation.[30]

For all their similarities, however, African-American evangelicals have been and are committed to the distinguishing feature of a "shared culture" and shared oppression that "binds together all black congregations distinguishing them from their white counterparts. There is a unique style of black worship" as well as other commonalities such as more confidence than white evangelicals in support for equal rights directed by the federal government.[31]

Scholars agree that among all evangelicals it is the distinctiveness of African-American worship that stands out as decisive. During the pivotal 1970s, as some church leaders thought African Americans and whites might desegregate in their church life to a greater degree than ever before, the former's worship became a fundamental symbol of its heritage and identity.[32] Along with its witness against racism, its leadership in urban ministry, and its demonstration that Christianity was not simply a white person's religion, African-American evangelicalism was in this decade creating its own personality. It had its own national organization, the National Black Evangelical Association (NBEA), founded in 1963. Since then it has come to serve as a clearinghouse of information, a coordinator of planning for future programs, a forum for discussion within the black community of common issues, and a symbol of affirmation in the faith espoused by its members.[33]

By the late 1970s, then, the evangelical movement so appealing to the mass media had become more than a household word in America. It had perhaps not replaced the aging mainline as the center of Protestant religious life, but it clearly had initiative, confidence, and optimism for continued growth. The national polling agencies gave support to this new outlook. In a very helpful study, *The Bible, Politics and Democracy*, Corwin Smidt and Lyman Kellstedt tabulated six studies measuring various phases of evangelical expression. The lowest estimate of the number of Americans considering themselves evangelical was 22.4 percent, the highest being 48.7 percent. The authors themselves endorsed the figure of about 30 percent.[34]

In 1978 the Gallup Poll responded to the growing general public interest with an extended investigation, reported in some detail. With a careful definition of "evangelical" as their criterion, they published their findings. They found that some 34 percent of the total population claimed they had undergone a born-again experience, a figure projecting to nearly 50 million Americans, 18 years old and over. Among only Protestants, some 48 percent stated they had known a born-again experience. Gallup added that within the denominational framework Baptists led the churches in people claiming a born-again experience (some 61 percent), while at the other end some 11 percent of Episcopalians acknowledged that event.[35] In a composite picture, the Gallup organization stated that evangelicals "are predominantly women—that is . . . 37 percent are male and 63 percent are female. They are also, for the most part, over 50 years old (57 percent), white (77 percent), live in the South (50 percent), and in the smallest towns or rural areas

(44 percent), have no political allegiance (86 percent are Independents), and are Protestant (86 percent)."[36]

As an addition to the study, Gallup noted certain problems inherent not only in their study but also in trying to create greater public understanding about a very diverse movement. Despite the widespread publicity about it, a large number of those polled could not define evangelicalism accurately; only 57 percent of those polled responded at all to even the first question the Gallup people asked, and many did so in vague terms. Despite this, "the image of evangelicals" was overwhelmingly favorable among those who responded, some 49 percent, while only 8 percent were negative. [37]

The problems within evangelicalism were located not only by the Gallup people but also by a small but increasing number of commentators within the evangelical community. These focused not on doctrine or scripture but on the manner in which the movement, in absorbing so much of its attention on popular religion, was perhaps not being faithful to its mandate to win the world. From its heritage of parachurch ministries, evangelicals had by about 1980 helped build some remarkably prominent programs: Young Life and Youth for Christ; InterVarsity, Navigators, and Campus Crusade; World Vision, the Christian Medical Society, Basic Youth Conflicts, and others. What emerged from the local parish was criticism that some of these and related groups led people away from the parish. Some parachurch leaders in turn suggested the congregations were not doing all they could for the cause. Observers asked: Might not a great deal of time and energy be unnecessarily spent in dealing with these issues rather than proclaiming the faith?[38]

In a related field, as religious television continued its phenomenal expansion, critics inside the movement started wondering whether this was indeed an unmixed blessing. J. Thomas Bissett, a religion media manager, in 1980 raised several crucial issues, the key one being, "How effective *is* religious broadcasting?" The research cited showed that religious broadcasting was reaching less than 4 percent of the total available radio and television network. He asked, "We are spending $2 billion a year to do *this*?" Bissett found such broadcasting was preaching to the choir, often overduplicating itself in local markets, unsure of its goals, and far too prone to emphasize fund-raising and viewer popularity at the expense of winning souls.[39]

Finally, perhaps the most extended critique of evangelical growth success of the 1970s was made by Jon Johnston, then a professor of Sociology at Pepperdine University and Fuller Theological Seminary and an ordained minister. At the decade's end his book *Will Evangelicalism Survive Its Own Popularity?* focused sharply on ingredients many had considered strengths but seemed in fact to be harming the cause. He praised the newfound popularity and acceptance of the movement. But then Johnston went on to blast the degree to which evangelicals had adapted much of their life-style to the larger world, focusing on one's immediate problems at the expense of world crises, taking material success as a sign of God's approval, uncritically accepting the latest fads in evangelism techniques, idolizing evangelical celebrity leaders, buying into the latest high technology innovations, and overspending on religious trinkets. He concluded that such technology was creating a new, highly undesirable spirituality driven by profits, blandness, and idolization of the patterns of success in the larger secular society.[40]

During the 1980s, evangelical popular religion both continued its rapid expansion in scope and size and also continued to attract considerable criticism from within and outside. On balance, the fears of overgrowth expressed by critics during the 1970s were largely ignored or only tacitly acknowledged. Some self-correction occurred during the later 1980s when three of the pioneer leaders, Oral Roberts, Jimmy Swaggart, and Jim Bakker, all worked themselves into highly objectionable situations concerning personal conduct or financial mismanagement.[41]

## THE NEW EVANGELICAL SUBCULTURE

On balance, after this housecleaning, the evangelical subculture, only a faraway dream some twenty years before, stood now as a major landmark on the American religious map. It rested fully on the 1980s achievements; the full range and complexity of popular religion now came into clear view. It embraced all the electronic media, much of the print media, involved itself with national values on a record-high level, chose to address its concerns to the ever-present threats to the family and the individual believer, and found the opportunity to expand its scope in a fresh way into the worlds of arts and letters. This final section outlines that story in its complexity and, as Wayne Elzey noted, its *incongruity*.[42] That is, during these years all the paradoxical, ironical, often contradictory themes of popular religion came into full public view: evangelical magicians, novelists, actors, cowboys, scientists, sculptors, athletes, beauty queens, stockbrokers, and the like; evangelical diets, money-making schemes, toys, trinket merchandise, shopping malls, Caribbean cruises, and more.

Evangelicals, however, despite their own critics, found the opportunity to find patterns of religious meaning in such popular phenomena. Popular religion, as it matured in the 1980s, taught them that "even though the world often works at cross-purposes and seems organized in contradictory ways, reality is finally neither unpredictable nor confusing. Popular religion works by reminding believers that meaning resides in the logical affinities one dimension of sensible experience has with another."[43] In a supreme incongruity, Elzey suggests, this popular religion absorbs the most recent high tech media marvels and the most up-to-date fads and ever-changing tastes in popular culture as proof "that things are as they always have been."[44] By contrast mainliners, while participating in some of these activities, chose not to identify them with the will of God. (Nor, of course, did all evangelicals.)

That prologue offers the observer equipped with lenses of irony and paradox an organizing principle to lead her or him through the world of recent evangelical popular religion. As the movement became more widely accepted, its participants in all their diversity showed their determination to understand just what it was they espoused. The question became: How could this faith be understood by themselves and by those outside their circles? A superb example of this growing self-awareness appeared as a photo essay in *Moody* in 1988, "Family Portrait: A Day in the Life of Evangelical America." By prior arrangement, fifty members of the organization "Christians in Photojournalism" took some 9,000 pictures on Easter Sunday; these were coordinated and printed in color in fourteen pages of the issue of July/August 1988.

Obviously Easter is the culminating day of faith for Christians, and in that sense this was no slice-of-ordinary-life photoessay. But it showed what evangelicals understood they should be doing; some were at sunrise services; some attended a musical-theatrical production at Midway Baptist, Dallas; some took communion; some with AIDS ministered to those with a homosexual life-style; some taught Sunday school; some talked about Christ to the homeless near an inner-city "Christian Outreach Appeal" in Long Beach, California. Charles Colson, converted Watergate convictee and founder of Prison Fellowship, visited men in jail; some of Youth with a Mission ministered to punk rockers in Hollywood; some led Bible studies in shelters for abused women; some visited residents in nursing homes.[45]

This self-consciousness appeared in measurable form in a wide-ranging *Gallup Report* (number 259) in 1987. There Kenneth Briggs found impressive the ability of evangelicalism to hold the loyalties of its participants, largely because it was able to keep "alive the choice of taking faith seriously."[46] By way of demographics, a poll made ten years after the poll cited earlier found that the profile of the individual evangelical would be "disproportionately Protestant, black, poor, and Southern." Forty-four percent of blacks call themselves evangelical, as compared to 31 percent of whites. Nearly four of ten evangelicals belong to households whose income is $15,000 or less, compared to about two in ten whose income is $40,000 and above. Nearly four in ten have not completed high school.[47]

Another important profile appearing at the same time, by Professor James Davison Hunter, suggested that evangelicalism was a "predominantly white, disproportional female religious phenomenon." The total population was older than among other religious bodies, and the clear majority was married, concentrated largely in the rural small-town South and similar areas in the mid-Atlantic and Midwest states. The evangelicals, as the statistics showed them, were "in the lower echelons of educational achievement income level, and occupational status . . . the lower middle and working classes." They also were solidly rooted in the denominational structure of American Protestantism.[48]

While a precisely accurate measurement of membership remained difficult to achieve among the experts, the same general pattern of growth persisted during the 1980s. During the previous decade, those church bodies joining the National Association of Evangelicals increased by 58 percent. Despite that, the NAE's executive director, Billy Melvin, suggested that still some 30 million evangelicals remained outside any national evangelical body.[49]

These numbers and those following are impersonal measurements standing as the quantitative evidence that popular religion, especially in the mass media, did expand in all its incongruity strongly in the 1980s. That is, the data here indicate that the opportunities for market growth continued to expand; the voluntary donations (as opposed to any government subsidy) grew; and the number of customers of books, magazines, videos, audiotapes, and films increased, in contrast to the 1970s. Undoubtedly the forces identified by Dean Kelley contributed cohesion and purpose to this growth. Also undoubtedly the greater skill and zeal of popular religion producers helped expand its range during this decade. It seemed, in fact, that very little overproduction of popular religion materials occurred, at least until the recession of the latter years of the decade. Entrepreneurs and artists kept producing, marketers kept selling, and consumers kept buying. Such at least is the commonsensical interpretation of these data.

For instance, the number of radio stations with a religious format increased from 1977 to 1987 some 22 percent, from 1,069 to 1,370 outlets. Television stations that programmed religion rose between 1982 and 1987 from 65 to 221, that is, by 71 percent. The number of Christian radio program producers increased during that decade some 33.1 percent, while in the last half of that time span the number of Christian television producers increased 32.4 percent.[50]

In May 1988, Arbitron Ratings listed the programs shown in Table 1.1 as the most popular syndicated religious programs.[51] Not included in the table are the many religious programs available only through cable systems. These grew rapidly, as did the entire cable system in the later 1980s. The 1988 data given in Table 1.2 show this expansion.[52]

Again, such statistics are only general indications; some televangelists knowingly greatly inflated their own estimate of their market size to impress their listeners and the general electronic media. Specialists for nearly two decades have studied and debated among themselves just how accurate and helpful such statistics are. No clear consensus to date has been established. Equally controversial has been the matter of aggressive, even allegedly misleading fund-raising techniques by several of the leading televangelists.

**Table 1.1**
**Top Television Programs, May 1988**

| | | |
|---|---|---|
| 1. | "Hour of Power," Robert Schuller | 1,394,000 homes |
| 2. | "World Tomorrow," Herbert Armstrong | 1,270,000 homes |
| 3. | "Jimmy Swaggart" | 923,000 homes |
| 4. | "Oral Roberts" | 635,000 homes |
| 5. | "Day of Discovery," Richard DeHaan | 514,000 homes |
| 6. | "Dr. James Kennedy" | 511,000 homes |
| 7. | "Ken Copeland" | 432,000 homes |
| 8. | "Old-Time Gospel Hour," Jerry Falwell | 410,000 homes |
| 9. | "The Promise of America" | 335,000 homes |
| 10. | "Fred K. Price" | 301,000 homes |
| 11. | "Insight" drama | 293,000 homes |
| 12. | "In Touch," Charles Stanley | 291,000 homes |
| 13. | "It Is Written," George Vandeman | 259,000 homes |
| 14. | "Larry Jones Presents" | 246,000 homes |
| 15. | "James Robison's Day of Restoration" | 238,000 homes |
| 16. | "The 700 Club" | 224,000 homes |
| 17. | "This Is the Life" | 201,000 homes |
| 18. | "Jimmy Swaggart—Daily" | 196,000 homes |
| 19. | "Christopher Close-Ups" | 167,000 homes |
| 20. | "Christian Lifestyles Magazine" | 161,000 homes |

Several studies have indicated that the issue has received considerable attention, but, in a realm where stringent government regulation seems unlikely, little has been achieved to establish national norms among broadcasters.[53]

No one has disputed the precipitous drop in revenue and status among most televangelistic giants brought on by the sex and financial scam scandals of Jim Bakker, Swaggart, and Roberts.[54] The major voice for mainline evangelicalism, *Christianity Today*, stepped into the disputed zone, realizing the potential dangers to the cause from uninformed viewers/donors. In two major research articles, its editors presented as much information as they could obtain from all reliable sources; some broadcasters such as Swaggart

**Table 1.2**
**Top Cable Systems**

| | | |
|---|---|---|
| 1. | Christian Broadcasting Network | 42.0 million subscribers |
| 2. | The Inspirational Network (formerly PTL) | 10.5 million |
| 3. | Trinity Broadcasting Network | 5.9 million |
| 4. | Eternal Word Television Network | 11.0 million |
| 5. | ACTS Satellite Network | 7.8 million |
| 6. | FamilyNet | 1.3 million |

refused to cooperate. A table the magazine editors titled "Taking the Plunge," in 1989, displayed this data, based on Arbitron figures, but without cable statistics (see Table 1.3).[55]

Eventually, all these programs except Swaggart's were able to recoup their earlier leadership positions in terms of households and receipts. The whole struggle, however, brought the efficacy of this form of popular religion into the public arena. *Christianity Today* also printed another major exchange of viewpoints and information, including the views of broadcasters such as Paul Crouch, founder of Trinity Broadcasting Network. He insisted that television, with all its exorbitant costs, impersonal technology, internal scandals, and the like, should nonetheless be considered a major source for evangelism. "The church should use any vehicle that has the potential to reach large numbers of people for Christ."

**Table 1.3**
**Televangelist Decline, 1986–1988**

| Programs | Households | | | | |
|---|---|---|---|---|---|
| | *2/86* | *2/87* | *2/88* | *5/88* | *7/88* |
| Swaggart | 2,298,000 | 2,161,000 | 1,961,000 | 923,000 | 836,000 |
| Schuller | 1,963,000 | 1,689,000 | 1,556,000 | 1,394,000 | 1,215,000 |
| Roberts | 1,269,000 | 1,149,000 | 627,000 | 635,000 | 561,000 |
| Falwell | 708,000 | 616,000 | 372,000 | 410,000 | 284,000 |
| Robertson | 527,000 | 444,000 | 271,000 | 224,000 | 191,000 |

The founder and director of the Institute for American Church Growth, Win Arn, in the same article answered that television had not persuaded very many people to become Christ's disciples to stand as responsible members of the church. He insisted, "In this, TV evangelism has failed." To Arn, television had a legitimate place in pre-evangelism but could not bridge the chasm between the local church and the broadcast medium. Religious faith needed people working on a one-to-one basis.[56]

## RADIO

In the other major electronic medium, radio, the pattern of growth closely paralleled that of television. Although its controversy was muted by comparison to the highly publicized "Gospelgate" stories, religious radio found itself also involved in considerable disagreement over aims and finances. Briefly just as the evangelical takeoff started, some 111 radio stations in 1973 were devoting at least twenty hours a week to religious programming (largely music and teaching). In three years, the number of stations rose to 341; six years later the total was 449, spread throughout most of the fifty states. One decade later, some 1,052 stations were broadcasting, and the number was still climbing. Glowing articles in trade journals such as *Religious Broadcasting* outlined the great opportunities in radio for evangelicals.[57]

**Table 1.4**
**The Top Ten Daily Evangelical Syndicated Radio Programs, Early 1988**

|  |  | Stations |
|---|---|---|
| 1. "Focus on the Family" | James Dobson | 744 |
| 2. "Thru the Bible" | J. Vernon McGee | 496 |
| 3. "Insight for Living" | Charles Swindoll | 481 |
| 4. "Back to the Bible" | Warren Wiersbe | 421 |
| 5. "In Touch" | Charles Stanley | 398 |
| 6. "Point of View" | Marlin Maddoux | 345 |
| 7. "Haven of Rest" | Paul Evans | 275 |
| 8. "Bible Radio Class" | Darrow Parker | 232 |
| 9. "Minirth-Meier Clinic" | Don Hawkins | 216 |
| 10. "Faith Seminar of the Air" | Kenneth Hagin | 207 |

**Table 1.5**
**The Top Ten Weekly Evangelical Syndicated Radio Programs**

|  |  | Stations |
|---|---|---|
| 1. "Lutheran Hour" | Oswald Hoffman/W. Schultz | 645 |
| 2. "Hour of Decision" | Billy Graham | 620 |
| 3. "Children's Bible Hour" | Charles Vander Meer | 592 |
| 4. "Revivaltime" | Dan Betzer (AoG) | 550 |
| 5. "Baptist Hour" | Southern Baptist Convention | 530 |
| 6. "Focus Weekend" | James Dobson | 510 |
| 7. "Unshackled!" | Pacific Garden Mission | 450 |
| 8. "Radio Bible Class" | Richard DeHaan | 439 |
| 9. "Moody Presents" | Moody Broadcasting | 410 |
| 10. "Questions & Answers" | J. Vernon McGee (deceased) | 380 |

Yet by 1990, as was true with television, it became clear that this medium was also preaching to the choir; like television, radio was not reaching the unconverted or the wider secular audience. It was in fact servicing the evangelical subculture very well and, like some religious television, showed signs of going even more commercial. Yet no one denied that religious radio served the evangelicals well. It had flexibility, the ability to adapt to local interests, a variety of formats for reaching several taste audiences, and strength to build loyal listeners accustomed to using radio in a very habituated manner. Tables 1.4, 1.5, and 1.6 suggest the scope of evangelical radio.[58] As

**Table 1.6**
**Radio Leaders' Income Growth (in millions of dollars)**

|  | 1984 | 1985 | 1986 | 1987 | 1988 |
|---|---|---|---|---|---|
| Insight for Living | 6.6 | 8.2 | 9.1 | 11.0 | 11.0 |
| Back to the Bible | 6.6 | 6.8 | 7.7 | 7.4 | 7.1 |

a further indication of strong growth in the late 1980s, Table 1.6 shows the increase in revenue for two of the leaders.

## PRINT

In a related field, that of print media, the evangelical subculture expanded its consumption of books and journals. It also, as with the electronic area, found itself embroiled in several conflicts, which indicates both the strength and the diffusion of aims for promoters of popular religion in these years.

Book publishing had been a major source of dissemination of information in the evangelical community throughout the first part of this century. Each major tradition (such as fundamentalist, Pentecostal, reformed, holiness) had at least one major publishing firm. However, most of these until about the late 1960s remained very small in production, limited to well-known subjects and favorite authors and generally of little appeal to the general evangelical reader. Then, during the first years of rapid growth, the publishing field took note and quickly responded with a variety of subjects and authors and marketing techniques that made a major contribution to evangelical growth. By the late 1980s some seventy specifically evangelical publishing houses were in business. In charge of marketing for these works were the approximately 6,000 independent religious bookstores. Something like 3,500 of these belonged to their national trade group, the Christian Booksellers Association (CBA). In 1984 these stores by themselves amassed gross sales of $1.25 billion.[59] Table 1.7 shows the rate of growth from 1967 through 1986.[60]

Among the bestselling authors in the 1980s were those who also had achieved notoriety through other media outlets: Pat Robertson, Charles Swindoll, Charles Colson, and James Dobson. Others included Bible trans-

**Table 1.7**
**Religious Book Sales in the United States, 1967–1986**

|  | Religious Book Sales, in millions of dollars | | Average Annual Growth for Previous Decade |
|---|---|---|---|
|  | *Yearly totals* | *In 1967 dollars* | |
| 1967 | 108 | 108 | |
| 1977 | 304 | 168 | 5.5% |
| 1986 | 685 | 209 | 2.7% |

lator Kenneth Taylor, cult expert Walter Martin, and social-relationships author Joyce Lansdorf; sales for each of them reached well into six figures.[61]

Evangelical book publishers (except those owned and subsidized by denominations) faced several perplexing problems, similar to those in other media. There was always the pressure of competition from the large independent houses such as Harper and Row (later HarperSanFrancisco) that also published some evangelical titles and had superior advertising and books of their own on the best-known bestseller lists. For a variety of reasons most evangelical titles, including such blockbusters as *The Late, Great Planet Earth* and *The Total Woman*, were not included in the definitive *New York Times* list, meaning a diminished opportunity for publisher and author to reach readers not directly familiar with offerings from only the evangelical houses.[62]

Within evangelical ranks the debates centered on three major problems. Many publishers seemed to be more interested in making profits than in providing a book ministry. Critics charged editors with favoring books that were brief and "zippy" at the expense of theological depth. Other critics criticized them for using an ever-increasing number of authors who were poor writers and for holding to a parochial viewpoint (preaching to the choir).[63]

Further, the world of journal and magazine publishing in the evangelical subculture during these years joined in general market-wide trends to improve sales: more sparkle in advertising, more dash and polish in packaging and subject matter—policies the secular houses were pursuing. By contrast to the media of television in which fewer than five broadcasters dominated the scene, in periodicals the trend was toward increasing specialization and diversity, a trend in harmony with that of secular magazine publishing. A few major voices spoke for the mainstream of evangelicalism: *Moody Monthly*, *Eternity*, *Christian Life*, *Christian Herald*, and the immensely influential *Christianity Today*. Evangelical magazine ministry provided a direct, flexible, often sophisticated understanding of popular religion and how it could serve the movement.[64]

By the decade's end evangelicalism had demonstrated in its many-faceted manner that it could provide both traditional and up to the minute styles of religious expression in the larger society. It had in fact become the major source of Protestant energy in the United States. The priorities of religious life could clearly be identified within evangelicalism. By contrast, with but few exceptions, most mainline churches had not significantly reversed a long-standing downward trend in membership and financial support.[65] By 1990 also the familiar pattern of widespread evangelical but only limited mainline utilization of popular religion themes and technology had continued. Indeed, evangelical trackers such as Larry Eskridge and others pointed to the growing size and influence of the movement's subculture. Especially obvious was the ongoing expansion of a "baptized" media alternative for evangelicals. Through its long-standing adaptation of the parachurch tradition, evangelicalism inspired the creation within its own ranks of many organizations in the larger secular culture, "an evangelical clone of nearly every secular organization, service, or product" allowing evangelicals to identify with both their own and the larger culture.[66] Through this process the full impact of popular religion on the rapid growth of evangelicalism made its presence clear.

For spokespersons within the tradition, such an identification proved that strength came with God's approval. The leaders—Pat Robertson, Oral Roberts, Paul Crouch of Trinity Broadcasting Network, and others—hailed the new technology as God-given. A leading observer, however, wondered about that.

American evangelicalism has produced its own rhetoric of technological salvation. Usually the rhetoric does not say that technology actually saves people from their sins or their spiritual death, but it does imply that the latest technologies are God's necessary tools for worldwide evangelization. In other words, the Lord has given humankind the media principally to fulfill the Great Commission of preaching Christ and baptizing the entire world in his name.[67]

The supporters were asking rhetorically: How could any instrument used for such purposes be anything but providential?

Increasingly in the 1980s, however, certain respected evangelical leaders came to regret and, frequently, to denounce the cloned subculture as being counterproductive to the aims of the faith. Noting the commendable "widespread passion for biblical orthodoxy," J. I. Packer bemoaned the result as only "minuscule" in changing America. The movement had become too much like the world, concentrating on individualist fulfillment, success, wealth, and "prizing ability over character," a sellout to secular humanism.[68]

Other reports suggested that evangelical televangelism as such had in the last analysis failed to convert very many persons. The several polling agencies showed studies pointing to a similar lack of improvement in certain categories of moral behavior and biblical literacy by the born-again population. For the entire American population the category of biblical literacy continued to draw critical attention with such statistics as eight in ten respondents claiming to be Christian but only four in ten knew that Jesus, according to the Bible, delivered the Sermon on the Mount. Many of the born-again who were polled pointed to the Ten Commandments as "valid rules for living today" but had difficulty recalling what those rules were.

Among evangelicals only 18 percent of the respondents stated they read the Bible daily; another 18 percent read it from between three to six times a day, the median duration of reading being twenty-two minutes. Some one-quarter of the born-again persons could not state where Jesus was born or whether Jonah was a part of the Bible.[69]

Other trends also pointed to at least a slowdown if not a halt in evangelical expansion by the last decade of the century. One bellwether sign of strength, the long-standing trend of increasing enrollment in and graduation from Bible colleges and institutes, at this point in time showed indications of a sharp slowdown. Officials of the American Association of Bible Colleges pointed out that the rapid growth of the 1970s could hardly be expected to continue and indeed had not done so. Other officials noted that curriculum programs popular twenty years earlier were now not working well among the new generation of students. Mostly the schools were attempting to improve the academic quality of their programs, leading them to shape policies to gain accreditation and cooperation with accredited four-year liberal arts colleges. All told, enrollment was down in 1990 some 15 percent from two decades earlier. As something of a postmortem explanation, Ronald Chadwick, director of the Grand Rapids (Michigan) School of Bible and Music told the Associated Press, "In the 60s and 70s, young people came to Bible colleges out of a deep sense of commitment to fulfill God's will. I think most 17-18-19 year olds today don't have the foggiest idea of what life is all about and where they are going."[70] Such a trend indicated that, in its determination to bring everyday life and religious faith into closer harmony, evangelical popular religion showed signs of slipping into accommodation to the world.

But the appearance of such evidence of slowdown within evangelical popular religion allows everyone interested at least an opportunity to bring together the many widely varying kinds of evidence, sort them into their various categories (as oversimplified as that process must be), compare them to earlier trends, and draw some conclusions about what has occurred during these last thirty years and why the lanes, paths, byways, avenues, and routes did crisscross, overlap, and lead the travelers on them into the destinations they reached. Such is the overall purpose of Parts II and III of this book.

## NOTES

1. See the discussions and documentation in Larry K. Eskridge, "Evangelical Broadcasting: Its Meaning for Evangelicals," in M. L. Bradbury and James B. Gilbert, eds., *Transforming Faith: The Sacred and Secular in Modern American History* (Westport, Conn.: Greenwood Press, 1989), pp. 127–39; Nancy Tatom Ammerman, *Baptist Battles: Social Change and Religious Beliefs in the Southern Baptist Convention* (New Brunswick, N.J.: Rutgers University Press, 1990), pp. 114–16; Grant Wacker, "Searching for Norman

Rockwell: Popular Evangelicalism in Contemporary America," in Leonard I. Sweet, ed., *The Evangelical Tradition* (Macon, Ga.: Mercer University Press, 1984), pp. 289–315.

2. David Harrington Watt, *A Transforming Faith: Explorations of Twentieth-Century American Evangelicalism* (New Brunswick, N.J.: Rutgers University Press, 1991), pp. 1–13; Phillip E. Hammond, *Religion and Personal Autonomy: The Third Disestablishment in America* (Columbia: University of South Carolina Press, 1992), passim.

3. Reinhold Niebuhr, *The Irony of American History* (New York: Scribners, 1952); readers will note my debt to Niebuhr here and elsewhere.

4. Joel A. Carpenter, "Youth for Christ and the New Evangelicals' Place in the Life of the Nation," in Sherrill Rowland, ed., *American Recoveries: Religion in the Life of the Nation* (Champaign: University of Illinois Press, 1989); see also the forty-five volume series of sources of fundamentalism in his *Fundamentalism in American Religion, 1880–1950* (New York: Garland, 1988).

5. Marshall Frady, *Billy Graham: A Parable of American Righteousness* (Boston: Little, Brown, 1979); William Martin, *A Prophet with Honor: The Billy Graham Story* (New York: William Morrow, 1991), and the review of it by Grant Wacker in the *Christian Century*, April 1, 1992, pp. 336–41; see the review of the Martin book by Quentin J. Schultze in *First Things*, February 1992, pp. 57–60.

6. See my discussion of this in *Holding Fast/Pressing On: Religion in America in the 1980s* (Westport, Conn.: Greenwood Press, 1990), pp. 1–12; see Joseph B. Tamney, *The Resilience of Christianity in the Modern World* (Albany: State University of New York Press, 1992), pp. 71–103.

7. George M. Marsden, *Reformulating Fundamentalism: Fuller Seminary and the New Evangelicalism* (Grand Rapids, Mich.: Eerdmans, 1987).

8. Richard Quebedeaux, "Conservative and Charismatic Developments in the Later Twentieth Century," in Charles H. Lippy and Peter W. Williams, eds., *Encyclopedia of the American Religious Experience*, vol. 3 (New York: Scribners, 1988), p. 964.

9. Ibid., pp. 965–66; see Appendix of this book.

10. George M. Marsden, *Understanding Fundamentalism and Evangelicalism* (Grand Rapids, Mich.: Eerdmans, 1991), pp. 62–82.

11. See my *Bold in the Spirit: Lutheran Charismatic Renewal in America Today* (Minneapolis: Augsburg, 1974) and my *The Holy Spirit in Today's Church* (Nashville, Tenn.: Abingdon, 1973).

12. Robert Ellwood, *One Way: The Jesus Movement and Its Meaning* (Englewood Cliffs, N.J.: Prentice-Hall, 1973); Joel Sherer, "Bill Bright," in Charles H. Lippy, ed., *Twentieth-Century Shapers of American Popular Religion* (Westport, Conn.: Greenwood Press, 1989), pp. 48–56.

13. Wacker, "Searching," pp. 297–315; Schultze's review of Martin, pp. 57–60.

14. Wacker, "Searching," pp. 297–302.

15. Dennis E. Owen, "Protestantism," in Charles Reagan Wilson and William Ferris, eds., *Encyclopedia of Southern Culture* (Chapel Hill: University of North Carolina Press, 1989), p. 1303; Robert Wuthnow, *The Restructuring of American Religion: Society and Faith since World War II* (Princeton: Princeton University Press, 1988), pp. 194–97.

16. Kenneth L. Woodward, "Born Again," *Newsweek*, October 2, 1976, pp. 68–76; Peter Clecak, *America's Quest for the Ideal Self: Dissent and Fulfillment in the 1960s and 1970s* (New York: Oxford University Press, 1983), p. 361, has a discussion of the vagaries involved with the interpretation of religion statistics; see also editorial, "The Year of the Evangelical," *Christianity Today*, October 20, 1976, pp. 80–81.

17. Ellwood, *One Way*, p. 5; Roy M. Anker, "Risky Business: Youth and the Entertain-

ment Business," in Roy M. Anker et al., eds., *Dancing in the Dark: Youth, Popular Culture, and the Electronic Media* (Grand Rapids, Mich.: Eerdmans, 1991), pp. 90–91.

18. Carol Flake, *Redemptorama: Culture, Politics, and the New Evangelicalism* (Garden City, N.Y.: Doubleday, 1984), pp. 171–74.

19. Ibid., pp. 172–94; Ellwood, *One Way*, p. 63; Judith S. Duke, *Religious Publications and Communications* (White Plains, N.Y.: Knowledge Industry Publications, 1981), pp. 181–95.

20. The Graham quote is in Bryan T. Clemens and Darrel Smith, *The Counselor and Religious Questioning and Conflicts* (Boston: Houghton Mifflin, 1973), pp. 13–15; Martin E. Marty, "The Making of a Magazine," *Christianity Today*, July 17, 1981, p. 945; Richard Quebedeaux, *I Found It! The Story of Bill Bright and Campus Crusade* (San Francisco: Harper and Row, 1979).

21. Quebedeaux, "Conservative Developments," pp. 967–68; R. P. Spittler, "Glossolalia," in Stanley M. Burgess and Gary B. McGee, eds., *Dictionary of Pentecostal and Charismatic Movements* (Grand Rapids, Mich.: Zondervan, 1988), pp. 335–51.

22. David Edwin Harrell, Jr., *All Things Are Possible: The Healing and Charismatic Revivals in Modern America* (Bloomington: Indiana University Press, 1975), pp. 225–39; Edith L. Blumhofer, "The 'Overcoming' Life: A Study in the Reformed Evangelical Contribution to Pentecostalism," *Pneuma*, 1 (Spring 1979): 7–19; Clecak, *America's Quest*, pp. 130–44.

23. A helpful summary is Elmer L. Towns, "Trends among Fundamentalists," *Christianity Today*, July 6, 1973, pp. 1032–35; news story, "Away from the Action and Back to Basics," *U.S. News & World Report*, April 11, 1977, pp. 58–62; see the seven-part series by Russell T. Hitt, "Evangelicals in Power," discussing evangelical growth in seven regions in the United States, printed in *Eternity* in 1977 and 1978; news story, "Our Nation As They See It: Ten Evangelicals Cite Their Reasons for Optimism But Also Voice Some Concerns," *Eternity*, July/August 1972, pp. 30–33, 70.

24. Robert Wuthnow, "Religious Movements and Counter-Movements in North America," in James Beckford, ed., *New Religious Movements and Rapid Social Change* (Newbury Park, Calif.: Sage, 1986), p. 18.

25. Ibid.; see his documentation.

26. Ibid.; for more information on the day schools, see Paul F. Parsons, *Inside America's Christian Schools* (Macon, Ga.: Mercer University Press, 1987).

27. George Gallup, Jr., and Jim Castelli, *The People's Religion: American Faith in the 90s* (New York: Macmillan, 1989), p. 17; see also Barry A. Kosmin, "Research Report: The National Survey of Religious Identification" (City University of New York, 1991, mimeographed study), pp. 4–12.

28. Duke, *Religious Publishing and Communications*, pp. 154–56; Robert Wuthnow, "Indices of Religious Resurgence in the United States," in Richard T. Antoun and Mary Elaine Hegland, eds., *Religious Resurgence: Contemporary Cases in Islam, Christianity, and Judaism* (Syracuse: Syracuse University Press, 1987), p. 19.

29. Duke, *Religious Publishing and Communications*, p. 154.

30. George Gallup, Jr., *Religion in America: The Gallup Poll Index 1977–78* (Princeton: Princeton Religion Research Center, 1978), p. 43; Julia Mitchell Corbett, *Religion in America* (Englewood Cliffs, N.J.: Prentice-Hall, 1990), pp. 267–68; Duke, *Religious Publishing and Communications*, pp. 40–41; see the statistics in "Tables," in Richard John Neuhaus, ed., *The Bible, Politics, and Democracy* (Grand Rapids, Mich.: Eerdmans, 1987), p. 135.

31. Hiawatha Bray, "A Separate Altar: Distinctions of the Black Churches," *Christianity Today*, September 19, 1986, pp. 21–22; Richard Quebedeaux, *The Worldly Evangelicals*

(New York: Harper and Row, 1978), pp. 156–59; James Earl Massey, "The Black Contribution to Evangelicalism," *TSF Bulletin*, November/December 1986, pp. 10–19.

32. Bray, "Separate Altar," p. 23; Quebedeaux, *Evangelicals*, pp. 156–59; Joseph R. Washington, Jr., "The Peculiar Peril and Promise of Black Folk Religion," in David Edwin Harrell, Jr., ed., *Varieties of Southern Evangelicalism* (Macon, Ga.: Mercer University Press, 1981), pp. 58–69.

33. *Christianity Today* carried several articles on the National Black Evangelical Association; see, for instance, those on April 25, 1975, pp. 758–59; June 27, 1980, pp. 784–85; July 11, 1986, pp. 30–32; May 6, 1987, pp. 20–23.

34. Corwin Smidt and Lyman Kellstedt, "Evangelicalism and Survey Research," in Neuhaus, *Bible*, pp. 81–102, 131–59.

35. Gallup, *Religion, 1977–78*, p. 41; on knowledge of the Bible, see George Gallup, Jr., and Sarah Jones, *100 Questions and Answers: Religion in America* (Princeton: Princeton Religion Research Center, 1989), pp. 40–43.

36. Ibid., p. 42; see the critique of the Gallup data in Neuhaus, *Bible*, pp. 160–61; for data on the 1970s see David Roozen, "What Hath the 70s Wrought?" in Jacques Constant, ed., *The Yearbook of the American and Canadian Churches* (Nashville, Tenn.: Abingdon, 1984), pp. 273–78.

37. Gallup, *Religion, 1977–78*, pp. 2–43.

38. Jerry W. White, *The Church and the Parachurch: An Uneasy Marriage* (Portland, Ore.: Multnomah, 1983), pp. 23–99; Richard G. Hutcheson, Jr., "Parachurch Organizations," in his *Mainline Churches and the Evangelicals* (Atlanta: John Knox, 1981), pp. 62–79; Stephen Board, "The Great Power Shift," *Eternity*, June 1979, pp. 17–21; editorial, *Christianity Today*, October 22, 1976, p. 13.

39. J. Thomas Bissett, "Radio Broadcasting: Assessing the State of the Art," *Christianity Today*, November 11, 1980, pp. 1486–89; see the replies to this article in the same issue by Pat Robertson, Jerry Falwell, Oral Roberts, and Jimmy Swaggart.

40. Jon Johnston, *Will Evangelicalism Survive Its Own Popularity?* (Grand Rapids, Mich.: Zondervan, 1980), p. 200; see the other critics he cites on pp. 38–39; a superb example of the new technology used is the material shown in the 1992 catalog distributed by Broadcast Electronics, Inc., 4100 N. 24th St., P.O. Box 3606, Quincy, IL 62305.

41. Steve Bruce, *Pray TV: Televangelism in America* (London: Routledge, 1990), pp. 114–39.

42. Wayne Elzey, "Popular Culture," in Lippy and Williams, *Encyclopedia*, vol. 3, pp. 1727–41.

43. Ibid., p. 1740.

44. Ibid.

45. Printed in *Moody Monthly* [since the 1980s known simply as *Moody*], July/August 1988, pp. 15–27.

46. Gallup, *Religion, 1977–78*, p. 4.

47. Ibid.

48. James Davison Hunter, *Evangelicalism: The Coming Generation* (Chicago: University of Chicago Press, 1987), pp. 58–60; The Barna Research Group, *Born Again: A Look at Christians in America* (Glendale, Calif.: The Barna Research Group, 1990), pp. 1–22.

49. News story, *Christianity Today*, April 9, 1990, pp. 52–53; see also Les Parrott III and Robin D. Perrin, "The New Denominations," *Christianity Today*, March 11, 1991, pp. 29–33.

50. Dan Nichols, "The Quiet Revolution in Christian Broadcasting," *Religious Broadcasting*, February 1987, p. 20; see Quentin J. Schultze, *Televangelism and American Culture* (Grand Rapids, Mich.: Baker Book House, 1991); and Bruce, *Pray TV*; Ben Armstrong,

"Religious Broadcasting Is Alive and Expanding," *Religious Broadcasting*, July/August 1987, p. 26; on televangelists see Tom W. Smith, "Are Conservative Churches Growing?" *Review of Religious Research*, 33, 4 (June 1992), pp. 313–17.

51. Carol Ward, *The Christian Sourcebook: A Comprehensive Guide to All Things Christian*, rev. ed. (New York: Ballantine Books, 1989), p. 226.

52. Ibid., p. 227; see the news story in *Broadcasting Magazine*, December 21, 1985, p. 38.

53. News story, *Los Angeles Times*, April 1, 1989, Part II, pp. 6–7; Nick Thorndike, "Electronic Church: Fearsome or Folly?" in Marshall W. Fishwick and Ray B. Browne, eds., *The God Pumpers: Religion in the Electronic Age* (Bowling Green, Ohio: Bowling Green University Press, 1987), pp. 174–82; Bruce, *Pray TV*, pp. 54–66; Schultze, "The Greening of the Gospel," in *Televangelism*, pp. 153–81; news story, *Christianity Today*, October 16, 1986, pp. 46–49; Stewart M. Hoover, "The Religious Television Audience: A Matter of Significance of Size?" in Robert Ableman and Stewart M. Hoover, eds., *Religious Television: Controversies and Conclusions* (Norwood, N.J.: Ablex Publishing Co., 1990), p. 109–29; Razelle Frankl, *Televangelism: The Marketing of Popular Religion* (Carbondale: Southern Illinois Press, 1987), pp. 132–34.

54. Charles E. Shepard, *Forgiven: The Rise and Fall of the PTL Ministry* (New York: Atlantic Monthly Press, 1989); Schultze, *Televangelism*, pp. 113–15; Bruce, *Pray TV*, pp. 198–212.

55. News story, "Surviving the Slump," *Christianity Today*, February 3, 1989, p. 33, see here for source documentation: this journal cites Arbitron; Gallup, *Religion, 1977–78*, has much data on public reaction to televangelists, see pp. 57–91; Ward, *Sourcebook*, p. 226.

56. Debate in *Christianity Today*, "Is TV Appropriate for Mass Evangelism?" October 16, 1987, p. 50; also see Garry D. Boddy and David Pritchard, "Is Religious Knowledge Gained from Religious Broadcasting?" *Journalism Quarterly*, 63 (Winter 1986): 840–44.

57. Quentin J. Schultze, "The Invisible Medium: Evangelical Radio," in Schultze, ed., *American Evangelicals and the Mass Media* (Grand Rapids, Mich.: Zondervan, 1990), p. 171; see the news story in *National and International Religion Report*, January 29, 1990, p. 8.

58. News story, *Religious Broadcasting*, April 1989, p. 44, see its source documentation; Jorstad, *Holding Fast/Pressing On*, p. 103; news story, *Christianity Today*, February 3, 1989, pp. 32–34.

59. See Donald K. Smith, *Creating Understanding: A Handbook for Christian Communication across Cultural Landscapes* (Grand Rapids, Mich.: Zondervan, 1991), for documentation; see also Leonard George Goss, ed., *Inside Religious Broadcasting: A Look Behind the Scenes* (Grand Rapids, Mich.: Zondervan, 1991).

60. See the documentation in John P. Ferre, "Searching for the Great Commission: Evangelical Book Publishing Since the 1970s," in Schultze, *American Evangelicals*, p. 100.

61. See the bestseller list, "Let There Be Books," in *Newsweek*, August 5, 1985, pp. 65–66; an update through 1988 is in Ward, *Sourcebook*, pp. 174–75.

62. Enola Borgh, "The Religious Press," *Arizona English Bulletin*, 17, 3 (1975): 172–76.

63. Ferre, "Searching," pp. 105–6.

64. Steven Board, "Moving the World with Magazines: A Survey of Evangelical Periodicals," in Schultze, *American Evangelicals*, pp. 119–42; see also the list in Ward, *Sourcebook*, pp. 194–218.

65. News story, *New York Times*, June 20, 1991, p. A11; news story, *Washington Post*, August 19, 1991, p. C11.

66. Eskridge, "Evangelical Broadcasting," pp. 131–32; see the review by J. Harold

Ellens of Ben Armstrong, *The Electric Church*, in *The Reformed Journal*, August 1982, pp. 25–26.

67. Schultze, *Televangelism*, p. 57; see here also pp. 34–35, 45–48, 62–63.

68. Editorial, *Christianity Today*, October 2, 1987, p. 15; see also Mike Yancolli, "The Loser of the Year," *The Door*, 1991, pp. 34–35; see also the editorial by Stephen Strang, *Charisma and Christian Life*, October 1990, p. 11; editorial, *Christianity Today*, August 7, 1987, pp. 12–13.

69. News item, *National and International Religion Report*, February 27, 1989, p. 8; news story, *National Christian Reporter*, January 18, 1991, p. 1; Princeton Religion Research Center, *Emerging Trends*, December 1987, pp. 2–4; news item, *Christian Century*, October 31, 1990, p. 990; news story, *Twin City Christian* (Minneapolis), February 11, 1990, p. 3A.

70. Interview with the Associated Press in the *Washington Post*, June 29, 1991, p. B7; see the documentation in Hunter, *Evangelicalism*, chs. 2–5; see also George Barna, *What Americans Believe* (Ventura, Calif.: Regal Books, 1991); James Lincoln Collier, *The Rise of Selfishness in America* (New York: Oxford University Press, 1991); see also the fascinating data in James Patterson, *The Day Americans Told the Truth: What People Really Believe about Everything That Really Matters* (New York: Prentice-Hall, 1991), pp. 199–206 on religion.

# Part II

# EVANGELICAL POPULAR RELIGION AND SOCIAL VALUES

The distinctive quality of evangelical popular religion is its openness to believing that the great, complex questions of life can be answered clearly and directly. From everyday parlance believers have testimonies and stories of "healed bodies and minds, ships coming in, prospering businesses, saved marriages—in short, a life where the shadows flee away," as defined by Leonard I. Sweet.[1] The lenses of irony and incongruity help only when they are understood to be tools that lead the believer to affirm the great truths of the faith. In evangelical vision, "whatsoever things are true, honorable, just, pure, lovely, excellent" cannot be limited to traditional qualities as found in the liturgically oriented Great Tradition as is the case with mainline values. Rather, the everyday, the ordinary experiences and maxims for living reflect the fact that Christians have at their command and disposal the resources for shadow-free living in the here and now.[2]

This quality underlies and unifies the various themes discussed in Part II, Social Values. In academic terms the unity here is that which is offered by considering the material as "social science," an imprecise term but one that at least by definition omits formal theological and ethicist discourse, the fine arts, and the humanities as well as the natural sciences.[3] Put another way, evangelicals pursue their commission by assuming that their social lives come together into a pattern that, although not always clear, will count in the long view for helping to achieve the advancement of the kingdom, as well as help make the United States more of a Christian society. In their earning of daily bread, in living with the inner self, in the female/male domain, in care-giving, and in watching the days draw nigh, evangelicals find patterns to understand and roads on which to travel. These are the trails we follow in Part II: economic, psychological, and sociological; by way of labels, they intertwine and overlap at almost every major point.

## NOTES

1. Leonard I. Sweet, "The 1960s: The Crises of Liberal Christianity and the Public Emergence of Evangelicalism," in George Marsden, ed., *Evangelicalism and Modern America* (Grand Rapids, Mich.: Eerdmans, 1985), p. 45.

2. See the sharply etched critique by Ronald A. Wells, "Whatever Happened to Frances Schaeffer?" *The Reformed Journal*, May 1983, pp. 10–13.

3. I am aware that this position will not win wide acceptance among postmodernists, deconstructionists, and semioticists.

# 2

# Earning Daily Bread:
# Problems and Possibilities

Evangelicals can be found in all categories of income level and career employment. There are rich and poor, specialist and generalist, wise and foolish, thrifty and profligate, ambitious and lazy. What stands as a very widely shared consensus of values among almost all is their loyalty to market capitalism as it has unfolded in the history of the United States. With but few exceptions they endorse the spirit of entrepreneurialism, the individual's right to earn and protect private property, the inherent importance of efficiency at all levels of economic life, the keeping of government regulation to a minimum amount of control, and the explicit wisdom demonstrated by allowing supply and demand to hold it all together.

Yet in their popular understanding, evangelicals also affirm the centrality of biblical wisdom, which contains specific teachings on the earning of daily bread and the distribution of wealth. Biblical wisdom embraces an explicit ethics of economic and social behavior that is binding on the rank and file. For them the crunch comes at this point because so much of American economic activity has not brought and cannot as it is practiced bring honor to the list of "whatsoever are honorable" qualities of a God-centered life.

The watcher does not detect a widespread unanimity of practice of shared values in this realm of popular social values. Over the centuries, in fact, Protestantism, including evangelicalism, in its diversity has undergone a profound transformation regarding earning one's living. Originally, as Max Weber delineated, it held to a model of an "inner-worldly asceticism," a moral code that insisted on the primacy of economic self-control, a preference for austerity over luxury, and a rigorous denial of instant gratification,

all of which focused the believer's preparation for the life in the hereafter
rather than the enjoyment of this world.[1] Older evangelical hymns such as
"Work for the Night Is Coming" or "Bringing in the Sheaves" well reflected
the popular evangelical understanding of dedicating in toto this part of life
to God. Popular maxims such as "the Devil has use for idle fingers" came to
be accepted as eternal wisdom, reflecting the evangelical preference for
frugality, sobriety, and efficiency.[2]

Over the centuries this economic ethic has undergone profound transformations. To be sure, evangelicals, especially fundamentalists and Pentecostalists, held fast to the older ascetic rejection of worldly amusements and idle
recreation.[3] But by the 1960s popular evangelical religion, J. Lawrence
Burkholder suggests, came to legitimate and express the values of American
culture, emerging as it did out of the upward mobility experienced by this
subculture following World War II. Many have aligned themselves with the
larger society in sharing the "deepest desires of this generation for freedom,
prosperity, enterprise, individualism, private ownership, family, and good,
clean living." These are grounded without irony or incongruity "in the law
of God," meaning that human aspirations and religious sanctions have
become one and the same.[4]

But the story was somewhat more complex for many. In the marketplace,
evangelicals slowly but clearly had to come to terms with what otherwise
seemed a fundamental anomaly: The Bible was written in a time when its
authors and their entire world stood far removed from the contemporary
bureaucratic organization and market-driven values of American capitalism.
How could an ancient economy be considered any kind of viable model or
collection of absolute dicta for today's world of economic life?

Among the enormous number of evangelical apologetics on this issue, that
by Edgar Norton seems representative as a voice for popular religion here.[5]
The Bible, he writes, clearly endorses the ownership of private property, "the
basic tenet of capitalism. The eighth commandment warns against stealing
property and the ninth commandment prohibits coveting that [property]
which belongs to one's neighbors." Norton says, "Both of these commandments imply private ownership of property. You cannot steal something
unless it belongs to someone else."[6] In Matthew 25 and Luke 19 are examples of private ownership; Christ talked about a man who owned a vineyard
and hired workers.

A second principle of capitalism, Norton points out, is "the freedom to
earn an income by means of using capital. Those who best use their capital
to meet the desires of consumers and society at large will be rewarded with
profits. Again the Bible speaks up for this principle. In both Old and New
Testament the rich and wealthy as such are not disparaged. Throughout the
Bible some great leaders such as Abraham, David, Joseph of Arimathea, and

Job all possessed great wealth." As to investment, the Matthew and Luke passages just cited show Jesus approved of the honest workers who invested their money and who worked wisely and hard and so would reap the benefits.[7]

Some people earn more than others simply because they have superior qualities of character such as endurance, intelligence, and leadership skills. "Those possessing such characteristics have a right to use those abilities in any way they choose, so long as the laws of the land are followed."[8] No amount of government regulation or interference in the economic life of the nation can change the inherent differences in people's talents. As for the poor, Christ had stated they would always be present.

The gradual acceptance by most evangelicals of popular support of American capitalism, however, generated considerable dissent and criticism from some outsider critics and some critics within the fold. Emerging as it did during the highly materialistic "decade of greed," the 1980s, this ethos was subjected during that decade to extensive disputation by evangelicals from several of its factions.[9] Evangelical writer Phillip Yancey argued that when Jesus praised the virtues of the poor, the oppressed, the hungry, and the mourners when he gave the Sermon on the Mount he was in fact criticizing those who stood to gain from amassing personal economic wealth. The more wealthy simply lost their need to depend on God in the way the poor came to depend. Faith involved more interdependence than the wealthy were willing to concede.[10]

Noted counselor/preacher Charles Swindoll commented that although accumulating wealth was not inherently wrong, it was wrong when it was not shared with others; he cited scripture: "Where your treasure is, there your heart will be."[11] Ivan A. Beals of the Church of the Nazarene put it more directly. Although the church had always seen the increase of wealth by a believer as "a sure sign of God's blessing . . . Christians must always choose between the way of the cross and worldly material goods." In blunt terms he stated that the followers of Christ must be willing to make the necessary sacrifices against all enemies including "materialistic capitalism." "Christians who promote business profits at the expense of the destitute choke the message of salvation through Jesus Christ."[12]

Finally, in talking of contemporary evangelical involvement in the larger society, noted evangelical commentator J. I. Packer let fly a stinging indictment of the use of popular norms by American evangelicals who were growing in number but had, in fact, sold out to secular humanist dogma:

Man-centeredness as a way of life, with God there to care for me; preoccupation with wealth, luxury, success, and lots of happy sex as means to my fulfillment; unconcern about self-denial, self-control, truthfulness, and modesty; high tolerance of moral lapses, with readiness to make excuses for ourselves and others in the name of charity; indifference to demands for personal and church discipline; prizing ability above character, and ducking out of personal responsibilities—is any of that Christian? The truth is that we [evangelicals] have met the secular humanist enemy, and ethnically, it is us. Shame on us? Yes, every time.[13]

That blast enveloped a wide variety of evangelicals but did not include them all. Within the ranks, a small but influential set of communities appeared during the 1960s as alternative expressions to the capitalism just described. Known as the Christian or evangelical "Left" these included the Sojourners community of Washington, D.C.; the program surrounding the monthly magazine *The Other Side* in Philadelphia; many within the Mennonite and related traditions; and a few dozen independent communities in both rural and urban areas. They shared the theological convictions of the larger evangelical family. But they chose other options regarding simple life-style, distribution of wealth, care of the oppressed and homeless, full equality for women, and careful avoidance of any ostentation in dress, abode, or other possessions. They were often the target of sharp criticism by mainstream evangelicals, who claimed the "Left" chose to embrace the latest or newest politically liberal causes or fads as they came along. Despite this and their small numbers, their publications, workshops, and persistence gave them a voice of influence and conscience that continues into the present.[14]

Evangelicals, in sum, shared a common dedication to the authority of scripture for economic matters. They differed very widely on how as individuals they should be able to apply the specifics to daily life situations or to claim financial success as proof that God had chosen to reward their efforts. A small but influential group of evangelical leaders in the early 1980s developed what became known as "prosperity theology" or the "health/wealth" school of conservative Protestant expression.[15]

What all evangelicals at the popular level did affirm, however, was the sanctity and blessing of the work ethic. Acknowledging that one could well become too successful by secular standards in earning daily bread, evangelicals stoutly believed God had nonetheless ordered humankind to honor Him by working hard, frugally, and carefully. To provide for one's own and one's community by such diligence has been a major teaching in evangelical religion. Through the popular periodicals, in other print media such as tracts, and through radio and television programming, the faithful are exhorted to do their very best, regardless of what job they hold. One writer asks, "Who, after all, can imagine Jesus turning out shoddy work? The biblical term for carpenter suggests a craftsman. . . . In small towns like Nazareth, there were village craftsmen, handymen who could repair a gate, build useful cabinets, or make a set of tables and chairs. That is the kind of work Jesus did. The drawers of the cabinets ran smoothly, the yokes were square, and the toys were sturdy and safe."[16]

With but few exceptions, the popular evangelical understanding of work requires the serving of God in the world of business. Over the decades writers, businessmen (I know of no evangelical businesswomen who have written on this subject), clergy, and laity have sought to discern just how the Bible teaches them to work effectively on the job. Dozens of such works are available and are considered by experts to be "an established genre of Christian business books . . . each an anecdotal account of Christians in the marketplace." They seek to convince the reader that being a devout believer leads to success in the business world; the proof is found in the many anecdotes given by the author.[17]

One of the most successful of these has been Larry Burkett, author and founder of Christian Financial Concepts (CFC), "the world's largest Christian financial counseling organization."[18] The themes developed there reflect popular religion at its clearest level. "I am not the first businessperson to discover the principles of business taught in God's Word. The use of the Bible as a business text in America goes back hundreds of years."[19] After becoming a Christian in his adult years, Burkett noted, "the one principle that caught my attention most vividly was that God's people should be debt-free." Once scriptural principles are followed, they start to win more converts. "Do the biblical principles of business work? Without question they do—over the long run."

The author notes these principles work for small, one-person business firms as well as for the largest enterprises. His organization moved from an annual budget of forty thousand dollars to over 3 million a year, debt free.[20] To help spread the word, CFC sends over seven thousand counselors to over five hundred seminars on "God's principles of handling money." Where, an observer can ask, would it lead? God had promised that those who obeyed his laws and commandments would receive God's prosperity beyond measure.[21]

Summarized and paraphrased briefly here, Burkett lays down these six principles:

1. Reflect Christ in your business practices
2. Be accountable; set up an accountability group
3. Provide a quality product at a fair price
4. Honor your creditors
5. Treat your employees fairly
6. Treat your customers fairly[22]

A more ebullient expression of market-driven popular religion is that by

James F. Hind, *The Heart and Soul of Effective Management: A Christian Approach to Managing and Motivating People*. Hind uses Christ and his teachings "as a role model—as a manager to emulate and follow." This led him to discover a new set of principles, "ones that breed productivity in people and make for effective management."[23] Hind consciously couched these teachings in the language of the business world. His studies led him to conclude that Jesus produced the most effective business operation of all times. With only a few men in only three years he organized Christianity, and today it has 1.5 billion "proponents and branches in all the world's 223 countries."[24]

Going on, Hind finds that Jesus's "key competitor was Satan, who tried to lure Him away from His Father's business with more lucrative offers." Jesus understood the strategy and countered with his own, locating and delegating his workers in Capernaum close to 100,000 potential workers. There he became "a positive thinker and doer. His words were solution-oriented, not problem-prone." He succeeded also because he was "a 'company man,' who identified the success of his life and mission with his obedience to the Father's will." Finally, Jesus succeeded with his plan to manage the disciples with "tough love." He "challenged and encouraged them to strive after obedience and excellence in carrying out His Kingdom mission. He never let a poor performance go unanswered."[25]

Aware that the risks involved in practices such as these could lead to trivialization of committed discipleship, several evangelicals in the academic world have attempted to lay down biblical principles and insights without the cultural baggage shown by Burkett or Hind. These works have become widely adopted in evangelical colleges in recent years. Their more nuanced and careful analyses point to the inherent tension involved between the academy and the larger evangelical world.[26]

Beyond such books, economic popular religion reached evangelicals through a variety of newsletters, regional seminars, reports, and other media information sources. This became a genre, as evangelicals modeled their specific programs after those of the larger corporate world. Since the 1960s, for instance, there emerged enterprises such as *Spiritual Fitness in Business*, a monthly newsletter that provided commentary, biblical insights, reviews, and information on both economic and social issues. Such included "Success," "Business Ethics," "Women at Work," "Facing Setbacks," and "Temptation," among others. The publication came out for just over seven years when "a hard look at the financial realities of the project" led it to close.[27]

A smaller outreach publication was that of financial adviser James L. Paris, with the *Christian Financial Times* of Sanford, Florida. It offered advice on investment plans, credit repair, and "God's will for your finances."

Another in the 1980s was the Omega Ministries of Medford, Oregon. Announcing that "God loves you, and has a wonderful plan for your bank account," its leader, Jim McKeever, sold for a $19 contribution his strategy materials for following God-honoring financial expansion.[28] In the same general category, the hugely successful Pentecostal/charismatic publishing firm with *Charisma* magazine of Lake Mary, Florida, publishes a monthly trade journal, *Christian Retailing*. It carries a variety of stories, reports, advice, advertising, and bestseller lists.[29]

Among these and others, the place of Christian Financial Concepts stands out with special influence. Founded in the mid-1970s it had by 1988 established some thirty programs to bring biblical principles to the world of finance. It provided training for some 3,000 laity who taught its materials in their local congregations. It successfully drew on the new technology for desktop publishing, filling its printed materials with capsule-size insights and insider information on the state and future of the economy. Its continuing success well illustrates how successfully it has united scripture and flourishing business practices.[30]

Another program, apparently the largest in the evangelical world, has been the Christian Management Institute. It espouses a specific, vigorously evangelical statement of faith as its prologue to its programs. Its corporate clientele comprises something of a who's who among evangelical ministries: the Billy Graham Evangelistic Association, Campus Crusade for Christ, Christian Broadcast Network, Fuller Theological Seminary, InterVarsity Christian Fellowship, The Navigators, Prison Fellowship Ministries, the Salvation Army, World Vision, Young Life, and Youth for Christ, among others. The institute started in 1976 in Los Angeles when some 220 Christian managers met to share their mutual problems and opportunities. Since then it has grown very quickly, having over 2,500 individual members representing 1,600 organizations in the fifty states and six overseas nations. It sponsors local, regional, and national workshops, seminars, retreats, fellowship network opportunities, newsletters, magazines, insurance programs, a savings program, a credit union, a VISA card, and a membership directory.[31]

Closely allied and very much a product of the evangelical resurgence in popular religion has been the appearance and continuance of the "Christian Yellow Pages" (CYP). Prepared for large urban markets, this directory publishes the names of a huge variety of firms who identify with evangelicalism. Perhaps no other single item in the world of business suggests the extent to which evangelicals see themselves as a distinctive subculture. It advises its readership to do selective buying, relying on these pages.

Two Jewish businessmen in Los Angeles, when told they could not advertise in the CYP, sued the publisher. Eventually the case was settled in favor of CYP. Its publisher there, David Llewellyn, explained to the public

**Table 2.1**
**Teachings on Wealth and Faith**

|  | Poverty | Stewardship | Prosperity |
|---|---|---|---|
| View of prosperity | Nonmaterialistic, disdain for possessions | Possessions are a trust given in varying proportions | Prosperity is the reward of the righteous |
| In a word, possessions are: | a curse | a privilege | a right |
| Scriptural reference | Luke 18:22 | Matt. 25:14–30 | Matt. 7:7, 8 |
| Mitigation | Prov. 21:20 In the house of the wise are stores of choice food and oil, but a foolish man devours all he has. | None | Prov. 23:4, 5 Don't wear yourself out to get rich. |
| Needs Met by | "carefree attitude" Don't worry—seek the kingdom first. Matt. 6:25–34 | "faithful administration" 1 Cor. 4:2 | "transaction" Tithe for a blessing. Matt. 3:10 |
| Concept | Rejecter | Steward | Owner |
| Attitude toward Poor | We are the poor. | We care. | We owe. |
| Preoccupation | Daily needs | Wisdom | Money |
| Attitude | Carefree Prov. 3:5, 6 | Faithful Luke 16:10, 11 | Driven Prov. 10:17 |

that its presence was to help born-again Christians establish fellowship in this form with each other. It would also, he stated, insure than an evangelical would be able to learn, by subtraction, that any potential firm he might shop at was not "Christian" and thus to be avoided. Professor Peter W. Williams, a close student of popular religion, commented on the CYP that evangelicalism was demonstrating an ambivalence over whether to " 'infiltrate' or simply to imitate the broader popular culture, while utilizing its techniques of advertising and distribution in all cases."[32]

In a different, practical expression of their faith, evangelicals searched for ways to remain biblically faithful in their personal and immediate family life. Spokespersons offered a vast array of options. Here was popular religion at its most explicit—articles using everyday parlance and imagery to convey deeper truths. Among the dozens of articles reflecting this understanding, an article by Patrick M. Morley sums up, as well as any one statement can, how the many admittedly confusing items about money found in the Bible can help the believer. The author states the Bible contains some 500 verses about prayer, but over 2,350 verses on handling money. What is clear beyond any doubt is Jesus's statement that a believer could not serve both God and money (Matthew 6:24, New International Version translation). There exists no middle ground.

But those thousands of scriptural truths still exist and attract considerable evangelical loyalty. From the Bible, one respected authority teaches, three general perspectives about relating wealth and faith can be discerned. All claim biblical authority, yet only one of the three stands clearly as the most faithful to evangelical understanding.[33] These three are summarized in Table 2.1. Column 1, "Poverty" and Column 3, "Prosperity" fall short of fully embodying the established truths of the born again. The teachings in Column 2, "Stewardship" clearly reflect those truths. Table 2.1 displays these teachings.[34] In sum, mainstream evangelicalism espouses the "stewardship" perspective while acknowledging other believers may hold differing perspectives.

## MERCHANDISE

The question of how "popular" or simplified the Christian witness should be appears also with the matter of explicitly religious merchandise: toys, wearing apparel, furniture, mementos, wristwatches, stamped candy, calendars, greeting cards, lapel pins, posters, coffee mugs—almost anything on which phrases such as "Jesus Saves" or similar short familiar messages can be stamped. Much of the merchandise, known widely among its critics as "Jesus Junk," was aimed at children with items such as "Jeannie, the Believer: The Christian Alternative to Barbie" or a "Christian Charm Course" advertised as a "proven way to reach girls for Christ."[35]

Easy to poke fun at because of their excesses and stereotypical imagery, religious merchandise and games have well suited the long-range goals of evangelicalism. Such products obviously would help teach the young to witness, would extol familiar virtues such as the nuclear family and traditional gender roles and, very important, would furnish reliable alternatives for evangelical parents looking for merchandise other than that which they found to be secularizing their children.

A huge array of programs, clubs, videos, curriculum lessons, and related items attempted to use general models from the larger culture with which the children were familiar: animals, sports heroes, dolls, and games; producers then infused these with explicitly Christian messages and symbols. Some toys were aimed directly at protecting children against what the manufacturer believed were occult practices aimed at converting youth to the side of Satan. For instance, "Spiritual Warfare" and "Dragonraid" were board games explicitly created to counteract the controversial "Dungeons and Dragons."[36] Clearly, popular religion preferences infused in both producers and consumers the desire to find in everyday life the opportunity to hold fast against powerful enemies.

Although widely criticized by many inside and outside of evangelicalism, proponents pointed out that they must be doing something right because such merchandise continued to sell briskly. Of the total estimated annual sales for all evangelical merchandise (including books and other items for adults), it was estimated "Jesus Junk" sold "only a small part of" the $3 billion total. The item most widely sold has been T-shirts with a great variety of Bible verses, slogans, maxims, logos, and similar references. These reflect the influence of visual communication: like television they can be viewed and understood at one glance; they rely on some kind of color or print scheme to attract instant attention; and they serve as a witness to the youth who were not in the evangelical community.[37]

What stood out clearly was the direct clash between the competing priorities and personal religious preferences of those supporting the sale of Jesus merchandise and those who found it in at least poor taste, if not worse. As suggested earlier, evangelicals fully support the market-driven form of entrepreneurial capitalism in the United States. When the Jesus people movement burst out, it carried with it much of what became the glorification of the accoutrements of the psychedelic counterculture, infusing the clothes, hairstyles, and other merchandise with evangelical symbols. Suddenly, with help from television and other mass media, this form of merchandise became big business, and outlet stores were soon glutted with a surplus of inventory. That meant the producers and retailers would have to find new ways to sell the overproduction and compete more vigorously with their competitors to do so.[38] This need led to what seemed to many to be less than Christian forms of business enterprise, such as the use of explicitly religious designs on one's personal bank checks, the introduction of a new sportswear apparel line named "Dunamis," the Greek word for "power," and aimed at "active Christians"—to name only two of the more controversial items.[39]

Caught up in the opportunity to advance one's faith through this form of merchandising, a small but eye-catching series of related programs appeared. Religious magazines such as *Charisma* carried ads for "Regina Royal Jelly," which, a buyer wrote, "gave me energy and stamina and turned my life around!" From Sherman, Texas, came "Allfoodtab" snacks sent out by Believers' Enterprises, Inc., to help weight reduction. A program, "Losing Yet Gaining" from Hazel Park, Michigan, offered a "Diet–Bible Study

Program," which combined in one series a study guide to help in both areas. In *Charisma* magazine a one-third page ad opened with a picture of a beautiful woman saying "Hello, Gorgeous," selling "Vitagenic Eye & Throat" oil based on recipes known to ancient Hebrew women.[40]

None flourished or came to raise the kinds of serious ethical and health questions that, by contrast, were brought up by a diet–weight reduction program calling itself a "Christian counterpart to national weight-watchers problems."[41] Known as "3D" (diet, discipline, and discipleship), this program started up in 1973, growing quickly to having programs in some 5,000 churches by autumn 1981. The leaders publicized many testimonials of satisfied participants, but reporters found a growing number of dissatisfied clients. Mainly the latter objected to "the emphasis . . . on sin and making you feel guilty [as if] that's the way you lose weight." Observers noted the influence of a nearby independent charismatic community, the Community of Jesus, located on Cape Cod. They found in sessions a "preoccupation with sin, especially attitudinal sins like jealousy, rebellion, willfulness, ideology, and haughtiness."[42] The program eventually passed away.

On a deeper level, as Robert Ellwood shows, popular religion was open to such excesses as these because of its openness to experiential validation of its religious instincts. Its practitioners could ignore the sarcastic ridicule of critics talking about its tacky quality, superficial aesthetics, and glorification of the mundane. Believers knew, following the logic of incongruity, that they had not sold out to a "consumer religion" but had involved themselves with such visible, tangible objects because these items were signs and triggers of their religious experiences and thus were self-validating. That is, such items were encapsulated symbols of prior religious experiences and understanding, which could be instantly evoked by seeing specific religious symbols "from childhood, from earlier spiritual stirrings, from the conventional lore of the religion."[43]

The means by which this merchandise was distributed suggests further the extent to which the use of popular religion helped broaden its appeal. Much of the material was sold via a rapidly growing number of catalog distributors. Dozens, if not hundreds, of such enterprises came into the business world during these years, offering quick service, toll-free orders, credit card charging, personal-attention service, and an eclectic variety of items.

A great amount of goods also came from what stood out as virtually a new creation of evangelicalism, the retail outlet, usually located in a shopping mall, that stocked an enormous variety of religious goods offered in a setting complete with religious Muzak. Some of the older mom-and-pop type of religious stores have survived, usually in small towns with little or no direct competition. The newer, more suburban stores have become merchandise marts with tastefully decorated merchandise islands and displays of books, greeting cards, audiocassettes, videocassettes, movies for rent, music scores, religious merchandise such as Jesus junk, pictures for wall hanging, serviettes for the dinner table, seasonal and holiday merchandise, a variety of religious gifts, posters, religious magazines, and the bestseller, the Bible.[44]

The retailers have access to a variety of sources of information to help their sales. Publication empires, such as *Charisma* out of Florida in its bimonthly *Christian Retailing*, offer specific pieces of advice, such as "Ten Deadly Merchandising Mistakes" or "Keeping Your Browsers Happy," that concern lighting, colors, carpet, and music.[45]

Retailers read that they too were offering a ministry. Nick Cavnar, a writer, told them:

After all, most customers of a Christian bookstore have more than price on their minds. They come to you because you offer a service they may not find anywhere else. You provide them a complete selection of Christian books, music, Bibles, Sunday school materials, and gift items to nourish and support their faith. You offer personal service to guide them to the right book or the right gift—and perhaps to offer a word of comfort or prayer or encouragement as well.[46]

What that ministry should focus on specifically, according to religious market research specialist George Barna, are the

key needs with which people are struggling:

personal relationships

the ability to communicate more effectively

finding a sense of purpose for living

understanding religion

gaining a sense of security[47]

Earlier in this chapter we looked at Protestant asceticism as reflecting the believers' understanding of the relationship between wealthy and worldly pleasures on the one hand and the one true faith on the other. What clearly emerged, with great acceleration since about 1960, with the takeoff of mass media technology has been what Martin E. Marty noted:

Being born again and turning the back on the world once meant leaving hedonism behind. Now, as a glance at the airport news stand offerings of the Christian Booksellers Association or at the televised displays of the Christian Broadcasters Associationists make apparent, religion justified self-centered leisure. Not only has the church begun to understand this shift; it is a major legitimator of it, for better or worse, for better and for worse.[48]

## NOTES

1. See James Davison Hunter, *Evangelicalism: The Coming Generation* (Chicago: University of Chicago Press, 1987), pp. 50–56.

2. Differences among evangelical elites regarding economic life are delineated in Craig M. Gay, *With Liberty and Justice for Whom? The Recent Evangelical Debate over Capitalism* (Grand Rapids, Mich.: Eerdmans, 1991).

3. See the review of Gay, *With Liberty*, by Amy L. Sherman in *First Things*, 20 (February 1992): 57–58.

4. J. Lawrence Burkholder, "Popular Evangelicalism: An Appraisal," in Clyde Krause et al., eds., *Evangelicalism and Anabaptism* (Scottdale, Pa.: Herald Press, 1979), pp. 29–30; see the "Books" section of *Christianity Today* for January 16, 1976, pp. 406–8.

5. Edgar Norton, "Is Capitalism Christian?" *Liberty Report*, Liberty University, October 1987, p. 36.

6. Ibid.

7. Ibid.

8. Ibid.

9. See the evaluation from the very citadel of capitalism, *Fortune* magazine, Myron Magnet, "The Money Society," July 6, 1987, pp. 26–31; James Lincoln Collier, *The Rise of Selfishness in America* (New York: Oxford University Press, 1991); Nicholaus Mills, ed., *Culture in an Age of Money: The Legacy of the 1980s in America* (Chicago: Ivan R. Dee, 1990).

10. Phillip Yancey, "The Peculiar Blessings of Poverty," *Christianity Today*, June 16, 1982, p. 72.

11. Charles Swindoll, "Winning the Battle over Greed," *Charisma and Christian Life*, October 1987, pp. 53–57; see the recent critique also in Michael Scott Horton, *Made in America: The Shaping of Modern American Evangelicalism* (Grand Rapids, Mich.: Baker Book House, 1991).

12. Ivan A. Beals, "Christianity's Affair with Capitalism," *Vital Christianity*, October 19, 1980, pp. 253–54.

13. See "From the Senior Editor," *Christianity Today*, October 2, 1987, p. 13.

14. See the Index for "The Other Side" and "Sojourners" in Robert Booth Fowler, *A New Engagement: Evangelical Political Thought, 1966–1976* (Grand Rapids, Mich.: Eerdmans, 1982); David E. Shi, *The Simple Lifestyle: Plain Living and High Thinking in American Culture* (New York: Oxford University Press, 1985).

15. Oral Roberts, *How I Learned Jesus Was Not Poor* (Altamonte Springs, Fla.: Creation House, 1989); Bruce Barron, *The Health and Wealth Gospel* (Downers Grove, Ill.: InterVarsity Press, 1987); Bruce Barron, "Rechristianizing America: The Reconstruction and Kingdom Now Movements in American Evangelical Christianity," Ph.D. dissertation, University of Pittsburgh, 1991 (Ann Arbor, Mich.: University Microfilms, 1991).

16. Bruce Shelley, "Why Work?" *Christianity Today*, July 14, 1989, pp. 20–22; Bruce Shelley, *The Gospel and the American Dream* (Portland, Ore.: Multnomah, 1989), pp. 75–115; Ben Patterson, "Work, Work, Work," *Charisma and Christian Life*, March 1988, pp. 57–58; Donna Day Loeven, "Reworking the Work Ethic," *The Other Side*, June 1983, pp. 10–12; Dennis Haack, *The Rest of Success: What the World Didn't Tell You about Having It All* (Downers Grove, Ill.: InterVarsity Press, 1989); Patrick M. Morley, *The Man in the Mirror: Solving the 24 Problems Men Face* (Brentwood, Tenn.: Wolgemuth and Hyatt, 1989); Hunter, *Evangelicalism*, pp. 154–61.

17. Book Review by Robert A. Case II, *Christianity Today*, May 14, 1990, p. 66.

18. On the dust-jacket blurb, Larry Burkett, *Business by the Book: The Complete Guide*

*of Biblical Principles for Business Men and Women* (Nashville, Tenn.: Thomas Nelson, 1990); Bob Chuvala, "Larry Burkett: From Rags to (Real) Riches," *Christian Herald*, March/April 1992, pp. 51–53.

19. Burkett, *Business*, p. 11.

20. Ibid., pp. 12–14.

21. Ibid., p. 15.

22. Ibid., pp. 16–26; Burkett's major book, *The Coming Economic Earthquake* (Chicago: Moody, 1992) was not available before this study was completed. Moody reported that in 1991 it did some $2 million in business with Burkett titles; "Spring Religious" column, *Publishers Weekly*, February 10, 1992, p. 31.

23. James F. Hind, *The Heart and Soul of Effective Management* (Wheaton, Ill.: Victor Books, 1989), p. 13.

24. Ibid., p. 14.

25. Ibid., pp. 35, 36, 50, 116.

26. Richard C. Chewing et al., eds., *Business through the Eyes of Faith* (San Francisco: Harper and Row, 1990); William W. Wells, *The Agony of Affluence* (Grand Rapids, Mich.: Zondervan Cantilever Books, 1989); Richard Chewing, ed., *Biblical Principles and Business: The Foundations* (Colorado Springs, Colo.: Nav Press, 1989).

27. *Spiritual Fitness in Business*, a newsletter from Probe Ministries, Inc., Richardson, Texas; February 1991, p. 24.

28. News story, *Christian Life*, March 1986, p. 11; news story, *Religious Broadcasting*, March 1988, p. 24; similar groups are Christian Business Men's Committee of USA, P.O. Box 3308, 1800 McCallie Ave., Chattanooga, TN 37404; Sherf Publications, Inc., P.O. Box 1089, Bel Air, MD 21014-7089; Personal Christianity, P.O. Box 549, Baldwin Park, CA 91706.

29. The address for *Charisma* is 600 Rinehart Road, Lake Mary, FL 32746.

30. The documentation here is in materials cited in notes 22 and 28; *Publishers Weekly*, February 10, 1992, p. 31; *Religious Broadcasting*, March 1988, p. 24.

31. Christian Ministries Management Institute, P.O. Box 4638, Diamond Bar, CA 91705.

32. Peter W. Williams, *Popular Religion in America*, Rev. ed. (Urbana: University of Illinois Press, Illini Books Edition, 1990), p. 193 n.181.

33. Patrick M. Morley, "The Gospel Truth about Money," *Charisma and Christian Life*, October 1988, pp. 64–69, especially pp. 67–68.

34. Ibid.; see the *Christianity Today* multitopic issue for May 12, 1989, pp. 27–40, entitled "The New Testament and Wealth"; major evangelical magazines such as *Today's Christian Woman* frequently carry stories such as Ron Blue, "Managing Your Money God's Way," 8, 6 (November/December 1986): 50–51; and advice in an omnibus column, "Super Guide" on related topics, including insurance, banking, borrowing money, and the like; see *Christian Woman*, 6, 1 (March/April 1984): 63–74.

35. Advertising, *Christianity Today*, November 8, 1974, p. 152; news story, *The Wittenburg Door*, 79 (1979): 6–7; Quentin J. Schultze, *Televangelism and American Culture: The Business of Popular Religion* (Grand Rapids, Mich.: Baker Book House, 1991), pp. 163–66.

36. David Porter, *Children at Risk: The Growing Threat of Bizarre Toys, Fantasy Games, TV, Movies, and Illicit Drugs* (Westchester, Ill.: Crossway Books, 1990); ads in *Liberty Report*, October 1987, p. 29; the magazine *Rainbows: The Magazine for Christian Children*, Tulsa, Okla.; news story, *Minneapolis Star Tribune*, February 4, 1988, p. 2A; the catalog of Praise Unlimited, Sarasota, Fla.

37. News story, *Cornerstone*, 9, 52, n.d., pp. 12–15 (*Cornerstone* does not date its issues); news story, *Christian Herald*, February 1985, p. 57; ad, *Charisma and Christian*

*Life*, October 1987, p. 2; evangelically inspired games are on Nintendo; *Christianity Today*, July 22, 1991, p. 1; ad for teen games in *Charisma and Christian Life*, October 1987, n.p.; news story, "Toys with Christian Values," *Fundamentalist Journal*, November 1987, p. 48; news story, *Minneapolis Star Tribune*, February 4, 1988, p. 3A.

38. News story, *Christianity Today*, January 2, 1981, p. 59; news story, *St. Paul Pioneer Press*, October 28, 1990, p. 5B; news story, *Christian Retailing*, April 15, 1989, p. 26; news story, *National Christian Reporter*, August 3, 1990, p. 4; see David Hazard, "Holy Hype! Marketing the Gospel in the 80s," *Eternity*, December 1985, pp. 32–41; Carol Flake, *Redemptorama* (Garden City, N.Y.: Doubleday, 1984), p. 159; Jon Johnston, *Will Evangelicalism Survive Its Own Success?* (Grand Rapids, Mich.: Zondervan, 1989), pp. 116–19.

39. News story, *Christian Herald*, November/December 1990, p. 51; the catalog of Dunamis, Woburn, Mass., in its advertising very closely resembles that of the apparel company Banana Republic; news story, *Christian Retailing*, May 15, 1989, p. 34; "Memo," Martin E. Marty, *Christian Century*, December 17, 1986, p. 1159; almost all of the issues of the *Wittenburg Door* after 1980 carry material on this general subject; see the evangelical merchandise catalog of Direct Access, Tulsa, Okla.

40. News story, *Charisma and Christian Life*, November 1990, p. 15; ibid., December 1990, p. 96; news story, *Christian Herald*, July/August 1987, p. 55; news story, *Christian Herald*, March 1987, pp. 60–61.

41. I follow here closely the reportage of Ron Enroth, "All Isn't Well in the Popular Christian Diet Program," *Christianity Today*, April 9, 1982, pp. 54–58.

42. Ibid., p. 57.

43. Robert Ellwood, *The History and Future of Faith: Religion Past, Present, and to Come* (New York: Crossroad, 1988), pp. 125–30; John Boonstra, "Mass Culture vs Popular Culture: Battle for Control of Everyday Life," *Radical Religion*, 3, 4 (June 1978): 15.

44. See Alice Chapin, *The Big Book of Great Gift Ideas* (Wheaton, Ill.: Tyndale House, 1991); Carol Ward, *The Christian Sourcebook: A Comprehensive Guide to All Things Christian*, rev. ed. (New York: Ballantine Books, 1989), pp. 53–67 on gift giving; Wayne Elzey, "Popular Culture," in Charles H. Lippy and Peter W. Williams, *Encyclopedia of the American Religious Experience*, vol. 3 (New York: Scribners, 1988), pp. 1730–35; Judith S. Duke, *Religious Publishing and Communications* (White Plains, N.Y.: Knowledge Industry Publications, 1981), pp. 134–47 on bookstores; Robert Walker, "Boom in Church Bookstores," *Christian Life*, January 1974, pp. 64–65; ad, *Virtue*, November/December 1990, p. 14; "Commentary," a column by John R. Olson in *Eternity*, December 1985, p. 56; Dale Goldsmith, "The Christian Bookstore: Caveat Emptor," *Quarterly Review*, Fall 1986, pp. 29–31; Will Norton, Jr., "Bookstores Grow Up," *Moody Monthly*, November 1971, pp. 32–33, 51.

45. *Christian Retailing*, June 1, 1989, pp. 15–17.

46. *Christian Retailing*, October 15, 1989, p. 11.

47. George Barna, commentary, in *Christian Retailing*, September 15, 1988, p. 14.

48. Martin E. Marty, "How the Church Has Changed in the Last Ten Years," *The Christian Ministry*, November 1979, p. 3.

# 3

# Popular Religion and the Self: Evangelical Options

From the perspective of time, those who follow the evangelical expression of faith find startling alterations in both behavior and content occurring within the fold shortly after the end of World War II. These are well summarized by a prominent pastor, Warren Wiersbe, with his copastor and son David in a question-and-answer article in *Leadership* magazine.

Interviewer: Why did people come to church in the fifties, and why do they come in 1990?

Warren: In the fifties they came because they were loyal. This was their church, so they were present on Sunday morning, Sunday evening, and Wednesday night. We would bring in an evangelist for two weeks, and we could guarantee a good crowd every night. Today, you can hardly get people out twice a weekend.

In the sixties, many people came to church because they were scared. The world was changing rapidly. Every value they held dear was threatened. They were puzzled about what was happening to young people.

In the relational seventies and eighties, people came to church because they needed a caring network. They hurt. Everybody I talk to carries some pain. Woe to that church that doesn't recognize people's need.[1]

Whereas a few decades earlier, doctrinal and familiar ethical questions dominated the pulpit topics, by 1990, David mentioned, "we have to talk about certain things; sexuality, abuse of various forms, alcoholism, suicide. Also, there is the issue of self-esteem. Who had heard of self-esteem thirty years ago?"[2]

In those earlier decades, the trackers discovered, American believers in all of the major religious groupings redefined the self and found in new ways that their faith had a great deal to do with their inner emotional and spiritual lives. With the onset of psychology in its many forms as both alternative to and supplement to familiar scriptural teachings, rank-and-file believers over these decades slowly moved into a mode of religious expression best described (by John F. Wilson here) as "privatization"; precepts "that maximize self-realization and personal growth and reward primary relationships" where "divine commandments are transformed into instrumental strategies for achieving personal satisfaction." This transformation was indeed something new in Christendom.[3]

Leaving behind their once-cherished posture as "fightin' fundies" ready to rebuff internal kinds of problems with scriptural quotes, evangelicals have come to accept, as one of several inner mental worlds, a course that helps greatly to hold back the forces of secularization in their lives. They insist through the logic of incongruity that there is one true faith which they must uphold in their lives.[4] Most have moved to embrace an outlook harmonious with much of the research from the expanding fields of psychology, accepting the fact that as human beings they have certain needs that can be met largely by cultivating such traits as joy, wholeness, health, and, for some, wealth.[5] For example, fewer sermons were being preached on hell, on the old Calvinistic teaching of total depravity, or on original sin.

Obviously not the concern only of evangelicals, this redirection of privatized, relational faith is largely a phenomenon that does not compete with the structured religious organizations. But it achieved its acceptance because it could "speak directly to the perceived religious needs and sensibilities of individuals, whatever their formal religious affiliation might be."[6] Religious faith has always been a unique (and highly personalized) blending of doctrine and teaching, ethics and morals, liturgy and sacrament, community and outreach, and in historical terms, "the care of the soul." It was this latter feature that came into such prominence in these years.

What quickly became apparent to laity and leaders alike was that the influx of such practices and ideas offered a very serious challenge to the belief that the inerrant Bible alone contained all the answers that God had chosen to reveal to humankind for dealing with their earthly struggles. Also much nonevangelical psychotherapy centered on working for healing with the seeker in a way that enhanced interpersonal relationships or personal development but seemed to glorify the pragmatic method of "whatever works for you" rather than obedience to fixed religious norms. Could the goals of therapy such as self-fulfillment, self-actualization, or self-improvement harmonize with the scriptural admonition that Christians should concern themselves with whatever is true, honorable, just, pure, lovely, and gracious? Might not the new relational emphasis lead people to become preoccupied with just themselves or their immediate relationships at the expense of winning the world for Christ? Might not they be more interested in building a pleasant personality than in developing a virtuous character?[7]

Substantial evidence suggested that by the mid-1980s some of these dangers had come into clear view among evangelicals. As explored by sociologist James Davison Hunter in 1983, statistical evidence indicates that a plethora of evangelical popular religion books had emerged, starting in the 1960s, and continued to proliferate. This clearly demonstrated a rapid growth in acceptance of the new outlook by the readers. Looking at the subjects of the books from the eight leading evangelical publishing houses appearing in the 1960s and 1970s, Hunter found that the record shows the totals given in Table 3.1.[8]

Within the evangelical world of academic scholarship, the growth of such interest both won considerable praise and attracted substantial doubt from the research specialists. In the popular journals an ever-increasing number of articles on problems of the self continued to appear.[9]

This tension turned up also among the laity, some of whom made their contributions to the debate. A homemaker, pastor's wife, and mother of five, Joan L. Jacobs, in 1974 offered a representative viewpoint in a plea for troubled evangelicals to see counselors who shared their faith. Recognizing that believers were called on to "be holy and blameless before Him," evangelicals, the author wrote, faced issues that blocked personal growth despite prayer, Bible study, worship, and fellowship. Often the battle was not, as the older tradition had taught, a clear-cut struggle against Satan or the world or the flesh "but the despairing conflict with an unknown enemy." The call of the Bible to love God "falls on deaf ears."[10]

With Jacobs the dilemma came when she and her husband could not agree on how to raise the children. She found resources to resolve the problem

**Table 3.1**
**Subjects of Evangelical Books**

| | |
|---|---|
| Emotional/psychological problems | 27.4 percent |
| Traditional theodicy | 12.2 percent |
| Emotional/psychological balance | 32.5 percent |
| Hedonism/narcissism | 27.9 percent |

through counseling with a like-minded evangelical specialist. She called on others to consider that same option, recognizing the danger of becoming in therapy obsessed with one's inner world at the expense of concern for others at home and globally.[11]

Up to the present day the issues of these two decades have continued to divide evangelicals. Over the years since World War II at least four major areas of controversy have continued to keep evangelicals searching for answers based on their priorities of faith and agenda for witnessing. With customary ironic overlapping, these are (1) the extent to which secular wisdom and saving biblical truths can be intertwined, (2) the potential for both good and bad results from the general field of psychotherapeutic counseling, (3) the opportunities for ministry in the field of healing and holistic faith, and (4) the ways in which the everyday lives and everyday problems of believers can be ministered to through the use of appropriate popular religious teachings.

On the first issue, gradually the larger evangelical community (with certain exceptions) has come to accept the blending of biblical truth and psychological insight. A few vocal critics continue to condemn all such efforts, but by the early 1990s their numbers attracted little attention.[12] The issue is not whether to make efforts to blend these sources, but what the results should be.

What continues both to attract and to befuddle those understanding the issues at the popular level is just how far they can extend the idea that God's saving truths can be uncovered by humans without explicit scriptural warranty. What of the possibilities of new and attractive therapies emerging, as they do, leading to a diminishing belief in the revealed, inerrant Bible? An influential writer, Professor Gary Collins, asks: "How do we respond to teachings about self-help, psychology, politics, education, health habits, and 'holistic healing' when the specific matter is not mentioned in the Bible and when most of us are not expert enough to distinguish the good points from the bad?"[13]

The very diversity and vigorous pride the entire evangelical community takes in its self-identification precludes reaching any one overarching consensus on the matter of scriptural authority. Evangelical scholars continue to contend with great dedication such biblical issues as the authenticity and authority of the books of the Bible and their internal and external consistency with each other and with the findings of secular scholarship. Such issues, of concern to evangelicals who embrace popular religion, are left to the specialists in scripture.

The matter of reconciling the Bible and contemporary psychology, however, is faced, if not permanently solved, by holding to the efficacy of one's born-again or second-baptism experience. From there, Elise Chase writes, regarding the absorption of the new psychological insights, one moves on to accept from the popularizer writers "behavioral and attitudinal guidelines for daily living, frequently taken from Paul's epistles to the early churches." In her research into the subject, giving it the title *Healing Faith*, Chase discovered that for some evangelicals this blending leads to a kind of "legalism," developing from these books of the Bible specific lists of behavioral dos and don'ts. At the same time, these new books, vastly popular among evangelical readers, teach them to be somewhat distrustful of "deeper, more intimate personal feelings," calling on the seeker to understand them as forces to be "mastered and controlled rather than explored in growing toward integration and understanding."[14]

Among other evangelicals, different forms of integration were being explored. In Columbia, Maryland, Walden Howard established a community, "Faith at Work," growing out of the earlier national parachurch program "Young Life." Asked directly about the issue of the authority of the Bible and the new therapies, he replied that he had developed a strategy of "triangulation": the first part being his own experience, the second being the Bible, the third being the local community. The members searched the scriptures for understanding together; "we take the Scripture each Sunday and we really come at it in practical ways. We role play it, move around, act it out."[15]

Always there lingered the suspicion by the rank and file that some of these new therapies might in essence contradict or undermine basic Christian truth.[16] With the immense popularity of advice giving on daily life such as raising children, marital strain, everyday stress, sexual feelings, all popularized immensely by daily newspaper columns and television talk shows, evangelicals turned to what became a new genre of spokespersons for the cause—media celebrities who understood both the new therapies and the deep religious feelings of their audiences.

Utilizing the advanced high technology available for communications, superstars such as Dr. James Dobson and the Reverend Chuck Swindoll and author Joyce Lansdorf, working outside any rigid denominational identification, became trusted interpreters of the ways in which secular wisdom and God's saving truths were one.[17] The first two had their own nationally syndicated radio programs, periodical newsletters, and audio and video cassettes and were widely popular speakers at national and regional conferences such as the Christian Booksellers Association and the National Religious Broadcasters' conferences. Lansdorf reached large numbers with her frequent books, articles, and lecture/workshop seminars.

In essence, they came to embody the most attractive features of the whole movement: nondenominational, populist, down to earth, yet rooted in the convictions of modern-day evangelicalism. Within that large framework, other individuals came to occupy positions of great influence for the rank and file within their respective traditions, including such leaders as Kenneth E. Hagin, Kenneth Copeland, Larry Lea, and John Wimber.[18]

## HEALING MINISTRY

What started to unfold in the 1970s and directly affected popular religion was the appearance within the larger community of a new emphasis on what was variously called "alternative medicine," "holistic medicine," and a catch-all term, "healing." Along with the boom in various popular therapeutic movements came a rapid increase in interest among evangelicals in health and healing issues. As evidence, *Publishers Weekly* continues to run theme issues devoted to the continuing growth potential for sales in this field. Such advice turns up in programs such as that of the Psychotherapy Book Club of Northvale, New Jersey, which offered, along with a monthly newsletter, a variety of titles in standard book club format covering the full range of healing, counseling, and the like.

Among therapeutic alternatives, the best known were Transactional Analysis, Gestalt Therapy, various body therapies such as Ida Rolf's Structural Integration, several human potential programs such as EST, William Glasser's Reality Therapy, and various therapies in art, dance, exercise, hypnosis, relaxation, biofeedback, and more. For the same general reasons, public interest in alternative and supplemental medical programs increased at great speed. Not simply a rejection of scientific medicine as practiced by the licensed physicians of the United States, holistic teachings argued that religious faith had a very important part in healing and in the general field of health. Each person involved with a client or patient has a specific role, including the physician, the psychologist, and the minister, because "God is a partner in the healing process. . .who helps make sure 'the spiritual dimensions' " are given adequate attention. It became a matter of cooperation between medicine and pastoral counseling.[19]

Alongside this came the rapid growth of Pentecostal and charismatic involvement in faith healing (a term many practitioners do not like but for which they have provided no adequate alternative). Long a part of the Pentecostal tradition, faith healing caught on because, as David Harrell suggests, for many poor Americans it was "the only readily available source of healing and health." In the 1970s and 1980s, it continued to be widely accepted there, along with increased popularity on certain television programs such as that led by Benny Hinn. Its classic pattern of expressions, as evidenced in services by such leaders as Oral Roberts, however, achieved very little acceptance within evangelical/fundamentalist circles.[20]

What apparently helped open those seekers to some aspects of the holistic/

therapeutic movement was both a reappraisal of long-held convictions about ultimate reality and a predictable response to the new influence of the mass media. On the first matter, Christopher Lasch suggests that the new advances in medical research and practices, along with a rise in the standard of living, led to the conclusion that "suffering plays no useful or necessary part in normal life; a tendency to define normal life precisely as the absence of suffering; even a willingness to insist that suffering has no right to exist." Americans, including evangelicals, came to believe that adversity could be harnessed by human control, thus weakening if not eliminating hardships long considered inevitable.[21]

The trend toward openness to mass media healing is explained plausibly by Professor Roger Lundin of Wheaton College, Wheaton, Illinois. Talking of a process he calls "evangelical culture-lag," he refers to the "evangelical habit of adopting the practices of 'secular' American culture soon after these have become established in, and thus made safe by, the society as a whole."[22] Thus by 1991 a major evangelical publishing house, Thomas Nelson, could bring out a major book, *The Better Life Institute Family Health Plan*, billed as "the FIRST comprehensive Family Diet, Exercise, and Health Plan for Body, Mind, and Spirit," with menus, recipes, exercises, health tips, testimonials by star professional athletes and coaches, and advice from positive-thinking preachers such as Robert Schuller and motivator Zig Zigler.[23]

Recognizing that such a movement, in all its complexity, has been unfolding, evangelical opinion shapers have been attempting to bring some measure of understanding to this expression of faith. That is, given the existence of the cultural-lag, me-too response, given the fact that the new therapies clearly lack a rootage in earlier evangelical language based fully on scripture, and given the reliance on learning these teachings through high tech mass media, evangelicals respond through the logic of incongruity with a "why not" reply. Why is it so hard for God to be working through such forms and styles; why should not God be understood as residing "in the logical affinities one dimension of sensible experience has with another"? What is at work, perhaps, is nothing less than modernizing the Kingdom of God.[24]

In more specific terms researchers have discovered that the rank and file among evangelicals respond in a variety of forms, perhaps the most important being small, informal support groups, largely evangelical and charismatic, exploring the many ways in which healing and holistic health can occur. Not attempting to substitute such experience for established medical practice, they meet for a variety of purposes and express their faith in a variety of ways. Perhaps the most widespread form is one that includes prayer, both silent and group oriented, in response to specific needs expressed to the group or from knowledge by members that a particular friend or family is in need of support.[25]

Such meetings also include voluntary testifying by members as to events occurring since the last meeting, about ways in which the member understood God was working healing in her or his life, and in expressions of continuing faith. Finally, many groups continue an ancient practice of laying on hands in a devotional manner as a means of expressing care and love for those in need, suggesting that through the hands the healing power of the Holy Spirit may be known, and making tactile the recipient's empowering to cope with future challenges.[26]

Across the country such practices receive support in a variety of settings, not only in evangelical but also in mainline and Roman Catholic circles. At times, some groups include all three. In small group meetings certain Pentecostal and charismatic worship forms appear, such as speaking and interpreting tongues. Such expressions tend to redefine traditional denominational lines rather clearly. In the Upper Midwest states a movement of "stunning proportions" involves such believers, who reach out to friends "to deepen their faith journeys."[27] A reporter found thousands of seekers meeting regularly for such growth opportunities. The fact that it was a ministry of the laity (and not of the ordained clergy) is an important ingredient, clearly in the heritage of the evangelical populist past.

At the same time this movement grows, reports from the organized, licensed mental health and counseling worlds indicate growing dissatisfaction; as a result of such alternatives, fewer clients are showing up for care from such professionals. Some of the decline, a *New York Times* story reported, is due to increasing costs created by the escalating costs from the new health maintenance programs. Also, psychiatrists and clinical psychologists are continuing their long-standing dispute over proper therapy, a controversy disillusioning to prospective clients, but also encouraged by a growing realization that more-direct and immediate benefits are obtained by many through the volunteer support group.[28]

In sum, the evangelical acceptance of the new therapeutic/wellness movement has demonstrated its willingness to keep abreast of certain secular trends, its concern to stay faithful to scriptural teachings, and its adaptability to the populist, high technology tenor of popular religion. Trackers may want more precision here in counting the number of persons involved and in finding documentable patterns. They may be able to do so when two other phases of the larger movement are seen, the huge popularity of both lay and clerical counseling, including "the 12-step movement," and the use of biblically inspired self-help therapy and advice for everyday living, the final two themes of this chapter.

## COUNSELING

The new psychological emphasis created several dilemmas for rank-and-file believers regarding the traditional pastoral role of counselor. There was the issue of which form of therapy should be pursued; *Christianity Today* in its 1988 issue on counseling outlined eight definably different approaches.[29] Now too believers, both lay and clerical, wondered whether or not involvement in such activity would really be worth the effort.

A pastor-writer, Eugene H. Peterson, stated the case directly, shedding light on how laity perceive the role of the minister. That role is often so frustratingly "invisible" compared to the work of, say, a carpenter. Counseling meant being involved with relieving anxiety, giving comfort, and confronting often immensely complicated problems.

Most of the people we deal with are dominated by a sense of self, not a sense of God. Insofar as we deal with their primary concern—the counseling, instructing, encouraging—they give us good marks in our *jobs* as pastors. Whether we deal with God or not, they don't much care. Flannery O'Connor describes one pastor in such circumstances as one part minister and three parts masseur.

It is very difficult to do one thing when most of the people around us are asking us to do something quite different, especially when these people are nice, intelligent, treat us with respect, and pay our salaries. We get up each morning and the telephone rings, people meet us, letters are addressed to us—often at a tempo of bewildering urgency. All of these calls and people and letters are from people who are asking us to do something for them, quite apart from any belief in God. That is, they come to us not because they are looking for God but because they are looking for a recommendation, or good advice, or an opportunity, and they vaguely suppose we might be qualified to give it to them.[30]

Peterson suggests that many people, including some pastors, believe that pastoral work is "mostly a matter of putting plastic flowers in people's drab lives—well-intentioned attempts to brighten a bad scene, not totally without use, but not real in any substantive or living sense." Another evangelical commented that people coming in for counsel often did not listen or understand, or attempt to try significantly to change their lives.[31]

Much of the confusion and tension exists because of the differences laity and pastors perceive in the uses of religious language, which rest on deeper issues, focusing on the Bible. It comes to people of faith through and in the languages of specific cultures. Those languages, obviously, were not scientific, as one commentator puts it, "but popular; the words were those of the common people. . . . The Bible thus has no comprehensive theory of psychotherapy or personality." As is true with the collision in recent years between secular therapies and evangelical interest in healing, so, too, the current jargon of psychotherapy has come into direct conflict with traditional biblical language with all its sense of transcendence and authority. It is a fair question whether the meaning of the scriptures undergoes some direct change, thereby losing some authority, when it is translated for laity understanding by specialists into the language of psychotherapy.[32]

For those asking such a question, the scriptures have some responses. From the Old Testament lament psalms comes a deep understanding of grief; from its wisdom literature, especially Proverbs, comes insight about premarital questions; and the parables in the Sermon on the Mount are understandable as counseling teachings for husband and wife.[33]

In another mode, Paul Pruyser has provided a framework for identifying biblical themes in psychotherapeutic language that blends teachings such as awareness of the holy, providence, faith, grace, repentance, communion, and sense of vocation with the words of the counselor. So too, Rev. Vernon Bittner has provided scriptural warranty for the twelve steps of recovery utilized by Alcoholics Anonymous (AA).[34]

It is in the area of recovery that an enormous growth of evangelical interest has occurred in recent years in the popular religion expression of counseling and rehabilitation. The issue of recovery from addiction stands as a vivid example of the interplay of the forces of religious faith at the center of this book. Thus they warrant extended discussion. Starting in the late 1980s, "a rage for recovery," as *Publishers Weekly* calls it, became strongly influential in counseling, support group, and psychotherapy circles. The new jargon word was "Twelve-Step" based on the AA program, the program being pursued by an estimated 15 million Americans in 500,000 recovery groups, with 100 million Americans related in one or another way to someone with addictive behavior.

Founded in 1935 the twelve-step system for alcoholics led to spinoffs for other forms of compulsive addiction. The takeoff of interest was not due to any sudden increase in alcoholism or other substance abuse but to a belief that somehow an established, respected program such as this, repackaged now in new language and expanded in scope, could help stem addictive behavior.[35]

The movement found a ready acceptance within evangelical bookstores and support programs. Recovery titles became the bestsellers at the Zondervan's 125 bookstores, outselling "religious fiction" and "oil-slicked Armageddon books" (meaning the war with Iraq and the End Times).

The union of the twelve-step program and evangelical faith occurred at the step in which the client acknowledges the presence and activity in her or his life of a "Higher Power" or "God as we understand Him."[36] This blend was a triumph for those therapists and seekers who came at their situation with a belief in a personal, loving God as espoused in Christian teaching. It also refuted some other evangelical critics who were suggesting that the whole twelve-step program had something of a New Age religion aura to it. More difficult to overcome was the conviction held by some evangelicals that addiction, in this case alcoholism, clearly must be understood as a sin, a moral defect, and thus not as any kind of spiritual, mental, or physical disease. Were it the latter, these critics argued, it would relieve the client from facing the stark reality that he or she had chosen to start drinking and must accept the responsibility for that choice rather than pass off the addiction as an affliction, like an infection, that was not a moral responsibility. In a brief summary, evangelical counselor Gary R. Collins concluded, "Today I'm less likely to criticize people like those who staggered home from Murphy's Tavern. Their drunkenness is sinful—but God forgives those who confess sin. Their alcoholism is a physical addiction, but that can be treated if they are willing to get help."[37]

The twelve-step program becomes something of a major breakthrough, even a transformation, in evangelical popular religion because it acknowledges that the born-again conversion experience and subsequent growth in holiness (the theological term is "sanctification") is no guarantee of improved, faith-inspired moral living. The editors of *Christianity Today* wrote, in launching a major theme issue on "Getting Free," "For many believers, 'Just trust in Jesus' has not been completely effective advice."[38]

The traditional understanding that the power of conversion is able to turn around the sincere seeker's life now becomes to its adherents the indispensable first step, but other kinds of support such as recovery programs flourishing in the secular world become indispensable also. Within church-related counseling programs, the twelve steps are reworded to make clear explicitly how powerful God's activity can become for the seeker. In that system "God's gift of salvation," an explicit Christian doctrine, stands as the first teaching; the second, equally orthodox, acknowledges the power of the Holy Spirit to "transform weaknesses into strengths." The believer then turns her or his life over to Christ, acknowledging that she or he has sinned and asking for transformation by Christ's power.[39]

The popular dimension comes into focus here because the recovery programs within evangelicalism rest on the personal decision of each client to accept responsibility without having to answer to any intermediate church-related official. It is popular in its foundations because it is oriented toward problem solving on an experiential more than an intellectual basis, acknowledging the power of unknown but strong powers in one's life, powers that cannot be controlled by rational, tradition-oriented answers.

Still, among popular religion watchers, such writers as Kenneth A. Myers wonder if the movement isn't too popular, oversimplified, too trendy. Myers writes that a term like "codependency" or "self-esteem" comes along and suddenly evangelicals and others discover they have that condition in their lives. Most important, these new converts are simply too self-centered. Once the client becomes proficient in using the steps, she or he becomes a "*technician* of the inner life," a reductionist standing apart from full dependence on the objective (already completed) redemptive work of Christ.[40]

Perhaps the most popular way of overcoming such fears is the work being done by writers and counselors such as Melody Beattie, Dale Ryan, and J. Keith Miller. In their own way they have become something close to celebrity stars such as Swindoll and Dobson. Willing to accept the situation that "There's enormous denial in the evangelical community about the need for recovery ministries," Ryan cites the steady growth of counseling centers, in a sense parachurch organizations dedicated to recovery.

Miller has developed a very loyal following in those same circles over the years for his writings, seminars, and counseling on major issues facing the believer in the pew. Since telling of his 1956 commitment and conversion experience, Miller has gone on to write ten more books on relationships, personal issues, and the life of faith. Still, he created a considerable stir in 1987 with his book *Sin: Overcoming the Ultimate Addiction*. It focused on the twelve-step programs and how he redefined sin to be an addiction, with the attendant behavior understood by compulsion, denial, and self-destruction.[41]

In 1991 Miller brought out a sequel, *Hunger for Healing: The Twelve Steps as a Classic Model for Christian Spiritual Growth*. This book went beyond earlier blendings of Christian teaching and twelve-step ideology by suggesting that the general twelve-step undertaking was much like the outreach of the first church in New Testament times: without a paid leader, without funds, without buildings, and without an organized missionary program. Thus he links the popular outreach of the expanding church to its nonhierarchical character and finds much the same in the history of AA and twelve-step therapy for commendation.[42]

Obviously the various psychotherapeutic ministries and the controversies over them and their teachings are still very much alive in evangelical circles today, precluding any opportunity to make a balanced evaluation.[43] What seems most appropriate to note here is that the critics have not produced an alternative therapy with a proven track record. The problem is that we can rarely know that a recovery or healing occurred because of this or that particular program, contrasted to one or more alternatives. The new Christian–AA alliance, to take the most talked-about current program, may enjoy success for a number of reasons; its adherents are convinced it is based on their understanding of the scriptures and of human nature. Whatever the outcome of the controversy, at least a sizeable segment of the evangelical community reaches out with popular religious understanding to deal with a mammoth social crisis of the day.

## SELF-HELP

That same understanding also dominates what we designate as our fourth topic within this chapter: scriptural/psychotherapeutic help for everyday problems, including the hard to define but ever present self-help movement. Here popular religious expression flourishes far from the specialist language, laboratory research, theoretical sophistication, and erudition of the experts. The keys to its popularity are its practicality, simplicity of understanding, and sense of being immediately relevant to personal and social needs. Anecdotal evidence suggests that these programs do best when they are led by laity and energized with spontaneity, vitality, and flexibility, rather than when they are informed and directed by recognized church leaders.

The forms for self-help religion are hard to categorize in any pattern for the tracker. Some are simply individuals with specific needs finding books or other media materials dealing with a matter of concern. A widespread social expression is the support groups that by their nature are well suited for religiously minded individuals. They are informal, sometimes regularly scheduled "for the direct purpose of caring, listening, and sharing." There the matters are not theological or concerns about liturgy or worship. The programs find ready acceptance among evangelicals and others because the participants are involved in one or more of these activities: showing love and care for others, helping to carry others' burdens, socializing on an egalitarian basis with each other, and meeting specific individual needs on a somewhat pragmatic basis.[44]

Such self-help activities have in one or more ways been a part of congregational and informal church life since its inception in this country. They came into their own shortly after World War II with the enormous proliferation of mass media carrying the sought-after messages to the growing population of listeners and viewers. At times they seemed (and seem) to be rephrased principles used in the American business world of sales, motivation, and self-understanding. Indeed, two major voices in American religious life, Norman Vincent Peale and Robert Schuller, explicitly make that connection.[45]

For example, two students of this form of popular religion find a significant connection between the American business penchant for technology and religious expression; they call it "spiritual technology." These include, in classic self-help form, several specific components: an instrumental attitude toward religion, an accompanying stress on technique, and a "magicalization of spiritual notions or principles." Little in self-help teachings gives much attention to other major religious themes such as self-introspection over one's sins, the meaning of suffering, and the demands of conscience. Those kinds of issues belong to another realm of religious understanding. That is, if religious faith is going to have meaning for believers, it should show them how to manage and endure their daily problems, offer solace when that is appropriate, and provide comfort in both the spiritual and material sense of that world. Americans, including evangelicals today, draw from a heritage here that emphasizes that believers should pray correctly, even scientifically, by using proven and tested methods, trusting that God hears and answers sincere prayers and will respond accordingly.[46]

Although often deplored by the evangelical academic world, this form of popular religion has received enormous promotion from the famous religious broadcaster Robert Schuller at his Crystal Cathedral in Anaheim, California, on his weekly "Hour of Power" program. Not in any programmatic way a part of the other televangelist movement, Schuller and his imitators concentrate on using proven techniques, books and other media, and small-group arrangements to help people help themselves.

Among evangelical readers, the most noticeable difference in acceptance of this form of popular religion is the enormous ongoing market for books of this genre. The trend-setting journal of the entire movement, *Christianity Today*, started in the 1970s to publish annual roundups with brief reviews of the new offerings. Entitled "More Psychological Insights," the stories made brief, largely informational summaries (as opposed to critical analyses) of self-help books for evangelicals.[47] Seekers reading the widely distributed *The Born Again Christian Catalog* (1979) are referred to works by such authors as Jay E. Adams, Ralph Keiper, Alphonse Calabrese, O. Quentin Hyder, Clyde Narramore, and others. "If these informal, self-help techniques don't work for you, the next step is to arrange to see a professional counselor, and the best counselor may be your pastor." Various "Christian psychotherapy clinics" around the world are also named, with addresses for inquiries.[48]

Among women writers the work of Joyce Lansdorf received wide acceptance in the 1970s and early 1980s. Dr. James C. Dobson in 1981 called her "the most effective articulator of women's concerns in the Christian community today."[49] Hers was a message aiming at women responding to the stirrings of the women's movement for greater acceptance and individual choice within the framework of traditional evangelical teaching. Her style was done in a more folksy, informal voice but with a clear moral urgency underlying its message for males and females to accept each other on biblically equal terms.[50] In a somewhat different vein, magazines such as *Today's Christian Woman* and its competitor, *Virtue*, offer a wide variety of self-help tips to readers. While not always related directly to scriptural authority, they appear in magazines such as these, which clearly reflect evangelical priorities. Here are stories and advice in the classic self-help mode about "resting in one's ruts," "working your network," developing checklists to keep tabs on household management, surviving the holidays, "ten tips for fitness," aerobics, "six ways to get more from what you read," "building self-esteem" "health-nutrition books for Christians," and the like. In the same mode, issues of the unofficial voice for evangelicalism, *United Evangelical Action (UEA)*, carry stories on "knowing yourself," "friend-to-friend helping," and "expectations."[51]

In summary, evangelicalism and the field of psychology, defined broadly as it is here, have found a variety of popular voices and agendas with which to edify the readers. A basic core of issues centering on everyday matters (as opposed to more complex issues discussed in the next chapter) keeps the faithful aware of how all of life is informed by one's faith if one only knows where to look. That incongruity and irony abound is considered a part of the fascination of finding God's will and how to follow it in everyday life, drawing on the accumulated commonsense wisdom of the faith.

## NOTES

1. "Is This My Father's World? An Interview with Warren and David Wiersbe," *Leadership: A Practical Journal for Church Leaders*, 10, 1 (Winter 1990): 20.

2. Ibid., p. 21; feature story, "Hey, I'm Terrific!" *Newsweek*, February 17, 1992, pp. 46–51.

3. John F. Wilson, "The Sociological Study of Religion," in Charles H. Lippy and Peter W. Williams, eds., *Encyclopedia of American Religious Experience*, vol. 1 (New York: Scribners, 1988), p. 28.

4. Mark Noll and D. G. Hart, "The Language of Zion: Presbyterian Devotional Literature in the Twentieth Century," in Milton Coalter, ed., *The Confessional Mosaic: Presbyterianism and Twentieth-Century Theology* (Louisville: John Knox/Westminster, 1990), pp. 187–207; Wade Clark Roof and William McKinney, *American Mainline Religion: Its Changing Shape and Future* (New Brunswick, N.J.: Rutgers University Press, 1987), pp. 7–8, 44–45, 53; Steve Bruce, *A House Divided: Protestantism, Schism, and Secularization* (London: Routledge, 1990), p. 176.

5. Charles H. Lippy, ed., "Introduction," *Twentieth-Century Shapers of American Popular Religion* (Westport, Conn.: Greenwood Press, 1989), p. xxiii; George M. Marsden, "Secular Humanism within the Church," *Christianity Today*, January 17, 1986, p. 15-I.

6. Ibid.

7. David Harrington Watt, *A Transforming Faith: Explorations of Twentieth-Century American Evangelicalism* (New Brunswick, N.J.: Rutgers University Press, 1991), pp. 137–54.

8. James Davison Hunter, *American Evangelicalism: Conservative Religion and the Quandary of Modernity* (New Brunswick, N.J.: Rutgers University Press, 1983), pp. 94–95; see his "Appendix Two" for information on his "Methodological Strategies," pp. 142–44.

9. See, for example, *The Journal of Christianity and Psychology*; *The Journal of Psychology and Theology*; *Christian Scholar's Review*; Stanton L. Jones, ed., *Psychology and the Christian Faith* (Grand Rapids, Mich.: Baker Book House, 1987); David G. Myers and Malcolm A. Jeeves, eds., *Psychology through the Eyes of Faith* (New York: Harper and Row, 1987); see also several books by Professor Gary R. Collins on this.

10. Joan L. Jacobs, "The Christian and the Headspreader," *Christianity Today*, February 1, 1974, pp. 492–94.

11. Ibid.

12. Gary R. Collins, "Saintly Snake Oil: Weighing Church Quackery," *Leadership*, 6, 2 (Spring 1985): 31; Paul Thigpen, "Sin, Sickness, or Something Else," *Charisma*, March 1992, pp. 48–51; editorial, "Demonizing the Head Doctors," *Christianity Today*, September 16, 1991, p. 21.

13. Collins, "Saintly Snake Oil," p. 31; Bob Passantino and Gretchen Passantino, *Witch Hunt* (Nashville, Tenn.: Thomas Nelson, 1990); Jack O. Balswick, "The Psychological Captivity of Evangelicalism," in William H. Swatos, ed., *Religious Society* (Westport, Conn.: Greenwood Press, 1987), pp. 141–52.

14. Elise Chase, *Healing Faith: An Annotated Bibliography of Christian Self-Help Books* (Westport, Conn.: Greenwood Press, 1985), p. xii.

15. "Unmasking: An Interview with Walden Howard," *Eternity*, August 1977, p. 12; see also the case study in Robert N. Bellah et al., *Habits of the Heart: Individualism and Commitment in American Life* (Berkeley: University of California Press, 1985), pp. 228–32.

16. Mark Kinzer, "Christian Identity and Social Change in Technological Society," in Peter Williamson and Kevin Perrotta, eds., *Christianity Confronts Modernity* (Ann Arbor, Mich.: Servant Books, 1981), pp. 28–29; Paul C. Vitz, *Psychology as Religion: The Cult of Self-Worship* (Grand Rapids, Mich.: Eerdmans, 1977).

17. See for example the stories in the May 3, 1991, and July 20, 1990, issues of *Publishers Weekly*.

18. Ibid.; for details see this author's forthcoming book on the history of the Third Wave of Pentecostalism.

19. Howard Clinebell, "Popular Therapeutic Movements and Psychologies," pp. 928–29; J. Patton, "Pastoral Counseling," pp. 849–85; J. L. Florell, "Holistic Health Care," pp. 1320–21; these are found in Rodney J. Hunter, ed., *Dictionary of Pastoral Care* (Nashville, Tenn.: Abingdon, 1990).

20. David Edwin Harrell, Jr., "Healing in Protestant America," in Harry L. Letterman, ed., *Health and Healing: Ministry of the Church* (Madison, Wisc.: Wheat Ridge Foundation, 1980), pp. 66, 71, 72; Florell, "Holistic Health Care," p. 320; Psychotherapy Book Club, 230 Livingston Street, P.O. Box 942, Northvale, NJ 07647-9970; through the ministry of Gloria Copeland some fifteen songs entitled "Healing Praise" are offered by Spectra, an evangelical distributor; *Charisma and Christian Life*, May 1992, p. 65; P. G. Chappell, "Healing Movements," in Stanley M. Burgess and Gary B. McGee, eds., *Dictionary of Pentecostal and Charismatic Movements* (Grand Rapids, Mich.: Zondervan, 1988), pp. 372–74; "Faith Healing," in David G. Benner, ed., *Baker Encyclopedia of Psychology* (Grand Rapids, Mich.: Baker Book House, 1985), pp. 389–91; a critical view is B. Van Drogt, "Holistic Health Issue," *SCP* [Spiritual Counterfeiters Project], 1977.

21. Christopher Lasch, "Engineering the Good Life: The Search for Perfection," *This World*, 26 (Summer 1989): 3.

22. Roger Lundin, "Deconstructing Theology," *The Reformed Journal*, January 1986, p. 15.

23. Steven M. Zifferblatt and Patricia M. Zifferblatt, eds., *The Better Life Institute Family Health Plan* (Nashville, Tenn.: Thomas Nelson, 1991).

24. Wayne Elzey, "Popular Culture," in Lippy and Williams, *Encyclopedia*, vol. 3, p. 1740; editorial, *Christianity Today*, September 16, 1991, p. 21.

25. Kathy K. Trier and Anson Shupe, "Prayer, Religiosity, and Healing in the Heartland, U.S.A.," *Review of Religious Research*, June 1991, pp. 51–56; an important, recent variation is discussed in Thomas Moore, *Care of the Soul: A Guide for Cultivating Depth and Sacredness in Everyday Life* (San Francisco: HarperCollins, 1992).

26. For materials used see, for example, the 1991 catalog of "Injoy," 2530 Jamacha Road, Suite D, El Cajon, CA 92019, which has a ten-part audiocassette series, "Starting Small

Groups in Your Churches," n.p.; see all of Meredith B. McGuire, *Ritual Healing in Suburban America* (New Brunswick, N.J.: Rutgers University Press, 1988); J. Rodman Williams, "Laying on of Hands," in Stanley M. Burgess and Gary B. McGee, eds., *Dictionary of Pentecostal and Charismatic Movements* (Grand Rapids, Mich.: Zondervan, 1988), pp. 535–37.

27. McGuire, *Ritual Healing*, pp. 19–21; many people (at Elderhostels, adult forums, etc.) have told me of the strong ecumenical spirit they sensed at such meetings; Kenneth L. Woodward, "A Time to Speak," *Newsweek*, December 17, 1990, pp. 50–56; news story by religion editor Martha Allen Sawyer, *Minneapolis Star Tribune*, June 24, 1990, p. 7B; news story, *New York Times*, May 17, 1990, pp. A1, B7; Mark A. Pearson, *Christian Healing: A Practical Guide* (Old Tappan, N.J.: Revell, 1990), pp. 77–99; see C. Samuel Storms, an evangelical writer, on *Healing and Holiness: A Biblical Response to the Faith-Healing Phenomenon* (Philadelphia: Reformed and Presbyterian Publishing, 1990).

28. News story, *New York Times*, May 17, 1990, pp. A1, B7; Pearson, ch. 5, "Sin, Sickness, Repentance," *Christian Healing*, pp. 77–99.

29. News story, "The Most Common Therapies," *Christianity Today*, April 8, 1988, p. 18; news story, *The Fundamentalist Journal*, January 1989, pp. 59–60.

30. Eugene H. Peterson, "Lashed to the Mast," *Leadership*, Summer 1986, pp. 53–54; among the many clinics one of the most prominent for evangelicals is Minirth-Meier Clinic, *Christianity Today*, December 16, 1991, p. 77; another is the Dr. Fred Gross Christian Therapy Program; still another group of facilities is the Rapha Centers, given endorsements by Jerry Falwell, Charles Stanley, Tom Landry, D. James Kennedy, Bill and Gloria Gaither, Gary Collins, and Beverly LaHaye, *Christianity Today*, May 18, 1992, p. 73; in the same issue see "Christian Counseling Centers Directory"; also, the theme issue on counseling in *Moody*, May 1991, pp. 13–21; ad in *Charisma and Christian Life*, June 1992, p. 8.

31. Peterson, "Lashed," pp. 53–54; Jack Boghosian, "The Biblical Basis for Strategic Approaches in Pastor Counseling," *Journal of Psychology and Theology*, 2, 2 (1983): 99–107; David A. Benner and Stuart L. Palmer, "Psychology and the Christian Faith," in Jones, *Psychology*, p. 171.

32. Robert H. Alberts, "Current Developments in Pastoral Care," *Word and World*, 6, 2 (Spring 1986): 211; Gary R. Collins, "The Pulpit and the Couch," *Christianity Today*, August 29, 1975, pp. 5–9.

33. See David M. Wulff, ed., *Psychology of Religion: Classic and Contemporary Views* (New York: John Wiley, 1991); Jones, *Psychology*; see the multivolume series "Resources for Christian Counseling," edited by Gary R. Collins, starting in 1977, Word Publishers, Waco, Texas.

34. D. Russell Bishop, "Psychology of Pastoral Ministry: Help or Hindrance?" *Journal of Psychology and Theology*, 17, 2 (1989): 154; Vernon Bittner, "Taking the 12 Steps," *Christianity Today*, December 9, 1988, p. 31.

35. Margaret Jones, "A Rage for Recovery," *Publishers Weekly*, November 23, 1990, pp. 16–24; William Griffin, "Religious Publishing," *Publishers Weekly*, May 3, 1991, pp. 16–27.

36. Griffin, "Religious Publishing."

37. Gary R. Collins, "Alcoholism: Sin or Disease?" *Christian Herald*, June 1988, pp. 16–19; Woodward, "A Time to Seek," *Newsweek*, December 17, 1990, p. 51.

38. "Introduction" to the *Christianity Today* Institute theme issue, "Getting Free," December 9, 1988, p. 99.

39. "Taking the 12 Steps to Church," *Christianity Today*, December 9, 1988, p. 31; see also in the same journal, Tim Stafford, "The Hidden Gospel of the 12 Steps," July 22, 1991, pp. 14–19; a critique of these is Wendy Kaminer, *I'm Dysfunctional, You're Dysfunctional:*

*The Recovery Movement and Other Self-Help Fashions* (Reading, Mass.: Addison-Wesley, 1992).

40. Editorial by Kenneth Myers, "Psychology," in the journal he edits, *Genesis*, February 1990, pp. 4–5; see also the commentary by R. J. Neuhaus in *First Things*, November 1990, p. 68; see also S. M. Tipton, "Sociology of Religion and Pastoral Care," in Hunter, *Dictionary*, p. 1200; news story, *Minneapolis Star Tribune*, November 25, 1990, pp. 1B, 8B.

41. Ryan quoted in Griffin, "Religious Publishing," p. 26; J. Keith Miller, *Sin: Overcoming the Ultimate Addiction* (San Francisco: Harper and Row, 1987), later retitled *Hope in the Fast Lane*; Richard G. Maudlin, "Addicts in the Pew," *Christianity Today*, July 22, 1991, p. 20; an excellent review of Miller is by Garrett E. Paul, *Lutheran Partners*, January/February 1989, pp. 37–39.

42. J. Keith Miller, *Hunger for Healing: The Twelve Steps as a Classic Model for Christian Spiritual Growth* (New York: HarperCollins, 1991), pp. 7–8; see Melinda Fish, *When Addiction Comes to the Church* (Old Tappan, N.J.: Revell, 1991); Mike Jeffries, "Christian Recovery Clinics," *Charisma*, March 1992, pp. 38–44, 48.

43. Three helpful discussions are Michael Scott Horton, *Made in America: The Shaping of Modern American Evangelicalism* (Grand Rapids, Mich.: Baker Book House, 1991); John F. MacArthur, *Our Sufficiency in Christ* (Waco, Tex.: Word, 1991); and Richard Rohr, "Why Does Psychology Always Win?" *Sojourners*, November 1991, pp. 10–15; see also the titles listed in Edith L. Blumhofer and Joel A. Carpenter, eds., *Twentieth-Century Evangelicalism: A Guide to the Sources* (New York: Garland, 1990), pp. 335–39.

44. Frank Riesman, "The New Self-Help Backlash," *Social Policy*, Summer 1990, pp. 422–48; Gary Collins, "Self-Help Psychologies," in Hunter, *Dictionary*, pp. 1135–36; Wendy Kaminer, "Saving Therapy: Exploring the Religious Self-Help Literature," *Theology Today*, Fall 1991, pp. 301–25.

45. K. Hanson, "Support Groups," in Hunter, *Dictionary*, p. 1243; Patricia Braus, "Selling Self Help," *American Demographics*, March 1992, pp. 48–53.

46. Louis Schneider and Sanford M. Dornbusch, *Popular Religion: Inspirational Books in America* (Chicago: University of Chicago Press, 1958), p. 60; Steven Starker, *Oracle at the Supermarket: The American Preoccupation with Self-Help Books* (New Brunswick, N.J.: Transaction Books, 1989), p. 158; Richard Quebedeaux, *By What Authority: The Rise of Personality Cults in American Christianity* (San Francisco: Harper and Row, 1982), pp. 1–16.

47. See, for example, Cecil B. Murphy, "Book Survey," *Christianity Today*, September 9, 1977, pp. 1252–56.

48. William Proctor, *The Born-Again Catalog: A Complete Sourcebook for Evangelicals* (New York: M. Evans, 1979), pp. 73–76; see the definitive listing and annotation in Chase, *Healing Faith*; see the news story in the *Minneapolis Star Tribune*, September 25, 1991, p. 7H.

49. Editorial, "Joyce Lansdorf: All about Women," *Christian Life*, November 1981, p. 21.

50. Bob Darden, "Joyce Lansdorf: Through the Pain," *Christian Life*, June 1985, pp. 29–34; in 1992 the Minirth-Meier program brought out a new magazine, *Today's Better Life: The Magazine of Spiritual, Physical, and Emotional Health* (Marion, Ohio); it is an excellent example of popular religion at its best.

51. See the "Table of Contents" in *UEA*, 38, 2 (Summer 1979), for the several stories.

# 4

# Sexuality, Marriage, and Family in Popular Religion

Although the evangelicals' concern with the self may seem rather far removed from their commitment to sharing their faith and converting the world, their participation in the world of social relationships embraces those goals in toto. Within the framework of popular religion they find themselves called to evangelize, to resist the forces of secularization, and to work for the Christianization of American society. Their expression of faith as found in ideas and practices in human sexuality, in singleness, in courtship and marriage, and in family life all bear directly on their highest priorities. Hence in this chapter we examine those topics as further evidence that with their heritage, their nondenominational loyalties, and their use of high technology and the mass media they exhibit a lively and many-sided understanding of bringing their faith into the everyday, popular expression of faith.

To carry out their goals, evangelicals in the last quarter century have given enormous amounts of time, commitment, and resources to fight off what they see as a concerted threat by nonbelievers dedicated to what has become known by its critics as "secular humanism." By this they mean a world-view devoid of any religious content that would in evangelical eyes, if empowered, eliminate any public reference to or reliance on a supreme being and absolute morality. Evangelicals fear such humanism will turn American life into a totally atheistic society, much like that of the former Soviet Union. Hence they resist such potential power by seeing to it that their faith commitments

are everywhere known and available for like-minded believers and any who
may wish to join them.

## EVANGELICAL RESPONSE

Historian Grant Wacker well captures the inspiration for evangelical
involvement in matters of sexuality and family life as a response to this peril.

the most lethal threat to the family. . .[is] the awful truth that the established
institutions of American society have determined to keep parents from controlling
the values of their adolescent children. . . . The literature of the movement leaves a
haunting impression that the rawest nerve of all is parents' fear that their kids will
grow up to scorn them.[1]

Added to this threat to America's most important institution for preserving
the faith, the nuclear family, have been the many expressions of drastic
deviation from traditional morality. These include the vast increase in
cohabitation, the soaring divorce rate, the greater public demonstration of
homosexual behavior, the ready accessibility of pornographic materials,
lewd language in commercial movies, mothers leaving infant children with
others to pursue their own careers, a decline in parental zeal for strict
discipline in rearing children, and the most controversial of all to evangelicals,
legal abortion.[2]

In the judgment of one of the leading evangelical commentators on family
matters, Dr. James Dobson, "We are watching the unraveling of a social
order," which has been nothing other than the sanctity of the traditional
family resting on long-standing moral consensus.[3]

Some experts outside the fold considered that many of these developments
deplored by evangelicals signified quite the opposite, that is, they meant an
increase in personal freedom and the right of expression. Others concluded
it was "hard to judge whether society is better or worse off under these relaxed
conditions."[4] Evangelicals, however, with but few exceptions, had no trouble
making their judgments about these perilous threats to their values. All that
was true, honorable, just, pure, lovely, and gracious was at stake; and the
new conditions could not be allowed to prevail.

At the same time within their own ranks, major questions emerged over
the meaning of sexuality, of gender roles, of the living out of being female
or male, of authority within the marriage, and of parental responsibilities. In
response to the ever-changing sociomoral climate both among their own
members and the society at large, new parachurch groups appeared.
Acknowledging that some form of reconsideration from the past regarding
such issues was needed, groups such as the Council on Biblical Manhood

and Womanhood (CBMW) and Christians for Biblical Equality (CBE) brought together considerable evangelical academic and parish-experienced leadership to focus on specific issues, attempting to inform and persuade readers about the scriptural teachings involved. Both presented multifaceted programs; the CBE for instance offering educational tours, guest speakers, and regional and national conferences as well as a variety of printed materials. The CBMW has focused more on its annual national conference and on distribution of what they call "our major book," *Recovering Biblical Manhood and Womanhood*, edited by John Piper and Wayne A. Grudem. These groups, emerging in the 1980s, found already on the scene two evangelical women's groups, the Evangelical and Ecumenical Women's Caucus (EEWC) and the Daughters of Sarah.[5] With but few exceptions, these groups consisted largely of those associated with the academic and church leadership worlds.

Further evidence of evangelical initiative in meeting the challenge posed by the secular feminist movement appeared with the debut of several magazines with an outreach using popular religion to circulate on the general reader market. The publishing empire of *Christianity Today* brought out a very polished, many-sided bimonthly, *Today's Christian Woman*. By January 1989, its distribution had reached 209,251. Another publisher in Oregon, backed by the major evangelical publisher David C. Cook, came into the same evangelical market with an equally well-planned bimonthly entitled *Virtue*. The separationist fundamentalist publishing firm Sword of the Lord, associated with the leadership of John R. Rice, countered with a smaller but carefully designed bimonthly alternative, *The Joyful Woman*. Another mass media evangelical giant, Word, Inc., of Waco, Texas, launched the "Word Women's Book Club," offering a variety of titles including inspiration, social concerns, and practical advice.[6]

That such publications found a ready market is evident in the results of a survey of the readers of *Today's Christian Woman*. With a 62.4 percent response, the statistics show that some 77 percent were married, 69 percent were between 25 and 49 years of age, some 31 percent had graduated from college, a very high 68 percent were employed outside the home, about 56 percent had children under 18 years of age, 31 percent belonged to a Bible study group, 40 percent taught Sunday school, 28 percent sang in their church choir, and 52 percent shopped six times or more a year in a Christian bookstore.[7]

## FEMALE AND MALE

Such continuing and diversified interest displays clearly the extent to which the influence of popular religion came to light. The issues were a combination of materials prepared both by experts and by the rank and file,

in an experienced general editorial policy understood by those standing apart
from the domain of academe or full-time religious organizations. The
professionals have spent considerable time utilizing specific biblical texts
buttressed by extensive scriptural scholarship to support their respective
positions. The reader of such magazines sees the issues of gender conflict,
authority, and the like in terms of how they play out in everyday life: whether it
would be practical to ordain women into the formal ministry; whether
"authority" (as used in the Bible) means the husband's will prevails;
whether any understanding of the religious and physical meaning of the sex
act outside of procreation is scriptural; and whether women's experience in
everyday life should command greater respect in shaping religious teaching
and understanding at the level of decision making in church and parachurch
organizations.

An evangelical feminist, Elouise Renich Fraser, crisply defines that issue,
focusing on femininity and masculinity:

Evangelical feminist theology, with its explicit attempt to join reflection on experience with reflection on God's self-revelation, exposes what has been happening all
along. Evangelical theologians have always relied heavily on experience in doing
theology. Hence, most theology has been written out of the male's experience of
God, the world, and others. The claim that these men are doing theology "from
above" becomes, then, an argument for the greater purity of their concepts and
propositions. Evangelical feminists say it is high time evangelicals face up to the
parochial, unimaginative thinking that is flooding our churches today.

We will be shamed by the revelation that our vociferous responses to women and
minorities are not really biblically or theologically based. Rather, they are a last-ditch
effort to hang on to what we know so well—the comfort and the power of
paternalism.[8]

At the heart of this judgment is the profound question of whether the
sexuality of females and males is such that one or the other must prevail,
given the teachings of the Bible, or, stated another way, that mutuality is a
noble but unrealizable ideal. If that is the case, then religion "from the bottom
up," the popular variety, must take second place to that shaped from above.

The latter is the thrust of the more conservative position from the CBMW
writers. Given their masculinity, males are to be responsible leaders, to be
the protectors and providers for women in ways appropriate to their unique
relationships. At the center of femininity, in this view, is a liberating capacity
when women come to receive, nurture, strengthen, affirm, and accept the
leadership of males in forms appropriate to scriptural teaching.[9]

From the pew came a voice searching for a course to follow between
"headship" and "equality of the sexes." Karen Burton Mains, a freelance
writer, concluded she could join neither camp because what she discovered

in her ponderings was the finality of paradox. "Truth often has this elusive quality. It refuses satisfaction like that which comes from a completed jigsaw puzzle on the dining room table. Somehow, the pieces don't all fit, and others are obviously missing." Sensing incongruity and irony at the heart of the controversy, she continues, how can Christ be both God and man, or how can believers be foreordained and responsible? These are mysteries and puzzles, which are beyond the final solution of a consensus agreeable to all.[10]

What stands out from the huge output of printed and media talk-show commentary on sexuality is that sex, as experienced by the partners, serves purposes beyond procreation. As suggested by Stanley J. Grenz, writing in the popular religion mode, sex is first "an expression of the self-giving of the marriage partners" (making clear here also that sex is permissible only within the bounds of marriage); second, that in this giving it is a "vivid reminder of the self-giving love of Christ for the church"; and finally that it "signifies an inward commitment," the sealing of faithfulness promised at the wedding. From experience coupled with the scripture, the sex act is understood not "as an accidental arrangement of the human species," but "related to our creation in the image of God!"[11]

The first book of the Bible, Genesis, Richard J. Foster states, "*affirms* the goodness of sex within marriage." "And the man and his wife were both naked, and were not ashamed (Gen. 2:25)." "The Old Testament book Song of Solomon *celebrates* that sexuality; the writing being a beautiful window into eros as it should be with four specific themes: intensity, restraint, mutuality, and permanence. In the New Testament these themes are affirmed and expanded by Jesus and the apostle Paul."[12]

Obviously, because mortal humans are the agencies to carry out such teachings, the results often leave them, including evangelicals, with questions of just *how* all this should be pursued. At this point the record of the evangelicals in all their diversity fully reflects the power of popular religion to contribute to the understanding of faith. Since its earliest years, reaching back into the eighteenth century, evangelicalism avoided any direct public discussion of the whole matter of technique. The old-time religion of fundamentalism and Pentecostalism (as well as most other Christians), left such subjects (when talked about at all) to the parents or friend or minister of the inquirers, with only vague, generalized books of advice and information made available.

Then came the awakening of the 1960s with its calls for greater freedom in every area of life, including sexual behavior. So also the movies, books, magazines, radio—the full gamut of the mass media offered far more sexually explicit products to the general public than ever before. (In 1952 a movie, *The Moon Is Blue*, was banned because it used the word "virgin.") Greater explicitness failed to turn up in evangelical books on the physical side of marriage, however, until one of the greatest bombshells in all of popular religion history exploded in 1974. This was, of course, the publication by born-again believer Marabel Morgan of *The Total Woman*. Widely acclaimed as a breakthrough for couples with a need for more information and encouragement to be erotic and just as widely denounced as being manipulative, sexist, and antifemale because it gave the female the greatest share of responsibility for "good sex," *The Total Woman* became a runaway bestseller, selling over 3 million copies by the end of the decade.[13]

As one commentator summed it up, Morgan "led the evangelical woman out of the romper room and into the bedroom." The book was an unabashed paean of praise for improving erotic sexual behavior, offering explicit techniques, games, and behavior patterns all endorsed by the aura of evangelical faith that women had not been able to find in print so readily before. It was experiential to the highest degree, drawing comments from outraged critics who called the "total woman" a skillful manipulator of male ego rather than a mutual sharer, to ribald humor such as Martin E. Marty's comment that her "costume fetish would dazzle Krafft-Ebing." This referred to Morgan's suggestions that wives dress in enticing costumes and find new locations for intercourse such as under tables and on trampolines and bales of hay.[14]

The success of the book also reflects the extent to which evangelicals were utilizing the most advanced mass media through high technology. The book, while at first banned in some evangelical bookstores, became a bestseller in those venues, with the legitimating quality of a religious bookstore being welcomed by the buyers. Morgan and some associates set up "Total Woman Seminars," daylong programs, sponsored largely by evangelical churches, in which women were encouraged to ask and share specific questions, receive advice about the issues, and find new ways to deal with age-old problems. Morgan, in the fashionable evangelical-hype style, became a media celebrity with her picture on covers of national news weeklies and commentary by such culturally conservative publications as the *National Review* and the *New York Times*. Hers was a manifesto, a how-to book, a true confession, and a call to greater openness in a time when evangelicals had long lagged behind other religionists in public consideration of so basic a part of human conduct.[15]

From that point on, the evangelical community, with certain exceptions, came more directly to terms with this complicated issue. Well-known writers in other fields started bringing out marriage manuals that offered clearly worded advice and counsel on technique. The best known of these was that by Tim and Beverly LaHaye, *The Act of Marriage: The Beauty of Sexual Love*, which quickly sold a million copies and by 1981 was in its thirty-first printing. Directed by evangelical assumptions, they found research supporting their assertion that those women with strong religious convictions were better able to enjoy physical sex than less committed believers. To the LaHayes, the born-again experience frees up the believer's conscience and thus removes "a common cause of orgasmic malfunction."[16]

As the books and debate continued, the expressions of popular faith in the magazines pursued the themes even more. Articles about "Questions Christians Are Asking about Sex" and explicit queries about pornographic movies as aids or about male impotence became commonplace in *Virtue, Today's Christian Woman*, and similar periodicals. The magazines engaged licensed clinical psychologists and marriage counselors as expert respondents to readers' questions. All the new realism, of course, could not settle the issue over headship versus equality, but it contributed a dimension and authority to the larger issues based on experience and everyday wisdom that remain a major contribution of popular religion.[17]

## WOMANHOOD AND MANHOOD

In a closely related area, evangelical popular religion found a widening outlet of interest in believers' exploring in several ways what it means to be a woman. Advice books and other counsel, of course, had over the years addressed this issue. But that was done in the context of the woman's being counseled in a specific social role as mate, mother, friend, or church worker and not within the realm of the female persona as such. Now as the women's movement continued its unfolding during the 1970s and 1980s, evangelical women considered more fully the notion that their experience as females was worthy of as serious consideration as that of males. Through a variety of workshops, seminars, and conferences, as well as a huge amount of printed material, they explored in church-related surroundings their feelings about spirituality, health, friendships with other women, and other topics new to the agendas of older evangelical women's groups.[18]

Closely associated with this came the greater openness of evangelical women to find ways to improve their physical appearance in terms of health, attire, and makeup. Having lived in that part of religious society that had banned or strongly denounced such interest as being immoral or worldly or frivolous, a major change occurred. In the 1970s and on to the present day evangelical women have responded to their new self-image with expressions of keeping up in these areas. The well-known Pentecostal preacher Marilyn Hickey wrote in 1987, "If a little make-up and darkening of the lashes will cover up some of our bad points and highlight our good ones, I don't think there is anything wrong with it. Likewise, I don't believe there is anything wrong with wearing an attractive outfit or having one's hair styled."[19]

The pentecostal Church of God approved a denomination-wide resolution at its national convention in 1988 acknowledging that wearing jewelry, using cosmetics, and attending movies could be compatible with personal holiness. The color advertisements in evangelical magazines over these years shows a progressively increasing use of such items of adornment by the women models. The journal *Virtue* engaged Joanne Wallace, president and founder of Image Improvement, as a regular columnist consultant on attire and related issues. The magazine carries features in each issue on clothing, personal health, and self-help improvement.[20]

By contrast, only a minuscule amount of such popular religious advice and news making is devoted to men. Only in the mid-eighties did advice articles appear about fathers taking more responsibility for childrearing, showing deep feelings more openly, modeling godly leadership, and answering questionnaire articles such as "Men—How Christ-like Are You?" A *Christianity Today* quarterly aimed at the popular audience, *Marriage Partnership*, once carried a special feature "Men and Marriage." It ran stories on fathers worrying that their job performance may suffer from the new emphasis on family life, a humor piece on belching, the joys of monogamous marriage, sexy males in the movies, and the joys of old clothes.[21]

In a related area, evangelical supercelebrity Charles Colson wrote a scathing attack on "unisexism—the intentional blurring of all distinctions between the genders, in almost every area; in professions, in fashions, and in human interaction." He attributed this to "an aggressive gay subculture" posing as a viable alternative life-style and glamorized by show-business celebrities and also to "an overzealous feminism eager to redress the injustices of past sexism." To Colson such behavior assaulted a basic truth established by God—the existence of male and female, masculine and feminine, providers and nurturers.[22] Although other popular evangelical journals avoided direct commentary on that theme, the general tenor of their articles show full support for Colson's ideas.

In sum, the themes of sexuality and gender characteristics have maintained their appeal for popular evangelical audiences to this day. Among religionist audiences their leap into explicit advice has been widely accepted by the rank and file, aided since the days of Morgan by comparable manuals authored by Charles and Martha Shedd, Ed and Gaye Wheat, and new editions of the work by the LaHayes.[23]

## SINGLEDOM

The same openness to the many sides of adult social life, including singledom, courtship, and marriage, also has come to be commonplace among the rank and file. Clearly, since its inception, evangelicalism in all its diversity has taught that adult life is fulfilled for virtually all believers through the institution of marriage and that although being single has been the necessary chosen situation for some, believers are expected to marry and replenish the earth.

Then as the women's movement in the 1960s expanded in different directions, a theme among some adherents dealing with the rewards and goodness of remaining single started to emerge. Various forms of "single adult ministry" have developed not so much as introduction ("the meatmarket") opportunities as to offer a place for believers without spouses or children (the latter constituting by tradition the core of congregational life); singles are offered "a place to belong." These ministries offer a variety of events such as open-forum discussions, Bible study, organized recreation, and support groups.[24] At the same time the opportunities for matchmaking continue through such programs as "Born-Again Singles Pen Pal and Correspondence Dating Service" and a dating service, among several nationally, in Los Angeles, "Equally Yoked." The latter was started out of a sense that congregational groups provided little opportunity for meeting prospective dates. From Christian Life Resources Publishers of Mesquite, Texas, comes a twelve-part video series, endorsed by Swindoll, known as "Successful Single Parenting."[25]

At a different level, a long-standing debate reaching back into the early twentieth-century debate over whether singles are somehow inferior or less than full persons compared to married believers has abated to some extent. For instance in 1975 Ruth Graham in writing against the ordination of women stated, "You name it, men are superior in all but two areas: women make the best wives and women make the best mothers!" To that a reader replied, "How sad it is, if I understand Ruth Graham correctly, that all single women are living second-class lives because God has not provided them with a husband and family."[26]

By the mid-1980s evangelicals were criticizing each other for making such comments and were in fact extolling the rewards of remaining single. Such a person "who has accepted him or herself as a child of God is in a unique position to reveal the wholeness of the individual, the completeness that is grounded in God's good creation." "Completeness in Christ, the new creation, is the fullness of life," "no longer judging completeness according to predetermined categories of masculinity and femininity or of marital status."[27]

Perhaps the popular understanding of singleness is best summed up by counselor Gary R. Collins. In talking to evangelical singles he suggests they focus on enjoying all that life has to offer where they are, pursuing a life of help and service to others, and pursuing those qualities that make for peace and happiness and thus reducing their anger and hostility. A happy single is one with a mature mind and spirit that enables him or her to "cope effectively with the tensions of life."[28]

## MARRIAGE

Singleness, however, as a universal practice would obviously mean the eventual cessation of the human race; that was not what God the Creator had in mind. Marriage in all of its several dimensions is understood to be central: for propagation to make available evangelists to win the world, for the enjoyment and rededication to faith the partners give each other, to be faithful to the teachings of the Bible, and in America to preserve Christian civilization against the forces of secular humanism.

Marriage as evangelicals understand it is for most persons simply pro-grammed into the biological, spiritual, and mental makeup of humankind. God intends that it be a blessing, a way of carrying out the divine mandates of the Bible, and a means of self-understanding. It has its share of incongruity also, because so often these noble ideals fall short of realization; yet no scriptural alternative to its role is known to humans. Through its imper-fections, its conflicts, its failures, marriage is a vehicle for serving God. A perfect God works through imperfect people, a condition rife with irony and paradox.

From its inception, evangelicals have maintained this special sanctity about marriage. In contemporary America, with the enormous changes occurring to the traditional teachings and practices of that institution, they face extremely difficult challenges to maintain that sanctity in light of the options available: liberalized divorce laws, cohabitation, easily accessible contraceptive devices, and the glamorization in the mass media of other life-styles than the nuclear family.

However, the adaptation by evangelicals themselves of high tech mass media suggests they are utilizing whatever acceptable means of communi-cation are available in their defense of marriage. Rank and file have readily accessible a wide selection of media. Through the parachurch outlets, a variety of marriage improvement seminars, clinics, support groups, and related items and opportunities exist for utilizing these materials. Only a minuscule number of examples can be cited here among the hundreds, perhaps thousands of evangelical materials readily accessible.

Some of these include a four-part film series, "Maximum Marriage," with counselor Tim Timmons. The subjects draw on the larger popular culture with titles such as "Why Marriage When You Can Live Together?" "The Eleven Battlegrounds of Marriage," "Why Are Women So Weird and Men So Strange?" and "How Do You Spell Relief?" Ligonier Ministries has available an audiocassette course with a study guide. Campus Crusade has an anthology approach, *Secrets of a Growing Marriage*, advertised as a "rich and practical treasury of marriage discoveries." The "Scriptural Counsel" organization offers an audiocassette album endorsed by superstars Charles Swindoll, James Dobson, and D. James Kennedy. The evangelical publishing houses continue to bring out a sizable number of the how-to-make-a-good-marriage-better genre titles.[29]

Again, although various viewpoints and emphases on these subjects flourish in different parts of evangelicalism, the popular expression of understanding is well exemplified by a major magazine published by Christianity, Today, Inc., entitled *Marriage Partnership*. As with *Today's Christian Woman*, its editors utilize a highly stylish, easily understood, multicolor format in harmony with other magazines known to the readers. This journal, obviously, addresses the issues with a coverage that indicates both the difficulties and the rewards in the spouse relationship (another of its magazines, discussed later, focuses on parenting). It offers practical advice, scriptural essays, humor, book reviews, counseling insights, role modeling by famous evangelical couples (such as Surgeon General Everett and Betty Koop), trivia information, a featured "Marriage Builders" plastic magazine wrapper serving as a study guide for the articles in that issue, and a vast array of advertisements of interest for this readership. These include books, records, films, and parachurch organizations such as the International Bible Society, along with Bible-study programs and gifts.

The magazine has its counterparts with other religious publishing firms. *Marriage Partners*, however, serves as something of a mirror reflecting evangelicalism's involvement with this expression of popular religion. It creates a network of information suggesting to the readers that what they are reading is what evangelical families around America are interested in and doing something about; it offers a forum for discussion of the issues the readers and editors consider worth airing; it offers an image in photographs, ads, and print of what the ideal evangelical marriage should look like and thus be emulated. It is in sum an item that serves as a starting point for various forms of counseling, support, and self-help groups and thereby creates a standard by which the participants can measure their own marriages. Utilizing celebrities in music, counseling, fiction, scriptural studies, and other advice, the magazine creates a norm that stands at the center of popular evangelical expression.

As with sexual counseling, evangelical popular religion brings to the world of marital experience a down-to-earth quality appealing to the everyday reader. The advice given focuses on drawing from common problems, familiar to the readers, and then finding solutions based on scripture and common sense. The advice also usually has a how-to quality about it, listing "Ten Guidelines" or "Seven Deadly Sins" for consideration. Reading through these suggests clearly that although "headship" as discussed earlier is of paramount importance when discussing the theology of a marriage, the practice of mutuality and compromise between equals dominates the advice given. The articles suggest that both "accept each other as you are," "do not dwell on faults," "recognize that differences in personality and temperament —to a large extent—can eventually be solved," "keep the sizzle in your marriage," and understand "the deadly art of criticism."[30]

## FAMILY

In evangelical faith among parents, the highest reward and most severe challenge to one's faith come together in raising one's family. It has always been such, and the conviction that to save society the family must continue points to its centrality as an expression of faith. The family, in fact, has always stood as the central agency through which supernatural grace is bestowed. When significant progress in human conduct is achieved, they believe, it will start first with the renewal of the family.[31]

Over the centuries in America, the evangelical family (as with all religious traditions) has undergone considerable change. In today's world children stay home away from full-time employment longer, much longer; they are more systematically studied (though not necessarily therefore better under-stood!) through formal research into childhood and adolescence; and they have become far more influenced in behavior by the outside larger society.[32]

That last development, as suggested earlier, helped feed the surge of new energy and growth within the general evangelical community starting in the 1970s. Parents fearful of what dangers lay in store for their children found evangelical commitment to orthodoxy, rectitude, and discipleship highly attractive as a foundation for educating their children in "the whole armor" of God, with instruction in what was right and wrong, God's revealed truths in the Bible, God's method of holding sinners accountable for their wrong-doings, and God's plan of reward for the faithful. Many parents believed education in morality and character building was no longer possible in the public schools, with the ending of public prayer and Bible reading and absorption into the curriculum of ingredients of secular humanism. Hence, those associations affiliated with evangelical, fundamentalist, and Pentecostal churches were teaching what they knew their children must learn.[33]

Beyond that, children are seen not only as the truthbearers of the future but as gifts, as blessings for the here and now. In raising them parents learn obviously how to love them and also by that experience how to love others and how by parenting "to see the world afresh." In an eloquent piece of writing Rodney Clapp pointed out, "It is children and others who kindle our imaginations in new and unexpected ways, enabling us to become the sort of people we could never have been without them. So, openness to children also signifies openness to the future, to the belief that *there is a future.*"[34]

A Christian family tells its members and the world that it believes there is more to the world than what is immediately accessible, that a future lies ahead, a situation that signifies they are not themselves the final word of God's revelation. Children are "sign gifts of the love of a God of gracious surprises, to whom we dare entrust not only our own future, but also that of our children."[35]

Obviously such commitments are also made by parents from the Judaic and other Christian faiths of the world. Where evangelical uniqueness unfolds is in the means and some of the specific teachings they enlist to defend and advance the faith and a Christian society. Evangelicals, as suggested earlier, enthusiastically embrace a variety of popular religion expressions, a situation of prime importance for the raising of the family. In their transdenominational location, they utilize an enormous variety of teaching programs, many of which are created by the high technology of the new media.

Again, Christianity Today, Inc., leads the field, here with its bimonthly magazine *Christian Parenting.* In clear, jargon-free language the writers create an atmosphere of showing parents that their problems are understood and can be resolved, if not eliminated. In a technological coup, they were the first to offer parents the opportunity to use touch telephones to learn more about a variety of products suitable for parenting. These included home school, parenting books, children's Bibles, greeting cards, Bible stories, and related items. (Many independent media distributors such as Family Tree of Colorado made available "informative, quick-to-read books . . . [to] support and encourage you as you strive to grow your teen-ager into a responsible, mature Christian adult.")[36]

A variety of Bibles adapted for several levels of child reading ability are distributed from major evangelical publishers. Parents could enroll in the "Family Bookshelf" of the *Christian Herald* suppliers, who offer a variety of self-help, inspirational, and fiction titles headed by Charles Swindoll, James Dobson, and Lloyd Ogilvie.[37] On the evangelical radio circuit certain broadcasters present specialized programs aimed at "the changing identities of the new evangelical man and woman"—those who are single, those who are remarried, those in dual-career families—and "above all . . . focus on the home."[38]

Something of a total synthesis for family life emerging out of the blend of media technology and faith is available in a year's planner-organizer publication much like a daily work planner. The organization named "Valdyme" has published an album-format book with places in it for photographs, activity coding, and a place for recording prayer concerns. It is aimed at family activity, with the code to be created by each family for such items as bill paying, sports, church, and baby-sitting. It is made available only through Christian retail stores, saving those retailers from having to compete with discount houses and neighborhood bookstores.[39]

Thus, through the media and from their own experiences evangelical parents become involved with their offspring, their church, and the larger world on a wide variety of fronts. Through readily accessible media, parents are given encouragement, inspiration, self-help tips, expert advice, direction, means of evaluation, and sources for additional information on a host of everyday problems such as postpartum blues, what to do when a child is found to be reading *Playboy*, and the like.

Typical popular religion insight is offered, again, by way of example, here from Gary Collins. Recognizing the agony of tensions within a family, he calls for its members, first, to give the care and nurture of the family a place of "prime importance" rather than letting the family adjust and adapt to the pressures of work, friends, and body maintenance. Second, using anecdotes and Bible stories, he calls on members to hold on to "balance," making commitments for Bible reading and family prayer and then insisting these be honored. Third is a call for open communication, by honest and loving means as being better than tears, outbursts of anger, and other negative messages.

Finally, Collins calls for a rededication to honoring the family by joining in activities with other families, clusters of fellow believers for recreation, Bible study, potluck meals, and worship. "Within the family, people of all ages should learn about God, about right or wrong, and about the importance of honesty, self-respect, hard work, and other traditional values."[40]

The realm of the popular is visible also in the response evangelicals make to conflicts developing between what they teach their children and what the latter often face in the larger society. This shows up often in ongoing battles between evangelical parents and local school boards or teachers' associations over the choice of textbooks and the content of sex education courses. With all the dangers lurking about, especially teen-age pregnancy, from today's permissive standards, parents have on the local and occasionally state level organized into evangelically led groups to protest specific texts. What has ensued is often a standoff among the involved groups; parents may transfer their children to religious day schools. On occasion specific school districts have allowed the child involved to be absent from class during the presentation of the sex education curriculum; in that way, the parents believe, they have preserved for their own religious freedom and right of choice the means of bringing up their children their way on so vital an issue.[41]

In summation, the convictions of evangelicals about the centrality of their social life leads them to engage the world directly, especially on the issues of rearing children in a hostile society. Their forms of response are varied;

the extent to which they utilize secular wisdom and advice alongside the lessons of scripture and their own heritage is likewise not of one cloth. Yet what seems to hold it all together among the various families within the tradition is the recognition of a common enemy and the absolute imperative of obeying God by obeying the commandments, usually, as the case studies show, at the expense of one's own ease and well-being.

To summarize Part II, for evangelicals in the worlds of social values and business, in cultivating one's sense of self and in social expression, the way is made simpler and more attractive by the infusion of popular religious ingredients. They enliven and legitimate the traditional teachings and commands of formal doctrine and church-centered faith. They can be validated or eliminated in everyday living experiences. They belong to those who find in popular religion the means to keep up the struggle in a world both hostile and indifferent to their convictions.

This conclusion, however, needs to be tested in the other major areas of everyday life for evangelicals, that which we classify as the media, literature, and music. There we have further opportunity to explore the ongoing appeal of our subject.

## NOTES

1. Grant Wacker, "Searching for Norman Rockwell: Popular Evangelicalism in Contemporary America," in Leonard I. Sweet, ed., *The Evangelical Tradition in America* (Macon, Ga.: Mercer University Press, 1984), p. 309.

2. See two publications by the Barna Research Group, George Barna, "Tables and Interpretation," *Born Again: A Look at Christians in America* (Glendale, Calif.: Barna Research Group, 1990), pp. 53–69, especially p. 66; and George Barna, *What Americans Believe: An Annual Survey of Values and Religious Views in the United States* (Ventura, Calif.: Regal Books, 1991), pp. 147–70.

3. News story profile on Dobson in the *New York Times*, June 5, 1990, p. A10; much of the Dobson material reaches evangelicals by radio, audio- and videocassettes, and by a monthly church insert bulletin published by Tyndale House, Wheaton, Ill., "Dr. James Dobson's Focus on the Family Bulletin."

4. Sar A. Levitan et al., eds., *What's Happening to the American Family: Tensions, Hopes, Results*, rev. ed. (Baltimore: Johns Hopkins University Press, 1988), p. 36; see also David Popone, "Breakup of the Family?" *USA Today* magazine, May 1991, pp. 50–53.

5. John Piper and Wayne A. Grudem, eds., *Recovering Biblical Manhood and Womanhood* (Westchester, Ill.: Crossway Books, 1991); CBE, 380 Lafayette Freeway, Suite 122, St. Paul, MN 55107-1216; CBMW, Box 317, Wheaton, IL 60189; EEWC, Box 209, Hadley, NY 12835; Daughters of Sarah, 3801 N. Keller, Chicago, IL 60641; see also news story, *Christianity Today*, October 16, 1987, p. 44; news story, *The Other Side*, December 18, 1986, pp. 25–27.

6. *Today's Christian Woman*, January/February 1989, p. 27; Carol Flake, *Redemptorama: Culture, Politics, and the New Evangelicalism* (Garden City, N.Y.: Doubleday, 1984), pp. 77–78.

7. Item in *Today's Christian Woman*, September/October 1984, n.p.

8. Elouise Renich Fraser, "Evangelical Feminism: The Threat of Its Survival," in David A. Fraser, ed., *Evangelicalism: Surviving Its Success* (St. Davids, Pa.: Eastern Baptist Theological Seminary, 1987), pp. 48–49.

9. Piper and Grudem, *Recovering Biblical Manhood and Womanhood*; see also George Sweeting, president, Moody Bible Institute, "Is the Church Unfair to Women?" *Moody Monthly*, March 1980, pp. 76–80.

10. Karen Burton Mains, "It's a Mystery to Me: Struggles with Sexual Ambiguity in the Church," *Christianity Today*, July 17, 1981, pp. 56–58; for considerably more quantified data on this general subject (which does not use "evangelical" as a variable) see James Patterson and Pewter Kim, *The Day Americans Told the Truth* (Englewood Cliffs, N.J.: Prentice-Hall, 1991), ch. 11, "The War between the Sexes," pp. 87–93.

11. Stanley J. Grenz, "What Is Sex For?" *Christianity Today*, June 12, 1987, pp. 22–23.

12. Richard J. Foster, "God's Gift of Sexuality: Celebration and Warning in the Context of Faith," *Sojourners*, July 1985, pp. 15–17.

13. See my *Evangelicals in the White House: The Cultural Maturation of Born Again Christianity, 1960–1981* (New York: Edwin Mellen, 1981), pp. 100–102; I follow David Watt, *A Transforming Faith*, pp. 131–36.

14. See Martin E. Marty, "Memo," *Christian Century*, December 8, 1976, p. 1111; Barbara Ehrenreich et al., "Fundamentalist Sex," in *Re-Making Love: The Feminization of Sex* (Garden City. N.Y.: Anchor, 1986), pp. 134–60, especially pp. 141–42; Krafft-Ebing was a nineteenth-century pioneer researcher and is the most widely known authority on sexual fetishes.

15. Richard Quebedeaux, *The Worldly Evangelicals* (San Francisco: Harper and Row, 1978), p. 77; Watt, *Faith*, pp. 131–36.

16. Peter Gardella, *Innocent Ecstasy: How Christianity Gave America an Ethic of Sexual Pleasure* (New York: Oxford University Press, 1986), pp. 155–58; Michael Leinesch, "Anxious Patriarchs: Authority and the Meaning of Masculinity in Christian Conservative Thought," *Journal of American Culture*, 13, 4 (Winter 1990): 47–55; Flake, *Redemptorama*, pp. 80–84; see the list of sex manuals in William Proctor, ed., *The Born-Again Christian Catalog* (Old Tappan, N.J.: Revell, 1979), pp. 90–93; Tim and Beverly LaHaye, *The Act of Marriage: The Beauty of Sexual Love* (Grand Rapids, Mich.: Zondervan, 1974).

17. Gardella, *Innocent Ecstasy*, pp. 155–58.

18. See Carol Kent, "Secret Passions of a Christian Woman," *Today's Christian Woman*, November/December 1990, pp. 60–63; Sharon Donahue, "Can a Woman Have It All?" *Today's Christian Woman*, July/August 1988, pp. 34–35; Debra Evans, *The Mystery of Womanhood* (Westchester, Ill.: Crossway Books, 1987); Judith Stacey and Susan Elizabeth Gerard, " 'We Are Not Doormats': The Influence of Feminism on Contemporary Evangelicals in the United States," in Faye Ginsburg and Anna Lowenhaupt Tsing, eds., *Uncertain Terms: Negotiating Gender in American Culture* (Boston: Beacon Press, 1990), pp. 98–117; editorial by Jamie Buckingham, "What Is Masculinity?" *Charisma and Christian Life*, October 1991, p. 100.

19. Marilyn Hickey, "Ask Marilyn," *Charisma*, February 1987, p. 13; Kenneth T. Wilson, "Should Women Wear Headcoverings?" *Bibliotheca Sacra*, 592, October/December 1991, pp. 442–62.

20. News story, *Washington Post*, August 13, 1988, p. B6; Peter Clecak, *America's Quest for the Ideal Self: Dissent and Fulfillment in the 1960s and 1970s* (New York: Oxford University Press, 1983), pp. 143–44; news story, *Christian Century*, August 17–24, 1988, pp. 725–26; Gigi Tchividdian, "Makeup for Inner Beauty," *The Christian Reader*, April 1987, pp. 6–11.

21. Editorial, Jamie Buckingham, *Charisma*, October 1991, p. 100; Len LeSourd, *Strong Men: Weak Men* (Old Tappan, N.J.: Revell, 1990); Cecil Murphy, *Mantalk: Resources for Exploring Male Issues* (Louisville: Presbyterian Publishing House, 1991); Fritz Neuen-huysen, "Dads Can Be Moms Too," *The Other Side*, January/February 1990, p. 72; Marga-ret J. Rinick, *Christian Men Who Hate Women* (Downers Grove, Ill.: InterVarsity, 1990); Phil Harnden, "I Never Saw Clark Kent Cry," *The Other Side*, March 1984, p. 30; see subsequent issues of this journal for several years for many, usually brief, items on this issue.

22. A reprint from Charles Colson, *Prison Journal Fellowship*, January 1991, n.p.; on the gay/lesbian theme see Scott Thuma, "Negotiating a Religious Identity: The Case of the Gay Evangelical," *Sociological Analysis*, 52, 4 (1991): 333–47.

23. See the news story by Kenneth L. Woodward, "The Bible in the Bedroom," *Newsweek*, February 1, 1982, p. 71.

24. Carolyn A. Koons and Michael J. Anthony, *Single Adult Passages: Uncharted Territories* (Grand Rapids, Mich.: Baker Book House, 1991); R. Michael Hoisington, "How You Can Start a Singles' Group," *Christian Life*, September 1985, pp. 67–72; R. O. Evans, "Single Persons and Pastoral Care and Counseling," in Rodney Hunter, ed., *Dictionary of Pastoral Care and Counseling* (Nashville, Tenn.: Abingdon, 1991), pp. 1181–83.

25. Ad in *Virtue*, November/December 1990, p. 98; news story, *Los Angeles Times*, August 6, 1988, Part 2, p. 6; Gary Richmond, "Successful Christian Parenting," Christian Life Resources, 427 N. Town East Blvd., Suite 106, Mesquite, TX 75150.

26. Ruth Graham, commentary in *Christianity Today*, June 6, 1975, p. 32; Elinor Gruen, "Reply to the Editor," *Christianity Today*, July 18, 1975, p. 17.

27. Bruce Yoder, "Singleness and Spirituality," *Studies in Formative Spirituality*, 6, 3 (1985): 412–13; Tim Stafford, "Beyond the Stiff Upper Lip," *Christianity Today*, Janu-ary 13, 1989, pp. 30–34.

28. Gary R. Collins, "Singleness," *Calm Down* (Chappaqua, N.Y.: Christian Herald Books, 1981), pp. 136–41.

29. Ad in *Christianity Today*, April 18, 1986, p. 9; ad in ibid., March 18, 1988, p. 49; news story in *World Wide Challenge* (Campus Crusade for Christ), 13, 2 (March/April 1986): n.p.

30. Alphonse Calabrese, "The Seven Deadly Sins of Christian Marriage," an article in Proctor, *Catalog*, pp. 85–86; Steve and Anne Chapon, "Five Ways to Keep the Sizzle in Your Marriage," *Christian Herald*, January 1985, p. 17; Craig Massey, "The Deadly Art of Criticism," *Moody*, May 1985, pp. 33–37; see the outstanding study by Nancy Tatom Ammerman, *Bible Believers: Fundamentalists in the Modern World* (New Brunswick, N.J.: Rutgers University Press, 1987), pp. 134–46.

31. See Watt, *A Transforming Faith*, pp. 86–91.

32. L. Schneider, "Family, Christian," in Hunter, *Dictionary*, p. 428; Steven Mintz and Susan Kellogg, *Domestic Revolution: A Social History of American Family Life* (New York: Free Press, 1988), pp. 202–3; Barna, *Born Again*, pp. 58–59; Robert Ableman and Stew-art M. Hoover, "The Portrayal of Family on Religious Television," in *Religious Television: Controversies and Conclusions* (Norwood, N.J.: Ablex Publishing, 1990), pp. 281–310.

33. See all of Eugene F. Provenzo, Jr., *Religious Fundamentalism and American Edu-cation: The Battle for the Public Schools* (Albany: State University of New York Press, 1990).

34. Rodney Clapp, "Is the 'Traditional' Family Biblical?" *Christianity Today*, Septem-ber 16, 1989, p. 277.

35. Ibid.; see also two pieces by James Davison Hunter, "Family," in *Culture Wars: The Struggle to Define America* (New York: Basic Books, 1991), pp. 176–96, and, with coauthor

Helen V. Stehlin, "Family: Toward Androgyny," in *Evangelicalism: The Coming Generation* (Chicago: University of Chicago Press, 1987), pp. 87–115.

36. Flyer Group Publishing Company, Loveland, Colorado, ad in *Christian Parenting*, May/June 1990, p. 5.

37. See Jim Manney, "James Dobson," *New Covenant*, September 1990, pp. 9–15.

38. Kay Kuzma, "Family Matters," *Religious Broadcasting*, February 1989, n.p.

39. News story, *Christian Retailing*, November 15, 1989, p. 29.

40. Collins, *Calm Down*, pp. 45–49.

41. See Martin E. Marty's newsletter, *Context*, August 15, 1990, pp. 2–3; Lee Grady, "The New X-Rated Textbooks," *Charisma and Christian Life*, March 1991, pp. 57–62; see the extensive section, "Sex Education in the Public Schools," in *The World and I*, September 1989, pp. 468–611; see also Judith Stacey, *Brave New Families: Stories of Domestic Upheaval in Late Twentieth Century America* (New York: Basic Books, 1990), where she focuses on the travails of two evangelical marriages/families; but also the critical review of this book by Christopher Lasch, "Books," *Commonweal*, February 22, 1991, pp. 135–38; see also the case study, R. Steven Warner, *New Wine in Old Wineskins: Evangelicals in a Small-Town Church* (Berkeley: University of California Press, 1988).

# Part III

# POPULAR RELIGION, THE MEDIA, LITERATURE, AND MUSIC

Pursuing the various roads and trails of popular religion, the tracker discovers both its arbitrariness and its predictability. The former emerges at times because what seem to be potentially nourishing and faithful expressions of the faith lead into thin clones of secular popular culture.[1] Predictability turns up as a regular feature because, by following the logic of incongruity, believers know what kind of content and style they will experience in their participation in popular religion. Certain evangelical opinion makers repeatedly attempted to introduce more unpredictable, often more sophisticated expressions of the fine arts into television, radio, literature, and music. But as the resurgence of the 1970s and 1980s slowed down during the early 1990s, the predictable quality of popular religion still prevailed, largely because that is simply what the greatest number of the rank and file preferred.[2]

In Part III we explore the reasons for the prevalence of the predictable forms of popular religion. We attempt to show that despite sharp criticism from elitist evangelical critics, the rank and file consumers choose in the print media, literature, and music those religious expressions shaped largely by the evangelicals' use of high technology.[3] Convincing quantitative evidence is found in the ongoing popularity among evangelicals of directories and guides describing products available in the humanities and the popular arts. Such materials include *The Christian Media Directory*, with over 4,500 listings of music, radio, video, film, and audio items, and *The Movie and Video Guide for Christian Families*, regularly updated.[4]

One evangelical critic, John Fisher, explains this preference. In his words, "the art of fromming" has come to prevail. Christian media and the arts, the religious versions of secular models, keep believers *from* having to face vulgar language, and vulgar literature, in brief, keeping them *from* straying from the true faith.[5] That preference, based by incongruity on verification in everyday life, leads evangelicals to prefer the more predictable and uncomplicated ways of staying in the faith, as seen in this section with television, film, video, radio, literature, and music including contemporary, performance, and hymnody.

## NOTES

1. Larry Eskridge, "Evangelical Broadcasting: Its Meaning for Evangelicals," in M. L. Bradbury and James B. Gilbert, eds., *Transforming Faith: The Sacred and Secular in Modern American History* (Westport, Conn.: Greenwood Press, 1989), pp. 127–33; Theodore Baehr, *Getting the Word Out* (San Francisco: Harper and Row, 1986); Joel Nederhood, "Communication: Is It Possible?" in David A. Fraser, ed., *Evangelicalism: Surviving Its Success* (St. Davids, Pa.: Eastern Baptist Theological Seminary, 1987), p. 80; Perry C. Cotham, "The Electronic Church," in Allene Stuart Phy, ed., *The Bible and Popular Culture in America* (Philadelphia: Fortress, 1985).

2. Steven R. Lawhead, *Turn Back the Night* (Westchester, Ill.: Crossway Books, 1985), pp. 123–26; Chuck Westerman, "A Confusion of Aims," *The Door*, 198, November/December 1989, pp. 68–69; Kenneth A. Myers, *All God's Children and Blue Suede Shoes: Christians and Popular Culture* (Westchester, Ill.: Crossway Books, 1989).

3. Charles H. Lippy, ed., *Twentieth-Century Shapers of American Popular Religion* (Westport, Conn.: Greenwood Press, 1989), pp. xxii–xxiii.

4. James Lloyd Group, Publishers, *The Christian Media Directory* (Nashville, Tenn.: Thomas Nelson, 1988); George Barna, *What Americans Believe* (Ventura, Calif.: Regal Books, 1991), pp. 30–31.

5. John Fisher, *Real Christians Don't Dance: The Art of Fromming* (Minneapolis: Bethany House, 1988), pp. 140–42.

# 5

# Popular Religion and the Transformation of Television

That the high technology of our day has produced a revolution of epochal dimensions in the mass media is a truism needing no further elaboration. Regarding popular religion, this upheaval is best understood as a transformation—of consciousness, understanding, language, and the response made by the faithful. No serious student in this field questions the sweep and power and potential for good or for woe from this revolution. An evangelical, Haddon Robinson, says,

Technology, which once served the faith, now overpowers it. Protestantism has always been "bookish," rational, ordered and individualistic. Now, however, Christians seem bewildered by the communications revolution. Television, VCRs, motion pictures, and even computers have moved us from a literate to a visual society. Traditionally, Christians have believed spiritual growth came through reading and studying the Bible. In a culture that cannot or will not read, the influence of the Bible in printed form will continue to slip.[1]

These attractive new forms of media, unavailable or in scarce supply to the rank and file until well into the twentieth century, are providing totally new means, writes Frank Dance, "of selecting, composing and sharing perspectives. New institutions of communications create new publics across boundaries of time, space, and social status. New patterns of information open opportunities for whole societies unknown before in history. Along with other dramatic changes, we have altered the symbolic environment that gives meaning and direction to humankind's activity."[2] So powerful have these forces become that commentators argue they have produced a new era in human history, not unlike that of the Reformation or the Age of Nationalism.[3]

Evangelicals obviously found in the electronic media, as statistics demonstrate, a highly congenial way to come to terms with the bewildering demands of faith in a secular world. Based on their transdenominational, parachurch tradition of populist, democratic priorities they have become highly receptive to the world of religion's television and radio programs, videotapes, magazines, and other items in the Christian "marketplace."[4] What such media accomplished was the enormous widening of accessibility to religious (among other) ideas, teachings, and alternative forms of expression to those currently being managed by the leadership elites of the time. Low-priced mass media make available to those otherwise standing outside the "Great Tradition" of scholarship and high literacy new or reaffirming expressions of what it means to be religious.

The differences between these two styles, the "Great" and the "Popular," can scarcely be overexaggerated. The older tradition focused on how slowly change in religious and other social institutional life really had unfolded over the years and on how complicated were the variety of ways religious priorities and participation affected other social institutions and forms of expression such as the arts, manners and styles of living, and family life.[5] Now, almost overnight, the accessible, affordable mass media made available in religious life the teachings of those who preached another way of knowing, that is, that of instant conversion, the urgency of attempting nothing less than the Christianization of America, and the necessity of trusting the religious lessons learned in everyday life.[6]

Within the ranks of evangelicalism, observers are arguing that the transformation has already occurred, that by studying the history of these decades one must conclude that even the "baby boomer church," consisting of the many born shortly after World War II, is being overtaken by the media-oriented "Pepsi Generation" (Sims's term) of the 1980s and 1990s. With the introduction of television into a child's earliest years, with the advent of the new Christian music, with Christian radio, video, and the rest of the electronic and print media marvels empowered and codified by computer wizardry, American evangelicalism, according to Jack Sims, is undergoing a profound transformation, based largely on the new media usage, from which no evasion or avoidance is possible or desirable.[7]

Nowhere is the unique blending of the central features of evangelical popular religion more vividly and convincingly discovered than in its adaptation of television, video, and film. As already seen, it has provided the leadership in programming, in technological innovation, and in marketing and evangelizing for the nation's religious community. It has ready access to the consciousness-altered audiences of the 1990s that did not exist thirty years before. The statistics from A. C. Nielsen show the average American household is now able to receive thirty-one channels. Sixty-eight percent of those households receive at least fifteen channels, 25 percent receive seven to fourteen channels, and just 7 percent can choose from fewer than seven channels. By 1989 some 92 million households owned television sets, almost double the 1960 total of 54 million. Of those 98 percent have color sets and 65 percent have more than one set. Over two-thirds of television households also own VCRs.[8]

Television came to such dominance in so short a time not only because of its newness but because of its accessibility. By contrast to many other leisure-time activities, it required no group participation; after its purchase it was very inexpensive to maintain; it required little or no sustained time or energy commitment over a longer period of time (contrasted to group sports, for example). It can be viewed in solitude, the choices from the menu are plentiful, and most viewers watch for hours on end "without finding the experience noxious or too tiring." Its rewards are a part of everyday life: relaxation, distraction, and amusement with minimal exertion.[9]

Its popularity shows up in the statistic that the average American home has the television turned on for 6.25 hours a day. Each person there views it for almost 4 hours daily, seven days a week. Research shows also that the average adult spends some 200 additional hours annually reading newspapers and the same amount reading magazines. But that same adult reads books just 10 hours a year.[10]

So vast a transformation in life has, of course, produced an enormous output of research by specialists on just why all this happened and what the effects are and could be for our future lives. Among the experts, Neil Postman suggests television triumphs over other media because of its "nondiscursive visual image." He puts forward these ideas. First, people *watch* television; they do not read it. Second, it is attractive because, as it consists of stories and pictures, its message is almost totally nonpropositional; it offers presentations of experiences, not comment about experience. In that way it remains largely irrefutable.

Third, television thus requires little sustained mental effort from the viewer. Fourth, it is by nature almost always entertaining. For financial reasons it must reach as wide a range of viewers/customers/supporters as possible and hence seeks for entertaining rather than unpleasant or unsuitable material for winning viewer loyalty.[11]

Whatever other features specialists may find, these features stand clearly as ingredients that make television viewing so popular. Given the nature of popular religion, with its involvement in everyday life, it seized upon television as its preferred medium. The union unfolded over the 1960s and

1970s, not without frequent and acrimonious dispute, and came into its own in the 1980s, the time frame utilized for the present analysis.

The disputes emerge because "televangelism" or "the electronic church," as it has come to be known, has offered viewers an opportunity for understanding and expressing their faith in a way enormously different from traditional congregational church life. Postman makes the point, "No dogma, terminology, logic, ritual, or tradition are called upon to burden the minds of the viewers, who are required only to respond to the charisma of the preacher."[12]

Certain leaders, however, find in it a God-given opportunity to evangelize the world. What clearly has developed here is a close, if initially confusing symbiosis of many secular television programs and religious television; the former in a very real sense are as fulfilling as certain traditional religious functions. For instance, commercial evening news programming is a ritual much like organized religion; it has icons such as portraying the common life and nature (e.g., Charles Kuralt's "On the Road"); at times it becomes iconoclastic as is the case with "60 Minutes," the televised Watergate hearings, and the promilitary presentation of the Persian Gulf war of 1991. Thus both religion and television have their everyday, well-known rituals, icons, and expressions of iconoclasm. Television, like religion, is integrating viewers into the belief system of American society.[13]

Likewise, evangelical observer Clifford G. Christians notes that for all their similarities television and religion differ over the central feature of transcendence, the permanent and eternal, the everlasting and heavenly dimension of religious faith. For all of its ability to make itself appealing through the use of intimacy, with its close-up camera shots of expressive faces, and its visual immediacy, in its ability to capture the immediate moment of occurrence, television in all its forms fails to bring home to the viewer any deep understanding of the eternal.[14]

Other critical judgments during the growth years expressed fears that some viewers would give up participating in their local churches in favor of watching the programs at home or would cut back on their financial support for the local parish. As research later documented, neither of these possibilities developed; viewers continued to attend and support their local churches.[15]

Although the viewing audience for religious television is very diverse in both its denominational and its social characteristics, it is clear the overwhelming number of viewers are in the evangelical/Pentecostal/fundamentalist/charismatic family. Despite efforts by mainline churches offering a religious program network entitled "VISN" to reach a wide audience, the broadcast and cable systems of popular religion discussed in chapter 1 continue to reflect the popular religion of the evangelicals.

As suggested, the evangelical drive to save America and the world for Christendom, with its emphasis on "ministerial action and congregational consumptionism," easily absorbs the popular television means of communication (see chapter 1). The tradition's heritage of populist preaching and informal worship services has proved fertile ground for the kinds of religious expression used by televangelists. That is, revivalist preachers of an earlier day, such as John Wesley or Charles Finney, knew how to use religion to attract the attention of sinners; so too, today's televangelists have similar know-how. Another similarity is the manner in which both earlier and contemporary revivalists have used mass meetings, with their attractiveness for coverage by the mass media, to persuade viewers at home of the need for prayer, preaching, and conversion.

The populist, democratic quality of evangelicalism of the past and of the present means that every person has the opportunity at any given moment for immediate salvation, and thus does not have to wait on the decisions of any church official or formal sacramental distribution. Also, such a conversion experience in evangelical understanding produces peace, joy, and, to some, material prosperity. Finally, the heavy emphasis placed by today's televangelists on raising funds is seen as a part of the opportunity to convert the world; for that opportunity no price is too great to pay. Televangelism is in the great tradition of superstar celebrities such as Charles G. Finney, Dwight L. Moody, Billy Sunday, and the contemporary leader, Billy Graham. With all its tradition and history, evangelicalism can easily absorb and enhance the features of preaching found in today's television ministry.[16]

These preachers are the ones whose innovations have been adapted to the demands of television. They knew how to replace intellectual features of the chosen message and use instead everyday parlance. They knew how to illustrate with story and anecdote, staying away from the more erudite and formally educated sermon, and they knew how to use body language and voice inflection to embellish and drive home their points. Finally, being often persons of "enormous ego and ambition who subscribe enthusiastically to the basic American values of success, competition, and progress," they offer role modeling and proof that the rags-to-riches theme is still thriving in middle America. Thus the popularity of the celebrity televangelists and other religious broadcasters stretches back to and runs from the beginnings of evangelicalism to the present.[17]

For all their similarities, the celebrity preachers and several of those of lesser fame reflected within their own ranks significant differences in programming and in personal styles of presentation. Media specialist William Martin finds that by the mid-1980s most religious telecasting came to the viewers in four different versions. First were the long-standing but decreasingly popular denominational and ecumenical programs such as

"Lamp unto My Feet," "This Is the Life," "Faith for Today," and "Herald of Truth." Their viewing audience was nationally between 200,000 and 500,000.

Second were the weekly worship services broadcast almost always by a local church for a local audience. These too, in light of escalating costs, have diminished in number. Third are the programs of the syndicated stars such as Graham, Rex Humbard, and Oral Roberts as well as Swaggart, Falwell, Robertson, James Robison, Kenneth Copeland, and Charles Stanley. Fourth are the programs working through the growing number of cable and satellite networks, such as those with the Family Network of Christian Broadcasting (Pat Robertson), and Trinity Broadcasting Network (Paul Crouch). Here are veritable smorgasbords of expression, everything from wrestlers for Jesus, doing physical deeds of prowess as testimony to their faith, and style shows with high-fashion clothes emblazoned with religious mottoes to the other extreme of the subdued, understated preaching of Lloyd Ogilvie and Jack Hayford.[18]

What stands out by the early 1990s is that televangelism continues, despite major setbacks, to be one of the major forms of evangelical popular religion. Also, given the constantly changing nature of the market and new economic pressures to produce funds, preachers are continually producing new programming of television evangelism, while holding to the traditional celebrity format.

To be specific, despite the huge drop in both revenue and public confidence because of the financial and sexual scandals of such blockbusters as Jim and Tammy Faye Bakker, Jimmy Swaggart, and Oral Roberts, the latter two remained on the air, even with diminished revenue. The other household names continued with new formats. Falwell ended the Moral Majority and greatly reduced other political exposure but kept his Sunday morning program. Robertson earlier had shifted CBN from twenty-four–hour religious programming to largely running old, tested favorites that include early sitcoms, Westerns, and adventure and war films.[19] Hence, by the time of this transition the viewing public could adjust to the fact that, although some of their trusted leaders had slipped badly, the popularity of religious television would continue to grow. Clearly such forms of ministry had not come to overshadow the appeal of orthodox doctrine, moral rectitude, and committed discipleship. But they had furnished the rank and file with an understanding and adjustment to the transforming power of this mass medium.

That understanding is strongly enhanced by the ability of broadcast television to create among its viewers a sense of a shared experience, of a commonality of similar everyday ways of knowing and sharing the faith. What united this very dispersed audience, geographically isolated from personal interchange, is the common experience and purpose of learning the faith and spreading its saving message.[20] Some specialists have suggested that it is not so much the message or the doctrine of a superstar preacher that makes her or him so popular as it is the "communicator style." Television audiences respond more to the highly intense, inspirational, fast speaking, body-language–oriented preacher seeking more to convert than to edify than to the more staid, expository kind of preacher.[21] Obviously the personalizing power of television with its close-up shots to display intensity, fervor, and commitment enhances that quality. But having acknowledged that, we need to explore here in some depth what specifically the televangelists do preach and how those themes are attuned to the viewer's understanding of the faith achieved through the medium of popular religion.

The television screen brings into the viewers' homes the visual statement of what the preachers are defining as a religious sanctuary. It makes colorfully vivid those objects and memories known to the believers such as pulpits, robed choirs, the cross, altars, organs, the Bible, hymn-singing, a responsive congregation, and the like.[22]

Media specialist William A. Fore demonstrates from his research what such symbols actually mean. For instance, the robe of the preacher indicates the authority held by that person; the presence of the pulpit and the Bible gives the same message of authority. When a celebrity preacher interviews a celebrity, it denotes the importance of success as a justification to hear that speaker; businessmen celebrity guests denote the importance of wealth.

The presence of several phone banks at a fund-raiser tells the viewers their calls are given personal attention. The televangelist who uses country-western music is saying religion can be fun; his or her "pulpit-thumping" appeals to emotions and entertainment. When the viewer is shown giveaway objects for which to write in, that viewer is being linked personally to the technological object of television.[23]

In the same format those who respond to the televangelists are themselves acknowledging their need to believe or are affirming a teaching being advocated by the televangelist. Fore points out the connections between "needs" and "appeals" to make that point. The need for amusement is met by, say, Jimmy Swaggart's humor and music; those needing to see authority exalted watch Jerry Falwell's television skills or Pat Robertson's forays into presidential politics. For the opposite effect, deflation, viewers can tune in the Bakker and Swaggart scandals. For sharing their religious feelings with others, viewers are invited to join the 700 Club or the PTL Club, becoming a "Prayer Partner."

To understand God's plans for each individual, the televangelists provide charts and proof texts printed on the screen. Unusually strong needs demanding fulfillment can be met by Swaggart's attacks on Roman Catholics or Robertson's on political or religious liberals. As role models, Robertson's suavity and Falwell's certainty on faith issues stand clear. Finally, for those needing to "believe in magic," Fore finds that need met by televangelist promises of healing, when requests are accompanied by donations.[24]

Among the directly religious topics on which these programs focus, the specific items considered depend upon the priorities unique to that particular community of faith and its leader; hence, Pentecostalists and charismatics spend considerable time on the gifts of the Holy Spirit, fundamentalists on doctrine and contending for the faith, and evangelicals on winning converts around the globe. The specialists tracking such specific priorities have found that the following topics appear the most frequently (in numerical order): God, Jesus, the Bible as a text, other uses of the Bible, sin, Satan, faith, healing, heaven, being "saved," being "born again," other religions, missionaries to foreign countries, the second coming of Christ, Hell, creation, the State of Israel, missionary programs in the United States, the supernatural, Armageddon, atheism, and the controversy over evolution.[25]

Throughout, the emphasis within evangelicalism remains on finding in scripture one or more proof texts to substantiate the teachings of the preacher. These stand in marked contrast to most mainline expository or confessional teachings, largely because of the two camps' different understandings of the nature of the Bible and of educational and other socialization experiences. Evangelicals believe the Bible is understandable and compelling because of its simplicity, a condition that leads to simple exposition in preaching.[26]

This kind of popular religion also embraces by contrast to mainline emphases, advocating the rewards and pleasures of obeying God in the here and now more than emphasizing self-denial and self-sacrifice. The prosperity theology of Oral Roberts, Jim Bakker, Kenneth Copeland, and others finds ready support as a "theology of glory" that upholds the benefits of faithful living, as opposed to "the theology of the cross" that emphasizes the sinful nature of humans in need of forgiveness throughout their lives.[27]

At the heart of the message is the priority given to the care shown by the all-powerful God to those who have come to faith. The social-outreach dimension to faithful living is secondary to the need to believe God is ready to and does answer individual prayer; God acts as "a benevolent resource" for the believer. Observers within and outside the evangelical world agree the key activity is that of conversion. In confronting God, individual seekers find the Creator unmistakably and overwhelmingly in the events of their lives. It is that last element—their lives, their everyday experiences—that keeps evangelicals believing that this personal God is at work in each of them.

That quality opens up the central feature of evangelical preaching and broadcasting, the necessity and the joy of personal testimony or witnessing to the faith. Both radio and television programs focus heavily on individuals telling their own life stories, such as how in a time of great crisis or doubt or fear they came to faith. This experience turns around their lives and sets them on a new course. The electronic and print media both offer large numbers of testimonies to which listeners and readers can easily relate and that they can confirm as true on the basis of their own experience.[28]

So central is conversion and witnessing to the thesis of this book that it merits additional discussion in some detail. A remarkably fresh interpretation (in a heavily crowded field of analysis) is offered by Professor William Hendricks. Acknowledging the presence of several different voices within the evangelical choir, he argues that the believers "agree among themselves more than they disagree."[29] He finds a dozen areas that, when considered together, stand as the essential message of the electronic church. He takes the titles from the two central books of the tradition, the Bible and the hymnal, the latter being an excellent source of insight into popular religion. By hearing the music and understanding the words of this tradition, Hendricks writes, the participant can better understand its theology; thus, the author here chooses certain gospel songs and hymns that are generally well known in that family.

First is "For the Bible Tells Me So," teaching that the Bible is self-explanatory; in the bumpersticker-style explanation: "God spoke it. The Bible declares it. I believe it. That settles it." Once a preacher announces "The Bible says," the question at hand is resolved. Second, "What He's done for others, He'll do for you," which translated into popular religion means the "triumph of experience." The Bible stands as the principle of authority but personal, everyday experience "is the substantive principle of authority." An evangelical hymn reads, "It is no secret what God can do. What He's done for others, He'll do for you." Those who have known this experience know it happened to them personally as individuals.[30]

Next comes "Trials dark on every hand," meaning God comes to be known through the shared experiences of believers. God stands on the side of those persons and is responsible for providential care through these trials and directs the seekers to individual redemption. However, fourth, not all problems are solved (as shown in the discussion of twelve-step seekers). So, as the hymn title reads, "It took a miracle." Here is further proof (beyond God's providential care of nature) that the believer is being cared for. In the popular testimony format of the media, miracles occur such as a woman on the way to have an abortion listening to a radio preacher talking about prolife as she was going out the door. She heard, changed her mind, and bore the child. Physical and mental healings with all their visual dramatic impact also have powerful appeal at the popular level.[31]

Fifth is "For sinners such as I"; believers fail to live up to God's providential care because they are by nature sinners. When life goes wrong or bad, the evangelical message finds sin and/or the work of Satan responsible for the setback. When God's will, clear and simple, is thwarted it is Satan who is to blame. At this point some seekers enter into the realm of demon possession, finding illnesses of various kinds being caused by the legions of Satan infecting the believer's life.

Sixth is "Let's just praise the Lord." When adversity strikes one's life, when bad things happen to believers, no explanation is needed; praising the Lord will do. "Positive affirmation in all and every desperate circumstance of life is the only appropriate response." In so doing, the born-again person helps strengthen her or his own faith and models this for others.[32]

Next, "Are there no foes for me to face?" When doubt or dissent appear, evangelical preachers find in their faith a prepared reply; all those negative qualities are of the Devil. Those outsiders whose lives seem to threaten the believers are seen as being of one cloth. As they are not for the faith, they are enemies; there can be no middle ground. Such an attitude is shown, for instance, in the categorization of those pursuing "secular humanism" such as teachers, broadcasters, journalists, liberal theology preachers, and the like. When such threats appear, the believer strengthens her or his courage, bears the cross, and endures the pain.[33]

Eighth, "Heaven came down and filled my soul." This is the familiar Christian doctrine of the atonement. God who became incarnate in Christ underwent crucifixion, death, and resurrection as payment or ransom for the sinner's otherwise condemned soul. This is the vicarious redemption, accepted on the popular level by faith in an act that cannot be repeated by human endeavor; it is supernatural.

Ninth, "What a friend we have in Jesus." The only incarnate expression of God on earth has been Christ, who continues to reign and work miracles. He is understood as a personal friend, helping believers, understanding believers, calling them to imitate him. Tenth, "Sweet, sweet Spirit." Here is the centrality of personal experience upheld as validating the believer's inner spiritual life. The Holy Spirit is the power that brings the seeker to repentance and conversion, working an individual miracle for the sincere believer. This Spirit is known by feeling, through a variety of emotions but always by the experience of feeling or sensing. Proof of this are the fruits of goodness, that appear when this Spirit is allowed to work in the believer. Those who may disagree at any important point within the community are probably without the Spirit. The actual workings out of this Spirit through the gifts of tongues, healing, exorcism, and the rest are the forces, as discussed earlier, that more than any other single feature divide the evangelical community.[34]

Eleventh, "When the roll is called up yonder" points to the teaching on the last things, the final days, the way in which God will conclude life on this planet and prepare the saved for the life hereafter. Most evangelicals believe that, prior to Christ's return, a great increase in evil and other works of Satan will spread across the globe. Christ with his army returns, defeats those forces in the battle of Armageddon, and prepares the way for the saved to enter heaven. Hendricks suggests, persuasively, that the timetable for these cataclysms is one of the most divisive issues among the evangelicals and hence is very rarely discussed in the media.[35]

Finally, "the family of God" refers to the doctrine of the church. With its tradition of populist, anti-intellectual expression, evangelicalists have allowed each participating family to claim some unique understanding of the complex variety of God's revelation. Hence they can live with one another knowing that no one has a monopoly on all truth. Further, they choose to present as their model of the true church one rooted in nostalgia, "recalling rural-religious America to the faith of ancestors" to create a Christian America in the here and now. By their music, code words, and insider symbols they find the faith of yesterday sufficient for the problems of tomorrow.[36] In the grandest of ironies, that faith, summed up in the hymn "The Little Brown Church in the Vale," is presented to the world by the most highly technical, sophisticated broadcast equipment available.[37]

## VIDEO AND FILM

Technological expertise, one of the major sources of evangelical growth, is dramatically exemplified by reference to two events. In 1985 Campus Crusade sponsored a videoconference attended by some 300,000 people at more than ninety sites in fifty-four nations through the connections of seven satellite "uplink" sites. The purpose was to conduct training and motivation sessions for volunteer evangelists to convert the world. Simultaneous translations were made in over thirty languages, and the telecasts were sent into some 9,000 United States cable systems, thirty broadcast systems, and national stations in other countries.[38]

Second, later in the 1980s the first "satellite-to-home Christian TV Network" in North America was put on the retail market. Sponsored by the Dominion Network, it offered to individual buyers a home dish and selector/receiver to bring into their living rooms a variety of evangelical programs. Its advertising came with the full endorsement of most of the televangelist stars: James Kennedy, Jerry Falwell, James Robison, Marilyn Hickey, Robert Schuller, Oral Roberts, Bill Bright, Kenneth and Gloria Copeland, and Tim and Beverly LaHaye.[39] Both illustrate the receptivity of evangelicalism to these opportunities for extending the faith and for informing the rank and file, with new tools and new strategies that had not been available before.[40]

The worlds of video and film offered the faithful another major opportunity to express their faith through the new media. Now the viewers could hear and see speakers (not just use radio) not available in this format before; they could see fields for harvesting souls in visual ways not open before; they could consider a vast variety of social and personal issues through a brand-new medium. These media, further, were readily accessible, often purchasable, and thus open for viewing at times convenient to the local audiences. Finally, these were produced by professional staffs "at a level of excellence that would be extremely difficult or impossible for any church staff to provide on its own."[41]

In less than twenty years the video ministry has become an integral part of the full range of services offered by evangelical congregations. In a major study of Protestant churches and video by Michael F. Korpi and Judith E. Saxton, over forty subject-matter categories were identified. Three major categories of user patterns became apparent. The first was the subject of interpersonal relationships, with some 27 percent of the reporting churches using one or more programs on the family, 26 percent sponsoring video on youth issues, and 14 percent on marriage. In the second category, personal growth and development, some 24 percent offered programs on Christian life and 16 percent focused on discipleship. In the final category, outreach, some 18 percent had programs on missions and evangelism, 4 percent on spiritual gifts, 4 percent on prophecy, and 3 percent on apologetics (advocacy of the faith).[42]

Of the churches surveyed, using the researchers' definitions, 80 percent of the general evangelical churches were using video and film. These were incorporated rapidly for several reasons: a number of large publishing houses such as Word, Inc., saw the potential and used its considerable assets to launch into this new ministry; parents saw the advantages of having whole-some and trustworthy programs available in this omnipresent medium for their children, who had the secular options readily accessible; the local congrega-tion could employ the expertise of James Dobson and Joyce Lansdorf, for instance, whose videos were presented to encourage direct local audience involvement; the distribution system was, by contrast to national television, in harmony with the evangelical practice of populist, decentralized adminis-tration. Many independent dealers set up centers—"Your One-Stop Christian Video Store"—with toll-free numbers, computerized billing, and credit card financing. Most denominations by the late 1980s had built rather complete inventories, giving the programs selected the sanction of each specific body even though most videos were and are nondenominational.[43] Most evangelical bookstores also carried a variety of religious titles. Some were also available in venues that carried the usual format of westerns, comedies, and drama.

Further information about these resources became accessible through the lengthening review columns in the nondenominational journals such as *Christianity Today, Charisma, Christian Herald, Moody,* and until its close, *Eternity.* Acknowledging that some of the materials were substandard in terms of quality of production and superficiality of teaching, the reviewers were making available the information viewers and congregations needed for their purchases. The popular theme became evident with such programs as one produced by World Wide Pictures (Billy Graham), "Home for Christmas," with music, down-home stories, and nostalgia about the season starring the likes of Cliff Barrows, George Beverly Shea, Johnny Cash, Evie Karlsson, and others.[44]

Much of the video footage is devoted to Bible studies, with experts such as Dr. James M. Boice and Donald Grey Barnhouse doing expository teaching. These give a local congregation, or an independent Bible-study group, the opportunity at times convenient to them to stay in touch with the thinking of recognized teachers. The format offers the opportunity for personal input and group reflection. One variation comes from the "RTS Outreach" ministry. It has a video, the "Baker's Bible Study," to which is added "The Fisherman Video Game" with some ninety minutes of discussion starters and questions set up on a competitive structure for the viewers. Drawing on the evangelical idea of being fishers of people, the program offers a more entertaining way of education and reflection than the older, formed into circle study groups.[45]

The videos are also made appealing because they offer at the local meeting place an opportunity to view the superstars. Sensing the potential in multimedia ministries, leaders such as Dobson, Charles Swindoll, J. Keith Miller, Joyce Lansdorf, and Anthony Campolo, to name but a few, moved into the media world with videos, radio, television, and print media. In a multimedia breakthrough Moody Videos combined several expressions into one tape: Maranatha Music and Moody Institute of Science together produced continuous scenes of the world of nature, backed by instrumental interpretations of hymns, followed by voices speaking selected scripture narrations. It encased features of high technology, popular expressions of affirmation, and opportunity for personal reflection in a way new to the religious community. It was also made available in audiocassette and compact disc.[46]

Finally, in the format of a book-a-month club, a "Family Video Club" enterprise appeared in the mid-1980s. Offering some 1,300 titles including classic cartoons for children ("Peanuts," "Winnie the Pooh"), instructional materials on body health, cooking, fishing, and nature films on national parks and foreign countries, it also made available religious music such as Sandi Patti, speakers such as Colson, Campolo, and Josh McDowell, and movies made by explicitly evangelical cinema companies.[47]

Acceptance of video has been much easier to achieve than the acceptance of the movies. Since their presence increased in the 1960s, evangelicals had maintained considerable resistance to and often total avoidance of the movies. The major reasons listed were their disapproval of the life-styles of the stars and objections to the emphasis on sex, violence, drinking, and gambling, all of which clashed with believers' convictions. Over the years many of the faithful rarely if at all attended the movie theatre.[48]

However, just as television and videos became dominant means of entertainment in American life, so too the movies have become a mainstay staple in that world. There simply was no closing out their availability to the curious or to young people tasting what their faith had taught to be forbidden. Beyond that, as the level of high technology improved the quality of movies in sound, lighting, editing, and the like, so too increasing numbers came to realize that they could use this medium for evangelizing, for recharging their own faith batteries, and for joint family entertainment and bonding. And, of course, the most influential of all spokesmen for evangelicalism, Billy Graham, was among the first to have his crusades placed on television and his media department start producing full-length movies with explicit Christian themes. Just as with video, evangelical magazines started carrying sometimes long reviews of the current fare of general movies. Some made by commercial companies outside evangelicalism, such as *The Dollmaker* and *Chariots of Fire* were praised for their strong affirmations of faith.

Also for family viewing, evangelicals recommended such older movies as *The Parent Trap, To Kill a Mockingbird, The Sound of Music, Meet Me in St. Louis, Singing in the Rain*, the cavalry trilogy of John Wayne, *The Searcher, Barrabas, The Trip to Bountiful*, and *Lilies of the Field*.[49]

Within the community itself, several evangelical educational film companies have continued to produce a variety of full-length features covering everything from famous church-history leaders to children's adventures to current social problems to film biographies of missionaries. The means of distribution are similar to those of videos, the higher costs of producing meaning that more rentals than purchases prevail. Finally, a major evangelical publisher, Thomas Nelson of Nashville, makes available a convenient resource. Edited by Ted Baehr, it is *The Movie and Video Guide for Christian Families*, first published in 1988 and updated since then. It includes the editor's estimate of a wide variety of films, both commercial and church related. It tells clearly what the readers might find offensive (violence, language, sexual behavior, and yoga, considered "magical thinking"). Various newsletters such as Baehr's *Movieguide* update the materials in this book.

All in all, the realm of television/film/video has proven to be one of the great instruments for popular religion. It harmonizes with the leisure-time, educational, and religious life-styles of most evangelicals and should continue to increase its influence even as new improvements in technology, such as high-resolution television, continue to keep Americans loyal to these media.

## NOTES

1. Haddon Robinson, "More 'Religion,' Less Impact," *Christianity Today*, January 17, 1986, p. 5-I.

2. Frank Dance, *Human Communications Theory* (Chicago: Holt, Rinehart and Winston, 1967), cited in Raymond Bailey, "The Mass Media and the Church," *Review and Expositor, Baptist Theological Journal*, 81, 1 (Winter 1984): 5.

3. Pierre Babin, *The New Era in Religious Communication* (Minneapolis: Augsburg Fortress, 1991), pp. 36–37.

4. Stewart M. Hoover, "Television Myth and Reality: The Role of Substantive Meaning of Spatiality," in James Carey, ed., *Media, Myth, and Narrative* (Newbury Park, Calif.: Sage, 1989), pp. 68–69; Robert Kubey and Mihaly Csikszentmihalyi, *Television and the Quality of Life: How Viewing Shapes Everyday Experience* (Hillsdale, N.J.: Laurence Erlbaum, 1990), pp. 181–221.

5. Ruel W. Tyson, "Journalism and Religion," in Mircea Eliade, ed., *The Encyclopedia of Religion*, vol. 8 (New York: Macmillan, 1987), p. 123.

6. See the argument of William Fore, *Mythmakers: Gospel, Culture, and the Media* (New York: Pilgrim Press, 1990), pp. 3–4.

7. Obviously this is a highly debatable interpretation, one well made by Jack Sims, "Baby Boomers: Time to Pass the Torch," *Christian Life*, January 1986, pp. 211–15.

8. *1990 Report on Television* (New York: A. C. Nielsen Company, 1991), pp. 2–17.

9. Kubey and Csikszentmihalyi, *Television*, p. 101.

10. Richard V. Peace, "The New Media Environment: Evangelicalism in a Visually Oriented Society," *Journal of the Academy of Evangelicalism in Theological Education*, 1 (1985–86): 36–37.

11. See also his point on deconstructing television texts; Neil Postman, "Engaging Students in the Great Conversation," *Phi Delta Kappan*, January 1983, pp. 310–16; Quentin J. Schultze, *Televangelism and American Culture* (Grand Rapids, Mich.: Baker Book House, 1991), pp. 15, 95, 212; Barry R. Litman and Elizabeth Bain, "The Viewership of Television Programming: A Multi-Disciplinary Analysis of Television," *Review of Religious Research*, 30, 4 (1988): 329–43; a helpful British viewpoint on American television is S.J.D. Green, "The Medium and the Message: Televangelism in America," *American Quarterly*, 44, 1 (March 1992): 136–45.

12. Neil Postman, *The Disappearance of Childhood* (New York: Delacorte Press, 1982), p. 116; Ronald A. Sarno, *Using Media in Religious Education* (Birmingham: Religious Education Press, 1987); see the recent critique by Quentin J. Schultze, Gregor T. Goethels, and Thomas E. Boomhine, "The Gospel According to TV," *Religious Broadcasting*, November 1991, pp. 10–19. Billy Graham criticized some televangelists for their activities once Russia became open for more missionaries' work. He found that several of them went there to raise money for their own use. They would take videos of their presence in Moscow and play these back in the United States for their own fund-raising without maintaining a program in Russia; news story, *Newsweek*, July 22, 1991, p. 49.

13. Gregor T. Goethels, *The TV Ritual: Worship at the Video Altar* (Boston: Beacon Press, 1981); John P. Ferre, *Religious Perspectives on Commercial Television in the United States* (Ames: Iowa State University Press, 1985, in the Critical Studies in the Mass Media Series, vol. 2), pp. 290–95.

14. Clifford G. Christians, "Redemptive Media as the Evangelical's Cultural Task," in Quentin J. Schultze, ed., *American Evangelicals and the Mass Media* (Grand Rapids, Mich.: Zondervan, 1990), pp. 331–56; Roy M. Anker, ed., *Dancing in the Dark: Youth, Culture,*

*and the Electronic Media* (Grand Rapids, Mich.: Eerdmans, 1991), pp. 47–55; William Kuhns, *The Electronic Gospel* (New York: Herder and Herder, 1969), p. 32.

15. Robert Wuthnow, "The Religious Significance of Religious Television," *Review of Religious Research*, 29, 2 (December 1987): 125–34; Peter G. Horsefield, *Religious Television: The American Experience* (New York: Longman, 1984), pp. 80–87; Stewart M. Hoover, "The Religious Television Audience: A Matter of Significance or Size?" in Robert Ableman and Stewart M. Hoover, eds., *Religious Television: Controversies and Conclusions* (Norwood, N.J.: Ablex Publishing Corporation, 1990), pp. 109–29.

16. Dennis E. Owen, "Protestantism," in Charles Reagan Wilson and William Ferris, eds., *Encyclopedia of Southern Culture* (Chapel Hill: University of North Carolina Press, 1989), p. 1303; I draw heavily here from Bill Leonard, "The Electronic Church: An Interpretive Essay," *Review and Expositor*, 81, 1 (Winter 1984): 44–45; Nathan Hatch, *The Democratization of American Christianity* (New Haven: Yale University Press, 1989), p. 14; Razelle Frankl, *Televangelism: The Marketing of Popular Religion* (Carbondale: Southern Illinois University Press, 1987), pp. 79–90; see especially her documentation.

17. Hatch, *Democratization of American Christianity*, pp. 8–12, 193–226; Schultze, "Keeping the Faith," in *American Evangelicals*, p. 35; William Martin, "Mass Communications," in Charles H. Lippy and Peter W. Williams, eds., *Encyclopedia of the American Religious Experience*, vol. 3 (New York: Scribners, 1988), pp. 1723–26.

18. Martin, "Mass Communications," pp. 1718–20.

19. News story on televangelists, *Wall Street Journal*, May 18, 1987, p. 6; James G. Hougland, "The Instability of Support for Televangelists: Public Reactions during a Time of Embarrassment," *Review of Religious Research*, 32, 1 (September 1990): 56–64; review essay by Garry Wills, *New York Review of Books*, December 21, 1989, pp. 20–26; Robert Ableman, "The Impact of the PTL Scandals on Religious Television Viewers," *Journal of Communications and Religion*, 2 (March 1988): 41–51.

20. Quentin J. Schultze, "Secular Television as Popular Religion," in Ableman and Hoover, *Religious Television*, p. 243; Chris Wright, "Preaching to the Converted: Conversion Language and the Constitution of the TV Evangelical Community," *The Sociological Review*, 37, 4 (November 1989): 734.

21. Kimberly Neuendorf and Robert Ableman, "Televangelism—A Look at Communicator Styles," *Journal of Religious Studies*, 13, 1 (1987): 41–59.

22. Richard G. Peterson, "Symbolism's 'New Spin,' " in Ray B. Browne et al., eds., *Dominant Symbols in Popular Culture* (Bowling Green, Ohio: Bowling Green State University Popular Press, 1990), pp. 49–58.

23. William F. Fore, *Mythmakers: Gospel, Culture, and the Media* (New York: Friendship Press, 1990), pp. 74–75.

24. Ibid., p. 77.

25. Robert Ableman and Kimberly Neuendorf, "Themes and Topics in Television Programming," *Review of Religious Research*, 29, 2 (December 1989): 152, based on their research explained in this article; William F. Fore, " 'Living Church' and 'Electronic Church' Compared," in Ableman and Hoover, *Television*, pp. 135–46.

26. William Martin, "Perspectives on the Electronic Church," in Samuel S. Hill, Jr., ed., *Varieties of Southern Religious Experience* (Baton Rouge: Louisiana State University Press, 1988), p. 78.

27. Bruce Barron, *The Health and Wealth Gospel* (Downers Grove, Ill.: InterVarsity, 1987); Michael Horton, ed., *The Agony of Deceit* (Chicago: Moody Press, 1990); Eugene F. Klug, "The Electronic Church," *Concordia Theological Quarterly*, 45 (October 1981): 261–80; Perry Cotham, "The Electronic Church," in Allene Stuart Phy, ed., *The Bible and Popular Culture* (Philadelphia: Fortress, 1985), p. 121; C. P. Wagner, "Church Growth," in

Stanley M. Burgess and Gary B. McGee, eds., *Dictionary of Pentecostal and Charismatic Movements* (Grand Rapids, Mich.: Zondervan, 1988), pp. 181–95.

28. Cotham, "Electronic Church," p. 121; see the examples cited in Margaret Poloma, *The Assemblies of God at the Crossroads: Charisma and Institutional Dilemmas* (Knoxville: University of Tennessee Press, 1989), pp. 219–51; see the testimonies by leading evangelicals Gloria Gaither, Jack Hayford, Joni Eareckson Tada, Jill Briscoe, Robert A. Cook, and Ted Engstrom in *Christian Herald*, February 1988, pp. 22–25.

29. William Hendricks, "The Theology of the Electronic Church," *Review and Expositor*, 81, 1 (Winter 1984): 62; see also the list in Jeffrey Hadden and Charles Swann, *Primetime Preachers: The Rising Power of Televangelism* (Reading, Mass.: Addison-Wesley, 1981), pp. 85–102; an important variation on these themes is Steve Bruce, "The Religion of Religious Television," *Pray TV: Televangelism in America* (London: Routledge, 1990), pp. 67–95.

30. Hendricks, "Theology," p. 63; alongside this read Wright, "Preaching to the Converted," pp. 733–60.

31. Hendricks, "Theology," p. 64.

32. Ibid., pp. 64–65.

33. Ibid., p. 65.

34. Ibid., pp. 67–68.

35. Ibid., p. 68.

36. Ibid., p. 69.

37. Steve Bruce, "Conclusions," *Pray TV*, pp. 233–40; Hendricks does not list "The Little Brown Church in the Vale."

38. News story, *Moody*, March 1986, p. 123; Carol R. Thiessen, "VCRs: Plugging into an Unexplored Medium," *Christianity Today*, January 23, 1981, pp. 97–98; Mellie Matula, "The Gospel Music Video a la Carman & Yake," *Religious Broadcasting*, April 1992, p. 10.

39. See their advertising materials from Dominion Video Satellite, P.O. Box 9060, Farmington Hills, MI 48108.

40. See ads in special advertising section, "Screening Room," *Christianity Today*, September 24, 1990, n.p.; Deirdre Boyle, "Video," in Eric Barnouw, ed., *International Encyclopedia of Communications*, vol. 4 (New York: Oxford University Press, 1989), pp. 282–87; Tom Neufer Emswiler, *A Complete Guide to Making the Most of Video in Religious Settings* (Normal, Ill.: Wesley Foundation, 1985), pp. vii–x, 1–4.

41. See the list of displayers in the annual preconvention issues of *Religious Broadcasting*; for example, February 1992, pp. 107–22; see the study by Michael K. Korpi and Judith E. Saxton, "Supporting the Status Quo: Film and Video Use in the Protestant Churches," a paper delivered at the Conference on Evangelicals, the Mass Media, and American Culture," Wheaton College, Fall 1988, in mimeograph, p. 4; I follow their material here closely; see Schultze, *Televangelism and American Culture*, pp. 239–40.

42. Korpi and Saxton, "Supporting the Status Quo," p. 181.

43. Ibid., pp. 18–19; see a special advertising section in *Christianity Today*, November 17, 1987, pp. 50–61; see the catalog on evangelical videos from Crown Ministries, Euclid, MN 56722; see also Emswiler, *Guide*, passim; Galaxy Communications makes available a wide variety of Bible videos, "The Living Book," which has enactments of Bible stories; Box 101, Blaine, WA 98230.

44. "Video," *Charisma*, February 1986, p. 9; David Baird, "Christian Video Needs to Grow in Quality," *Christian Herald*, November 12, 1991, p. 9.

45. "RTS Outreach," Ellenwood, GA 30049.

46. News story, *Christianity Today*, August 5, 1983, pp. 29–36.

47. Mark Coppengh, "A Christian Perspective on Film," in Leland Ryken, ed., *The*

*Christian Imagination: Essays on Literature and the Arts* (Grand Rapids, Mich.: Baker Book House, 1981), pp. 288–302; news story, *Charisma*, April 1987, p. 44; see also the Barna Research Group, *VCRs and the American Way of Life* (Glendale, Calif.: Barna Research, 1990); see Entertainment Plus, P.O. Box 9550, Jackson, MS 39202; Donald J. Drew, *Images of Man: A Critique of Contemporary Cinema* (Downers Grove, Ill.: InterVarsity, 1974).

48. See Gordon Lindley, "Should Christians Attend the Movies?" in *The Voices of Healing*, Dallas, 1964, listed in Paul A. Soukup, *Communication and Theology: Introduction and Review of the Literature* (London: World Association for Christian Communication, 1983), p. 233; Ken Wales, "Can Any Good Thing Come Out of Hollywood?" *Christianity Today*, September 21, 1984, pp. 19–25.

49. See as early as January 1969, *Moody Monthly*, pp. 36–44, a feature on "Media"; the most famous of the World Wide movies has been *The Restless One*, 1965; see Anne Henderson Hart, "What Makes a Film Christian?" *Eternity*, June 1982, pp. 19–21; review, *Christian Herald*, September 1987, pp. 38–40; evangelical student filmmaking is discussed in "Portrait," *The Chronicle of Higher Education*, October 30, 1991, p. A5.

# 6

# Popular Religion and the Radio: Those Who Have Ears

In the ongoing tension between "holding fast" and "pressing on," between preserving the past and being open to the future, evangelicals, along with other religionists, claim that the pillars of their faith, the fundamentals, do not change even though the ever-changing media for their transmission must be in constant change.[1] Nowhere is this more evident than in the world of radio as it interacts with popular religion. Evangelicals and radio have been allied since the earliest days of this medium. From the first days of broadcasting evangelicals seized the opportunities for carrying out the Great Commission and turned radio into one of their principal means of communication. Over the years they have come to dominate the religious broadcasting airwaves. The format until the 1960s consisted largely of carrying worship services, inspirational messages with some music, and considerable Bible study. Since then, as suggested in chapter 1, radio programming has matched the pattern of combined bold experimentation and predictability so characteristic of most of popular religion. This chapter examines the main issues and expressions of faith involved in that transformation, a situation that contains the same kind of incongruity as do the upheavals in religious television.

Radio was, and is, ideally suited to the evangelical community for a variety of reasons. Its comparatively low cost of producing and low cost for receivers made it available to the widest audience; most households today own several sets, to which one must add their presence in the automobile, the workplace, and the school. Radio can meet local needs more easily than broadcast television, thus creating strong loyalty from those closest by. It is highly flexible in its formatting, being able to change a program or a longer scheduled block of time almost instantly in contrast to the long lead time necessary to produce most major television programs. For the same reason, radio can offer more in-depth coverage to news and other stories than television which usually offers highly condensed versions of fast-breaking stories. Radio has the attractiveness of the call-in program, with any person being able to challenge or support the star of the program. (A few television stations have these, limited almost exclusively to sports.) By contrast to television where costs make it necessary to reach a very wide audience, radio can specialize on one area of religious life, again building a loyal constituency. Thus, from its populist heritage, its transdenominational outreach, and its ready use of new technology, radio proved to be a fertile ground for evangelical seeding.[2]

Today, however, with the widening opportunities appearing within popular religion to express faith in varied ways, evangelical radio reflects much of the diversity, even serious conflict, within its own community on how believers should follow the biblical mandate to honor whatever is just, pure, lovely, and the rest. Both arbitrariness and experimentation find full, perhaps fuller expression in evangelical radio than in television because the high cost of the latter keeps it largely bland and heavily trendy. Radio meanwhile can, for reasons discussed hereafter, reflect the growing differences within evangelicalism, what some trackers call its "tribalization." As the use of high tech media expands and becomes more accessible and the targeting of specific listener markets becomes more accurate, the several subcultures within evangelicalism find in it a major means of holding fast to their particular forms of religious expression.

The field of radio today is divided largely into these categories: (1) traditional worship, suited to local or regional preferences, helping hold loyal supporters; (2) religious information radio, consisting mostly of evangelical interpretations of current public and social issues; (3) the ever-popular Bible studies; and (4) a rich mixture of various forms of music and inspirational programs.[3] No longer is evangelical radio limited to its initial and creative format as perfected by such early pioneer giants as C. E. Fuller, Walter Maier, and the young Billy Graham. That format consisted of preaching, some familiar hymn singing, and then brief requests for support.

Although these three leaders over some four decades were the true builders of evangelical radio, their format today has been transformed by the station owners to broadcast a vast variety of programs to carefully targeted audiences, made clear by sophisticated demographic analysis. Today with each group ("tribe") having its own tastes, the directors of radio are attempting to identify with greater precision the listening preferences of each audience and to fine-tune the various programs to match their expectations. That change from the old-time broadcasting is in fact the source of the tension; instead of one gospel message with one general cluster of hymns and praise music being transmitted, now a vast variety of programs go out based on careful market demographics.[4]

As a case in point, one trade association in the field, the Gospel Music Association (GMA), finds itself trying to capture the essence of evangelical popular religion within its genre. As with television and rock music, the GMA has the option of adapting more secular, market-driven policies in hope of broadening the base of its appeal. Others in this field, as observers point out, "believe that gospel music should stay with its own Mother Church—the Christian community—even if it means living in the shadow of the mainstream recording industry and playing second fiddle to popular music." To them, gospel music must always be ministry before marketing.[5]

Thus the original thrust of evangelical radio has broadened to penetrate the huge market consisting of those who have little or no background in popular religion but who, advocates hope, would be attracted by this appealing medium. The conflict here emerges, as with television, over what constitutes religious programming. For some, the old-time religion with hymns such as "How Great Thou Art" captures the essence of the radio music they want to hear. Others find that form of music too dated and out of touch; their preference is for sounds akin to much of today's "praise" and religious rock. Preaching and worship services find the same kind of division with the traditional tastes running up against contemporary "joyful noises."[6]

Various trade associations such as the Gospel Music Association and the inclusive National Religious Broadcasters (NRB) attempt to be helpful with leadership, advice, and market research for all participating members. In terms of popular religious preference, the NRB annual convention awards list for meritorious services serves as an accurate mirror of this eclecticism. To the Religious Broadcasting Hall of Fame by 1987 had been named Walter A. Maier of "The Lutheran Hour," Charles E. Fuller of "The Old Fashioned Revival Hour," Paul Radar of radio evangelism fame, Paul Myers of "First Mate Bob, Haven of Rest" notoriety, Billy Graham, Richard M. DeHaan of "Radio Bible Class," Jerry Falwell, Theodore Epp of "Back to the Bible," Pat Robertson, and the leader of the Assemblies of God, Thomas F. Zimmerman. The "Award of Merit" was given to a wide variety of programs, from "Tip to Teens" to "Inside Russia" to "The Pat Boone Show" and the "Sanctity of Human Life Week." These are the equivalents of the Oscars and Grammys in the larger entertainment world.[7]

Evangelical radio thus reflects the diversity and the unity of the movement, suited as it is to local loyalties and specialization. Its rapid growth in the 1980s confirms its ongoing popularity and ability to meet the interests of the listeners. What evangelical radio apparently has more difficulty in reaching is a consensus understanding of what will achieve the goals of evangelization and the Christianizing of American society.

Those goals are difficult to achieve for a variety of reasons. Radio broadcasting is in several ways an act of faith; the response through mail and donations is but only one way of learning whether radio is effective in spreading its message. Beyond that, its programming strategies help watchers understand how its listeners understand the ways radio expresses their faith. To be specific, for the largely music stations the broadcasters, as is the case with the larger secular community of radio broadcasters, have decided to specialize in the type of music that is beamed out. The major categories are "Inspirational/MOR [middle of the road]," "Southern Gospel," "CHR [Christian Contemporary Hits]," "Traditional/Sacred," and "Beautiful" [or "lite"].[8] In all of these categories, the broadcasters draw on a variety of market research studies that denote which age, income, education, gender, and location data suggest which group will listen to what evangelical artists and support the advertisers on those shows.

These data suggest a profile of the listener as follows: Those who prefer music programs are more numerous than those who prefer news/information programs, with the latter having a much greater tendency to turn off those programs after only brief listening than adherents of music. However, as the news/information programs are able to attract higher revenues from sponsors, the numbers of their listeners are less important. The largest single listening group is the category of 18- to 49-year-old males, largely because they are the "drive audience," that is, they listen to the radio when driving to and from work daily. More women listen during the evening than do men. Women, at home, listen more to evangelical radio in the afternoon. The number of programs broadcast during the evenings and overnight is about one-third as large as daytime broadcasting.

Finally, the statistics show the radio market is growing steadily among younger audiences, reaching sizable numbers in the 12- to 24-year-old bracket. Barna Research shows Christian music to be most popular in the 45 to 64 age bracket. Within that category it ranks as most popular for radio listening among 48 percent of non–college graduate adults; most popular for listening among 76 percent of African Americans; most popular among 51 percent of rural residents, and most popular among 50 percent of southern and southwestern state residents. The largest single religious segment listening to Christian music are the born again. Much the same demographic pattern holds for those listening to Christian preaching.[9]

Among stations that offer a mixed series of programs, no single pattern other than that of eclecticism prevails. Given the large number of stations, it becomes clear no systematic research is available to show major trends in broadcasting; hence, the evidence cited here must remain anecdotal. For example, with the evangelical station listened to most frequently by this writer, KUXL, Twin Cities, one discovers the pluses of radio broadcasting made evident. Radio listening creates very strong daily habits, centered of course around the listener's time schedule. As old favorites remain in the same position over long periods of time, listeners know when to tune in. New programs are up against this kind of loyalty and at times fail to be renewed because they are not able to attract the numbers to match the standards and favorites. Thus the Charles Swindolls, James Dobsons, James Kennedys, and Marlin Maddouxes are fixed in place on the time schedule. (On other stations one also finds such multimedia favorites as Phyllis Schlafly, Sandi Patti's children's program, and Jack Hayford.) Interspersed on KUXL are inspirational music, news broadcasts, programs on world evangelism, homemaking, and call-in programs. Specialized programs include "Minneapolis Latinos," "International Prison Ministry," and the "Minneapolis Urban League." Sunday programs are mostly worship and inspiration oriented, again with a wide variety of selections.[10]

Of the greatest importance is the understanding of the purchase habits and preferences of the audiences. Unless potential advertisers know that through this invisible medium the audiences they want to reach are in fact listening, they do not support this form of broadcasting. Although the list of industries making products bought by evangelicals changes over the years, by 1988 the following were listed as the "Top 20 Prospects for Christian Radio." Prepared by the Simmons Market Research Bureau, the data show evangelicals "are more disposed to support certain types of businesses over others." In alphabetical order these are (wearing) apparel, appliances, audio/video, automotive, baby products and toys, banking, chiropractors, computers, florists, groceries, hardware and home centers, health foods and vitamins, insurance, lawn and garden, motorcycles, pharmaceuticals, restaurants and fast food, sewing, shoes, and sports gear.[11]

Arguably, the only item here that might not harmonize directly with the consumption patterns of the nuclear family so central to evangelicals would be that of motorcycles. The commentator here notes that only record-album buyers (not evangelical) are more likely to purchase motorcycles than "Christian decision makers. Overall the Christian radio audience is 25 percent more likely to buy cycles than the average American."[12]

Radio advertisers and broadcasters outside the world of evangelical radio realize that listeners use this medium as a background to doing something else, such as reading, housekeeping, pursuing hobbies, and the like. In religious radio, researchers therefore carry out detailed additional research asking whether listeners do tune in to hear the specific theme or teaching. The answers generally are a carefully guarded affirmative; on evangelical radio, market specialists say, the "listeners deliberately tune in for the message." In other words, "Christian audiences will listen to a Christian station not just because it represents a sound which they *prefer*, but rather represents what they *are*. Christian radio listeners *do* listen because they *are* Christian."[13]

On those stations neither largely music nor eclectic, the call-in, news/information format attracts a sizable portion of the evangelical public. Much of the interest here arises from the conviction of many evangelicals that the commercial news/information media, both radio and television, are heavily biased in favor of a politically liberal, religiously indifferent viewpoint. Evangelical critics assert that little if any news about the American religious world is heard on these media, unless it is about televangelist sexual or financial scandals or internal disputations among mainliners over controversial issues such as the ordination of homosexuals. Hence, evangelicals conclude, there exists a genuine need for reliable, informed programming focused on religious news from their world and giving editorial comment on larger public matters with a less liberal-biased perspective.[14]

Further, the ongoing popularity of talk shows with call-in formats opens the lines of communication for direct interchange between spokespersons and rank-and-file believers. This format has an intrinsic human-nature kind of interest, especially when the questioning gets sharp, the comments sarcastic, and the tempers heated. By contrast to much of the moderate to bland, noncontroversial theology and religious thought expressed on evangelical televangelism, the news/information call-in format is invariably lively, sharp, and even acrimonious for its specific audience. That kind of drama has its own appeal not available elsewhere.

With the news/information programs, the superstar format prevails to about the same degree in radio as in television. The names of Stuart McBirnie and David Breese, for instance, have strong evangelical listener recognition and loyal support. Perhaps the best known is Marlin Maddoux on his program "Point of View," heard on about 25 percent of all evangelical radio stations.[15] The show is largely commentary and editorial. Maddoux has also presented a straightforward news program, "USA RADIO PROJECT," avoiding the insertion of evangelical comment. The media empire at Moody Bible Institute in 1990 had formats for radio listeners to participate in two-way broadcasting; their format includes Swindoll, Dobson, Graham, Hal Lindsey, and others. In 1990, however, Moody revamped its structure, plugging in with Maddoux as market pressures continued to scramble the older patterns. So also, Pat Robertson's media center offers a twenty-four-hour-a-day satellite radio service that has music, news, and inspiration. From Virginia, Jerry Falwell's Liberty Federation offers a three-minute news commentary over evangelical stations. It carries interviews with Falwell and other prominent conservative leaders.[16]

Again, as with the music and eclectic stations, no nationwide research exists showing clear patterns of development and decline. The variety of evangelical radio is as extensive as the interests of the listeners. One specific format, however, does stand out vividly. With its built-in advantage of local interest, evangelical call-in radio that focuses on pending city political matters, local school problems, indigenous social problems, and the like is extremely popular in many areas.

Another format, aimed more at entertainment-form edification seems popular. This concentrates in a more lighthearted way on contests, especially picking up on the current popularity of evangelical board games and trivia tests. The announcers present questions or "name that tune" or "name the writer" puzzles and award to winners the likes of books or albums for the first to call in the correct answer. Other contests focus on world leaders, knowledge of the Bible, Bible characters, and past and present evangelical leaders. Evangelical broadcasters, characteristically, are aware of the advantages of including people other than experts and celebrities in programming. "The common person is sometimes easier to identify with than our supposed 'stars.' "[17]

Unquestionably, the most dramatic and apparently most popular format for talk radio is listeners' testimonials or witness as to how and why their faith marked a major turning point in their lives. Evangelical culture critic Phillip Yancey, a frequent guest interviewee, makes a telling comment, "On secular stations, callers were obsessed with one question: 'How can a loving God permit so much suffering?' On Christian stations, the callers were obsessed with the opposite: 'Yes, God directly causes suffering, and here's why.' " Yancey found such call-ins would preface their stories with the statement, "I've never told this to anyone before."[18] That kind of spontaneous format obviously draws and holds listeners' attention.

Among the several with national or regional notoriety, that of Bob Larson of Denver clearly exemplifies the expression of popular religion through this medium. Hard to classify by any familiar category because he covers so vast an array of topics, Larson has become something of a celebrity because of his ability to encourage people to bring their private misfortunes (often stark tragedies) onto the airwaves and invoke prayers for support. He has through a combination of aggressive and sympathetic interviews made his program a model for others.

After starting up in 1983, Larson and his staff within a short time completed research on some 500 subjects, "anorexia to yoga." These are but a few of the subjects: New Age religion, Jehovah's Witnesses, hypnosis, abortion, cults, reincarnation, Amway, UFOs, movies, Mormonism, Masonry, AIDS, heavy-metal music, sex education, gay/lesbian churches, Satanism, movies, the Ku Klux Klan, and religious fanatics.[19]

The centerpiece of the show is the saved-from-disaster testimony, such as that from seekers talked out of joining Scientology, those asking Larson for prayers to be delivered from Satanism, or the woman on her way out the door for an abortion who listened by chance to Larson, changed her mind, and had the child. The following is a story by Larson printed in one of his fund-raising letters. Kelley's husband had left her. She had been horribly abused and so found no reason to go on living. Next to her phone lay a loaded revolver. But before she pulled the trigger, Kelley called "Talkback" with Bob Larson. He wrote, "I talked with her and shared the joy of Christ in the midst of her despair."[20]

Larson's staff also produce books based on their research and the audiences' interests, centering on the hot-button topics of the time: rock music, cults, drugs, and so on. Shorter tracts summing up the advice given on the radio are also offered to the public. In most cases Larson tries to stay in touch with interviewees through a program, "Project Follow-Up," to counsel those in need.

Not without his critics, especially over fund-raising tactics, Larson continues to pursue a grass-roots, true-to-life format with a substantial audience. He attributes his success to a realization that although a large portion of his audience is not evangelical, probably non-Christian in the traditional sense, they need to talk anonymously with one who has created a sense of caring. His positions have at times offended other conservative Christians, a condition he acknowledges, while suggesting they turn off his program. He finds its success thriving amid "diverse opinions, strongly expressed viewpoints and provocative subject matter." Such programming addresses age-old problems, known throughout human history, through state-of-the-art satellite technology by which people can ask questions and ask for help in ways that were not available before.[21] It is an example of popular religion to be at its most appealing among rank and file.

The major risk of such programming, as the critics point out, is that its appeal arises more from the sensationalist, often entertaining and emotional problem than from the religious message. Just as Quentin J. Schultze has found with high-voltage televangelism, call-in radio flourishes when it is spontaneous, expressive, and dramatic. By its nature, it cannot do any kind of deep doctrinal probing; audiences may not remember the brief answers delivered by the host.[22] Call-in also has popular appeal because it so attractively combines thought and feeling, finding areas of commonalty of experience within a very diverse audience. In its confrontational mode, call-in radio can lapse into communicating the primacy of emotion over thought. Such a medium encourages audiences to experience a program rather than to reflect on it.[23]

In summary, radio in its several forms points to the diverging expressions of popular religion, a situation that seems to be growing rather than unifying. As critics mention, this condition means that radio preaches to the faithful, stands firmly in the evangelical subculture, and seems poised to take on increasingly profitable aspects of commercial success at the expense of the old-time faith. That prediction makes the enormous amount of money invested in radio something of a risk, which observers feel is not a wise use of money.[24] Because little evidence exists that evangelical radio produces decisions for Christ, perhaps it could best turn its considerable potential to finding new ways to achieve that. On the other hand, those who listen to and support it will continue to do so without worrying over whether Christian radio lacks identity or a common purpose; radio is an intensely personal medium and seems destined to continue to thrive.

## NOTES

1. See my definitions of the terms used here in *Holding Fast/Pressing On: Religion in America in the 1980s* (Westport, Conn.: Greenwood Press, 1990), pp. xi–xii.

2. Dennis N. Voskuil, "The Power of the Air: Evangelicals and the Rise of Religious Broadcasting," in Quentin J. Schultze, ed., *American Evangelicals and the Mass Media* (Grand Rapids, Mich.: Zondervan, 1990), pp. 69–95; Schultze, "The Wireless Gospel," *Christianity Today*, January 15, 1988, pp. 18–23; Russell Franzen, "The Broadcaster as Servant," *Religious Broadcasting*, July/August 1985, pp. 22–23; Jim Pennington, "Refiner's Fire," on Christian radio, *Christianity Today*, June 29, 1979, pp. 32–33.

3. Gary Crossland, "The Changing Face of Christian Radio," *Religious Broadcasting*, September 1988, pp. 12–13, 35; see the wide variety of responses made to the show "Nightsounds" in the article by Bill Pearce, "Music," *Religious Broadcasting*, November 1976, pp. 34–35.

4. Crossland, "The Changing Face"; Crossland, "Understanding Broadcasting," *Religious Broadcasting*, September 1988, pp. 12–13; Crossland, "Understanding the Average Christian Media Consumer," *Religious Broadcasting*, March 1992, pp. 42–43; Quentin J. Schultze, "The Invisible Medium: Evangelical Radio," in Schultze, *Mass Media*, pp. 171–95; for some superb examples on how this plays out through Crossland's organization, Soma Communications, Dallas, Texas, see its occasional publication, "Tri-S Media Report."

5. Quentin J. Schultze and William D. Romanowski, "Praising God in Opryland," *The Reformed Journal*, November 1989, p. 10.

6. Schultze, "Invisible Medium," pp. 171–95.

7. News story, *Religious Broadcasting*, September 1987, p. 28; Ben Armstrong, "In Defense of the Electric Church," *Moody Monthly*, January 1981, pp. 24–26.

8. Bob Augsburg, "On the Air," *Religious Broadcasting*, September 1988, pp. 38–39.

9. Gary Crossland, "How Do Various Christian Formats Compare?" *Religious Broadcasting*, December 1988, pp. 16–17; George Barna, *What Americans Believe* (Ventura, Calif.: Regal Books, 1991), pp. 130–35.

10. This is from the KUXL-FM schedule printed in *Twin City Christian*, February 11, 1988, p. 21; news story, *Religious Broadcasting*, December 1987, p. 34; the monthly newsletter from Church on the Way, "Living Way Ministries," Van Nuys, California; other excellent case studies are those described in the publications of WVCY-FM, Milwaukee,

which affiliates with the "VCY America" network, and the materials from the "USA Radio Network" publications, Dallas, Texas.

11. Gary Crossland, "Twenty Top Prospects for Christian Radio," *Religious Broadcasting*, October 1987, pp. 16–17.

12. Ibid., p. 17; see this audience income profile in Crossland, "Radio," *Religious Broadcasting*, March 1985, pp. 28–29; see also Crossland, "Market Place," *Religious Broadcasting*, April 1983, p. 21.

13. Jorstad, *Holding Fast*, pp. 100–103; Gary Crossland, "Where Christian Radio Excels," *Religious Broadcasting* , June 1986, pp. 17–18, emphasis in original.

14. Marvin Olasky, *Prodigal Press: The Anti-Christian Bias of the American News Media* (Westchester, Ill.: Crossway Books, 1989); ad, *Religious Broadcasting*, February 1986, pp. 46–47.

15. John Adams, "Christian Radio and the News," *Religious Broadcasting*, February 1988, pp. 84, 88; Jonathan Peterson, "Hard News and Christian Mission," *Religious Broadcasting*, March 1985, pp. 26–27.

16. Ad, *Religious Broadcasting*, November 1985, p. 21; ad, ibid., July/August 1987, p. 8; ad, ibid., March 1987, p. 23.

17. Chris Fabry, "Reach Out and Touch Someone," *Religious Broadcasting*, March 1989, p. 16; USA Radio, "Telling It the Way It Is," *Religious Broadcasting*, January 1992, p. 52.

18. Phillip Yancey, "Sound Bites from Never-never Land," *Christianity Today*, April 21, 1989, p. 56.

19. Bob Larson Ministries, Box 36A, Denver, CO 80236.

20. Daniel J. Nichols, "Christian Radio: A Lot of Talk," *Religious Broadcasting*, September 1984, pp. 16–17; Larson Ministries fund-raising letter, August 1987, p. 2.

21. News item, *National and International Religion Report*, March 13, 1989, p. 6; see news story, *Christianity Today*, March 3, 1989, pp. 47–48; Larson, "Talk Radio," *Religious Broadcasting*, October 1987, pp. 22–23.

22. See the critique by W. R. Olney, "A Case against the Spots," *Religious Broadcasting*, May 1975, p. 21; M. Anthony Carr, "Church Advertising: Competing with the Big Boys," *Religious Broadcasting*, March 1992, pp. 20–21; Jim Pennington, "Christian Radio: Breaking out of the Gospel Ghetto," *Christianity Today*, June 29, 1979, pp. 32–33.

23. Mark Holton, "Evangelical Broadcasting: Preaching to the Choir," *Christian Century*, April 12, 1989, pp. 375–76.

24. Schultze, "Invisible Medium," pp. 171–95.

# 7

# Popular Religion and the Print Media: Those Who Have Eyes

In contrast to television, which in the United States after World War II started with no previous experience, the evangelical print media had long been a staple in evangelical ministry to outsiders and for the believers. But, in synchronicity with electronic media, evangelical books and magazines during the boom years reached a much larger and more diverse clientele. Its growth pattern paralleled that of television and radio in that it took risks by adapting high tech innovations, diversification of product, and careful attention to what the readers told the publishers they wanted to read. Such is the stuff of popular religion.

However, print requires a mode of absorption different from that of television and radio. It is essentially private; it is silent; it requires especially in fiction the active participation of the reader's visual imagination to create a viable image of the printed word. It is active, not passive; it requires for coherence an effort at logical connection. As columnist George F. Will suggests, the print media, by contrast to almost all television, are able to communicate qualities crucial to mature religious understanding—irony, ambivalence, and paradox.[1]

Some evangelical media investigators, such as Jack Sims, argue that the transformation in consciousness created by television and related technology has relegated reading to a secondary position in the evangelical world of ministry.[2] However, even though the enormous growth in evangelical publishing of the 1970s and 1980s seems to have slowed considerably, evidence such as that presented by George Barna and others suggests that reading for recreation and edification may be on the upswing again. What publishers, including those in the evangelical world, are discovering is more sophisticated and reliable means by which to determine what the public will purchase and read. Like so much else in American life, specialization has also come to dominate this market.

In book publishing the buzzword is "genre," a specific type of writing known to the reader, such as "western," "science fiction," "fantasy," "romance," or "who done it?" What genre specialization achieves is what both readers and publishers want, a clear statement of content so that both sides know what is involved. Today, as in all mass media, print genres overlap and change as befits high technology innovative power.[3]

In a major survey, many American readers (39 percent of the total sample) stated that they have a favorite author, living or dead. These include Stephen King, Danielle Steele, Louis L'Amour, Sidney Sheldon, James Michener, V. C. Andrews, and those considered the "classics": Charles Dickens, Mark Twain, Ernest Hemingway, John Steinbeck, and William Shakespeare. This preference obviously opens the door for evangelicals to join in the trend.[4]

Loyal to the Bible, which is a part of the print media, evangelicals have found in genre publishing trends a major means of expressing their faith. Indeed, the historical record shows that shortly after the printing press was invented, making possible widespread reading of the Bible, the Protestant Reformation unfolded, as one predictable result. As denominations emerged later, most found a great interest in promoting their respective positions through the printed word, available to everyone (not just the educated elite), usually at low cost, and accessible at all times of the day (not just during church or library hours). Printed matter allowed for the more critical, comparative form of studying the different statements of belief and practice of each emerging denomination; it proved to be an ideal vehicle for the transmission of popular religion.[5]

Evangelical publishing took off in a major fashion in the 1970s. As market research increased in sophistication and advertising took on a more glitzy, up-to-the-minute character (compared to the drabber look of earlier evangelical publications), various demographic components were matched to specific genres; by age (obviously there always had been books just for children); by region, ethnic loyalty, race, education level, and related items.[6]

The same pattern prevailed also in the enormous increase of publication of the Bible itself. Whereas before most households bought the King James version, now a plethora of new, more brightly translated versions appeared, giving bookstores the staple item they needed to help move the rest of their inventories by increasing their customer traffic.[7]

In a brief summary after making an exhaustive study of the field, one expert wrote, "Changing audiences and new techniques in publishing and retailing are persuading many Christian publishers and booksellers to re-examine their assumptions and procedures. Better market research, editorial flexibility in recasting the timeless message in relevant form and the contemporary idiom, and more aggressive outreach to hitherto unresponsive audiences appear to be essential."[8] While critics within the community suggested that much of the genre style was more "formula" writing than ennobling literature, the readership for popular writing continues to grow.[9]

Supporters of popular religion books and magazines point out that these media well serve the faith; they can lead a person to make a decision for Christ, they can edify a new believer or jolt another out of complacency, comfort a believer in distress or reinforce one's witness. A person can return to a meaningful book at a time of her own choice. It can be transported anywhere. Further, books have the ability to take their readers, often those with little or no knowledge of the faith, step by step through the essential directions of seeking, assuming that the readers need a patient guide rather than the instant flash of electronic media.[10]

In terms of subject matter, evangelicals are reading books oriented to these general genre boundaries: (1) the highly experience-oriented, true-life stories of those who became celebrities, such as Nicky Cruz, Joni Eareckson Tada, and Catherine Marshall; and (2) a specific style of writing, a narrative style applying "the techniques of good fiction" to true stories, the leading example being Charles Colson's story of his conversion, *Born Again*.[11] (3) Another genre that produced the all-time, nonfiction bestseller in evangelical circles, Hal Lindsey's *The Late, Great Planet Earth*, is that of "end time" books. These find ready audiences, including books that focused on the Middle East during the hundred-hour Persian Gulf War. (4) Conflicts facing families and individuals with personal problems spawned a seemingly unending variety of self-help, specific-advice books. Finally, (5) as in the secular market, came what turned into a blockbuster genre known as the Christian romance novel, with sales by leading authors totaling well into the millions of copies.[12]

As with television and radio, the evangelical adaptation of high technology helped make possible this proliferation. Besides the credit cards and toll-free numbers, customers found that they could obtain a book within a few days by calling a wholesaler. Gospel Light Publications, for instance, by 1986 had in place a system that typed telephone orders into a computer terminal, leading to the works being shipped within twenty-four hours. A second technique was having sales representatives talk by telephone with the smaller, independent firms; a third group called specific congregations known by records kept of their purchases for their specific interests. In such a way the firm could guarantee an interested buyer immediate delivery, thus forestalling losing such a person or church to a competitor. Gospel Light also sends out "video catalog tapes," which make available on one tape its upcoming line of titles.[13]

Other ways of informing customers include the widespread use of catalogs, considered by some to be the most successful means. Specific firms, such as Baker Book House or specific bookstore conglomerates such as Northwestern Books of the Upper Midwest, present a variety of printed listings. Another major source of advertising for books is having them reviewed in the major nondenominational magazines. After a rather reluctant start, all the major ones—*Christianity Today, Christian Herald, Charisma, Moody*, and when in business *Eternity* and *Christian Life*—carried regular reviews of books the editors thought important or for which large sales have indicated an interest among the rank and file. For several years in the 1970s and 1980s *Christianity Today* carried a regular feature on the arts, "The Refiner's Fire," which carried extended reviews on writers considered leaders in the world of general religious expression: C. S. Lewis, J.R.R. Tolkein, Samuel Beckett, and Alexander Solzhenitsyn, obviously not within the evangelical genre. A considerable number of books are sold through the several book clubs offered by certain magazines. In brief, through advanced high technology and market analysis, evangelical publishers have made available to readers an immense diversity of titles, varying greatly in quality of writing and depth of insight, to be sure, but yet readily accessible.[14]

## THE BIBLE

The most accessible and central book of course is the Bible. It has as many uses for evangelicals (and all other Christians) as there are human dimensions to life. In popular religion evangelicals have attempted to "confer a religious meaning on nearly every dimension of the private sector, creating, as it were, a sacred world from the bottom up. . . . For each and every creation of popular culture there ought to be a religious equivalent."[15]

The Bible serves evangelicals in so many ways that no single list could capture the total scope of its omnipresence. It encompasses wisdom on health, marriage counseling, child rearing, care for the aging, managing one's wealth, in-law relations, building houses, planting crops, courting, warfare, peacemaking, tithing, wearing apparel and hairstyling, animal husbandry, and discerning the natural weather, among dozens of other specific everyday phenomena.

One can find in other ancient literature similar kinds of wisdom. The Hebrew and Christian Bibles, however, as witnessed to by all the families of evangelicalism, claim to be the revelation of the one and only God of the entire universe and as such stand as the final authority in all matters of life. To evangelicals, they contain the history of the Jewish people, testifying to the power and steadfastness of Jehovah. They contain also the story of the Incarnation of God on earth in the person of Jesus of Nazareth, whose appearance and ministry and resurrection forever transformed the course of human history. This witness is indispensably central to all evangelicals. And since the apostolic age the Bible has stood as the manifesto legitimizing the appearance and expansion of the thousands of various denominations and other church bodies.[16]

As suggested, for most of its history, evangelicals of all varieties accepted the 1611 King James Version and its later equivalent, the 1901 American Standard Version. Shortly after World War II mainline scholars associated with the World and National Council of Churches brought their expertise to bear on a new translation, known as the Revised Standard Version, which appeared in toto in 1952. In the mid-1950s a religion print editor, Kenneth N. Taylor, started during his daily train commute to work a rewriting of the scriptures, in his words, "thought by thought." By 1970 the work was completed, a paraphrased version known as *The Living Bible*.[17] It soon became an all-time bestseller, millions of copies being purchased in all areas of the world.

Besides its impact on a reader's religious life, the Taylor version helped open the gates for dozens of other evangelical scholar-translators seeking to make the Bible as intelligible as possible to a world they found drifting from the moorings of traditional religion. By 1988 one of the leading print distributors, Spring Arbor of Michigan, produced a study showing the "best-selling Bible translations," acknowledging that it did not stock every Bible available but that it held some 2,800 versions of Bibles, and Testaments and portions of the same. See Table 7.1 for volume of Bible sales.[18]

With the introduction of computer word processing, evangelicals have been at the forefront in adapting for software programs the various versions, along with the Concordances and the original Greek and Hebrew versions for both the scholar and the everyday reader. Other software programs include opportunities for Bible learning, memory drill, games centered around Bible stories, graphics and maps, and other concordance aids. Meanwhile, the mainline bodies made ready for the public a new revised standard version of the Bible, which appeared in 1990. Publisher rules prohibited a release of total print run figures.[19]

To add to their popular appeal, publishers have added a huge variety of paraphernalia to the various editions. The color range for covers includes the traditional black, brown, and white, to which are now added chocolate, indigo, crimson, and lollipop, along with eight shades of black. Bindings are available in a variety of animal skins, including horse, goat, seal, calf, leopard, and water buffalo. One version offers an easy-to-clean "real bluejean denim, with simulated stitched pockets and a 'Good News' patch on the

**Table 7.1**
**Bible Sales**

| Version (by title) | January–June 1988 (% of total sales of Bibles during those months) |
|---|---|
| New International Version | 31.6 |
| King James Version | 23.1 |
| Living Bible | 12.6 |
| New King James | 8.8 |
| New American Bible | 4.5 |
| New American Standard | 4.0 |
| Today's English | 3.6 |
| New Century Version/Int'l Children's Version | 2.2 |
| Parallel Bibles | 1.8 |
| Revised Standard Version | 1.5 |
| Other English Versions | 1.4 |
| Spanish Bibles | 1.4 |
| Amplified Bible | 1.3 |
| Jerusalem/New Jerusalem | .9 |
| Foreign Language | .9 |
| Interlinear Bibles | .6 |

front." Various editions are available for awards in church programs, for business executives, for teaching by pictures, and for the blind and the deaf. These are standard items sent out to contributors by radio and television broadcasters and accompanied by study guides.[20]

## CHRISTIAN BOOKSELLERS ASSOCIATION AND NATIONAL RELIGIOUS BROADCASTERS

To coordinate and promote this vast array of electronic and print media, several major national trade associations have emerged during the resurgent years, the most influential being the Christian Booksellers Association and the National Religious Broadcasters. Each focuses primarily on its titled specialty, but considerable overlap exists on the local, regional, and national levels. Similar to such associations in other professions, these two serve the world of popular religion primarily as clearinghouses for information, as forums for problem solving especially for new entrepreneurs, and as award givers that declare leaders and rank and file alike just what and who are considered the outstanding exponents of each genre of popular religion. Evangelicals who may not have direct access to the various kinds of music or novels or radio learn from such lists what is thriving on the religious market.

Beyond that, the associations' adaptation of high technology shows how skillfully they have understood the importance of interdependence of one medium on another. For example, Sandi Patti, superstar vocalist, also has audio- and videocassettes as well as tracts and wide popularity on radio. At regional and national conventions the everpresent James Dobson and Charles Swindoll meet the buyers. The producers of their media programs show those buyers the means by which print, radio, television, and guest speaking at appropriate national conferences indicate what the rank and file are endorsing now.

These organizations and smaller ones such as the Evangelical Christian Publishers Association (ECPA) serve also as excellent examples of the much greater sophistication the evangelicals have brought to bear on distributing popular religion in the last three decades. Each year, observers note, the displays become more glitzy and larger, the competition more intense, the hype of skilled public relations more sophisticated, just as market research and high-powered advertising have intensified in television, radio, and print.[21] Obviously, it would be unfair to suggest here that such extravaganzas somehow represent the essence and core of all evangelical popular religion; they do not. Leaders are aware of the often sharp criticisms made by like-minded believers and are also aware that the entrepreneurial spirit is much a part of their own tradition. That excesses (with tacky religious material items, for instance) exist is not so much a surprise as it is an embarrassment for those who call for whatever is just, pure, and lovely.

## LEADING WRITERS

As in radio where, as we have seen, there is no single pattern for trackers to identify, so too in the reading of books do choices vary widely and elude simple patternization. Rather than to try to summarize here all the prominent themes, we look at the work of three of the superstar bestseller writers, each representing a distinctive genre and each clearly reflective of the manner in which popular religion supplements doctrine, ethics, and discipleship in evangelical life. These three are the novelist Janette Oke, the writer Frank

Peretti, and the "end times" commentator Hal Lindsey. These three are household names among evangelical bookreaders.

A long-established genre in fiction is the romantic novel.[22] Centering around the most powerful of all human emotions, love in its many expressions, this type of novel is readily understood for what it can do for the reader. Although a few (*Anna Karenina*, for instance) have become great literature, most are read to meet the more immediate interests of entertainment, escape, and perhaps reinforcement of existing values and ideals, mostly by adult women.[23] Their appeal centers around the ability of the writer to convince the reader that her inner emotions as a female are understood, appreciated, and celebrated. The time spent reading a novel is meant to be time spent for one's self: silent, active, furnishing pictures from one's own experience. Knowing that the readers are almost exclusively female, the writer is free to develop these themes without worry that male disapproval may cut into critical acclaim or sales.[24]

Within the world of evangelicalism, the romantic novel as a blockbuster item selling into the tens of millions of copies did not emerge until the resurgence years of the 1970s. Perhaps the first high-quality novel was that in 1978 by Shirley Nelson, *The Last Year of the War*, published by Harper and Row. It dealt in a realistic way with the desires of a young woman to come to terms with unrequited love and the difficulties of witnessing effectively and learning to accept the stormy character of one's internal spiritual life.[25]

Such writing helped overcome earlier-expressed worries by evangelical editors that fiction writing within the fold had only a limited future. What was needed was a recognition that the genre had its own built-in appeal, one that had not yet been tapped. Then, just as in the larger society, the huge successes of historical romances took off, as evangelical authors such as Janette Oke started to produce more enduring work. Mass-market producers came out with formula romances in the Harlequin, Candlelight, and similar series. The readers could find these readily in special displays, indicating in popular culture fashion these were predictable, clear, and celebrative of the everyday world of ordinary experience. However, although these series centered almost entirely on one solution to the central woman's problems, that of attaching herself to a dominant male, "sugar-coated sexism," the same is not true in the novels of Oke, Debbie Macomber, Susan Feldhake, and other well-known evangelicals.[26]

Oke's first book, *Love Comes Softly*, came out in 1979 and became a great hit, to the surprise of evangelical market specialists, within that community of readers. Since then she has been writing almost two books a year, producing eighteen titles by 1991 in three series, Love Comes Softly, The Canadian West, and Seasons of the Heart, with a total sales for Bethany

House Publishers of over 8 million copies.[27] That success has been followed widely, with varying levels of sales success, by other evangelical publishers and trade publishers with special evangelical lines, such as Ballantine with its Epiphany series.[28]

The Oke phenomenon rests on several standard items indigenous to success in this genre: careful but not overly detailed historical research, a clear focus on how the woman/mother herself grows spiritually by a nurturing career in homemaking, and an affirmation that traditional evangelical family values are, even when seriously threatened or seemingly impractical, the eternal verities that God has given humankind for direction and fulfillment. The key virtue seems to be patience with the understanding through religious faith that all things will work to the good of those who follow God's way for them. Always the emotions are expressed in a slightly understated manner, allowing the reader to furnish the warmth of feeling suggested by the writer.

Oke's formula helps draw the reader into a more personal identification with the story, set as it almost always is in the historic past, of about fifty to one hundred years ago. By this historical perspective, Oke is saying that, although today's world may be in constant flux and turmoil, human nature has not changed; that all that is true and good and permanent still abides; and that we have to accept certain outward changes in life, but be ready to stand fast for those commitments that appear true through the living of each day, the finding of religious meaning in ordinary experience. The major female figure demonstrates a simple, familiar ability to speak with God in such situations, a trait that obviously provides strong resources for the vicissitudes of raising children, supporting an overworked husband, coping with unregenerate or catty neighbors, and generally surviving the rugged climate of life without the benefits of today's homemaker technology. It is true Oke does not challenge traditional gender roles, that the "hegemony" of males remains intact. But a sense of mutuality, based on deep respect between wife and husband, also emerges, a quality that is perhaps the most attractive feature of Oke's writing.

Working in a totally different genre, that of science fiction demonology, Frank Peretti has produced the bestseller work of the contemporary age, *This Present Darkness* (1986), and its sequel, *Piercing the Darkness* (1991). To the amazement of his publisher, Crossway Books, and a goodly number of critics, the works have been selling in six-digit quantities into the 1990s. These works and his Cooper Kids Adventure Series are already in boxed form and on audiocassette; the author has become a star on the evangelical talk show circuit. In an interview Peretti explained that the idea for the books came from what he perceived to be the rapid, insidious, and demonic spread of New Age religion.[29] A minister in the Assemblies of God (one step down from being an ordained pastor) and an occasional writer, he found all through

American society, including church life, "ominous symptoms of spiritual warfare, neo-paganism, demonic activity, heretical teachings."[30]

Using what he called a "creative fictional treatment" Peretti presented in these works long stories set in recognizable small towns in which the demons and evil spirits are not visible but "what we all know to be a reality."[31] As a student of the Bible he concluded that the situation demanded scripture-based information to convince first himself and then his readers that these demons have parahuman characteristics such as free will, emotions, and self-awareness. To aid the reader in understanding them, Peretti portrayed them in the traditional sci-fi/demon genre fashion: one was a

black hunching figure, sulfurous breath, bat wings. . . . He was like a high-strung little gargoyle, his hide a slimy, bottomless black, his body thin and spiderlike; half humanoid, half animal, totally demon. Two huge yellow cat-eyes bulged out of his face, darting to and fro, peering, searching. His breath came in short, sulfurous gasps, visible as glowing yellow vapor.[32]

Such descriptions, of course, harmonize fully with traditional popular culture images of such imaginations. From early medieval art to today's newspaper cartoons (such as "The Far Side"), much of the public accepts such characterizations as being as close to factual accuracy as is humanly possible.[33]

Such creatures Peretti finds at work tearing away at the fabric of Christian society in the name of New Age liberation and peace. Just as Jesus cast out demons, so too Peretti uses this genre to embolden believers to do the same. Aware of the excesses often found in this genre and among witch and demon hunters, Peretti carefully wrote in what he thought was "demonization" or "oppression" of people but not "demon possession." In his works, such demonization comes in varying degrees, from mild temptation to potential control over one's life by the devil.[34]

The stories are vividly sketched, often gut-wrenching struggles as decent people seem to understand what is happening to their town, this named Ashton. The godly identify with the powerful forces of Tal, the evil ones with those of Rafar. The embattled are the more threatened and bewildered because the demons appear in everyday life, as do the angels. They travel about in normal ways, they shop at the supermarkets, they interact in familiar ways. In clear popular religion fashion, the author keeps the story moving in a direction in which the reader knows the faithful will triumph. The conclusion is predictable, but is not reached without titanic struggles, which are presented to be both episodic and a part of everyday life, the tension between the mundane and the sacred that is indigenous to religious insight.

Unquestionably Peretti's success comes from his writing capacities and because it is made clear he is talking about specific manifestations of New

Age such as the highly publicized Church Universal and Triumphant with its remarkable leader, Elizabeth Clare Prophet. Her claims at omniscience and visions for the new world order strike many rank and file as the first stages of the Last Days, the coming of the Anti-Christ. So too, the often highly publicized news stories in the mass media over alleged satanic activity lead readers to try to understand such behavior from the work of an author who is clearly sympathetic to their beliefs that such evil is flourishing throughout the world, and in their own locales. Finally, sales flourished because, after the manuscript had been rejected by some fourteen publishers, Crossway accepted the book, gave it strong publicity, and publicized its endorsement by such celebrities as Amy Grant.[35]

The two Peretti books have become major staples in the evangelical community. Their sales indicate a huge acceptance by readers. But major reservations and criticisms also abound. To some the works are "the 'bible of spiritual warfare' for a number of Christians today"; to others they present simply wrong-headed, often dangerous teaching on the nature of the spiritual world and the redeeming work of Christ.[36] Distributed largely through the infrastructure of religious bookstores, the books suggest not only how word-of-mouth advertising can help create a blockbuster but also how strong the interest and concerns are that this current age may well be the expression of medieval and early modern fantasies about the ultimate nature of good and evil in this life.[37]

The other representative genre, not fiction, but a clearly established form within evangelical/Pentecostal/fundamentalist/charismatic circles is End Times or Last Days prophecy exposition. From the earliest days of the Christian church in Jerusalem, when believers expected the Lord to return to destroy the evil ones and inaugurate at that point the promise of eternal life, and down to the present day, whole religious movements and mountains of writing and research have sought to discern the signs of the times. Elaborate systems of interpretation by students of the Bible and of other religions have found and continue to find wide interest in this subject, about which so much interest but so little verifiable evidence exists.

Out of the Jesus movement on the West Coast in the 1960s, Hal Lindsey started his research working as a minister in the "Light and Power" community of Westwood, California.[38] A graduate of Dallas Theological Seminary, which has a strong emphasis on eschatology, the study of the doctrines of the End Times, Lindsey in 1970 produced the greatest bestseller of the decade, *The Late, Great Planet Earth*, with sales by 1990 well over 20 million, followed by six other books covering the same general field.[39] He is also in the 1990s a popular analyst for the Trinity Broadcast Network of television and has a radio program.

The work caught on undoubtedly because some of the predictions made, as evangelicals understood them, with the absolute authority of God as author of the Bible in the unfolding of history, seemed to be coming true after World War II. The events of world history proved to them that what the imminent–End Times people over the centuries had been preaching was literally taking place, validating their claim to understand the Bible in their professed manner. This was especially true with the Jews returning to the homeland State of Israel in 1948. For decades evangelicals of various schools had been preaching that God had promised this would occur; then, it actually took place. This meant, in defiance of the critics who scoffed at such prognosticators, that the promises and predictions of the Bible were occurring right now, in the present time. Thus the Bible, as it was being explained by those with the insights of a Lindsey, was trustworthy despite what the agnostics and indifferent may claim. Thus a world that seemed to be moving quickly toward self-destruction by nuclear warfare or nationalist terrorism or sexual immorality was in fact in the hands of the God who still ruled.[40]

This historical trustworthiness is the central theme of *The Late, Great Planet Earth*. Lindsey avoids giving any specific date when the last days will come. He does state clearly that, with the Jews back in Jerusalem to rebuild the ancient temple on its historic site, all the conditions for Jesus to come bodily with his army to defeat Satan and his army in the Battle of Armageddon will be fulfilled. It will only be a matter of time. The book has appeal also because of its specificity; Lindsey looks at the globe's trouble spots and finds, usually in some passage in Daniel or Ezekiel from the Old Testament or from the book of Revelations in the New Testament, an explanation as to what the situation is in this age and what this means to believers for the future. The analyses are made in a folksy manner, clearly attempting to avoid old-fashioned Doomsday rhetoric.

Understanding his audience's absorption with popular culture, Lindsey explains how he came to find the formula for such success. "I'd imagine that I was sitting across the table from a young person—a cynical, irreligious person—and I'd try to convince him that the Bible prophecies were true. If you can make a young person understand, then the others will understand, too."[41]

Beyond that, the book has an unmistakable anti-Russian, anti-Communist dimension to it, with identifiable references suggesting the last great battles for dominion over this world will come out of that area, which is officially anti-Christian. In a time of great national and world concern for nuclear destruction, this explanation of the trustworthiness of fulfilling scripture found ready acceptance. At some point in his time as governor of California, Ronald Reagan publicly agreed with the basic thrust of the Lindsey scenario.

However, as with Peretti, significant numbers of evangelical critics found large and small reasons to reject such predictions. Some found it too simplistic, too willing to believe that specific events in ancient history were occurring to be fulfilled exactly at this point in history; some found a willingness to skip over or minimize other complex eschatological texts; some argued that such end times prophecies had flourished for centuries and none had materialized; this one seemed no different from the others. No matter to the many readers; such as Nathan Hatch concludes, the popularity of *Late, Great Planet*, outselling all other paperbacks in the 1970s, "is testimony to the confidence American evangelicals still have that the truth is simple and open to all."[42]

One final surge of evangelical End Times popular religion burst across the book-world scene. In early 1991 the United States attacked Iraq over its invasion of Kuwait, in "Operation Desert Storm." That event produced a storm of its own with the readership of the rank and file, who started to purchase in huge numbers books by like-minded believers explaining how this war fit into the timetable for the Last Days. Publishers searched through old backlists and encouraged well-known authors to bring out fresh interpretations of this battle. For instance, a Dallas Seminary professor, Charles H. Dyer, found with coauthor Angela Elwell Hunt that their book *The Rise of Babylon: Sign of the End Times* had sold over a half million copies. Zondervan, one of the publisher giants, discovered that the purchase of at least 1.5 million copies of their title *Armageddon, Oil and the Middle East*, by John Walvoord, also of Dallas Seminary, had caught them by surprise. These and related titles did not claim that Desert Storm meant the Last Days were here but suggested that the whole struggle reaffirmed the traditional teaching that Last Days activities would be very intense and decisive in the Middle East.[43]

To date, no comprehensive evangelical expository book of the End Times genre has appeared on the meaning of the collapse of the Union of Soviet Socialist Republics, the upheavals in the Balkans, the reunification of Germany, and related issues. The issues are frequently discussed on such televangelist talk shows as that of Pat Robertson, Paul Crouch, and John Annkerburg; undoubtedly the rank and file would welcome authoritative teachings on these events, as profoundly worldshaking and transforming as any other upheaval of recent centuries. The market is there; perhaps by the time this book reaches the market, such teaching will be available.

## MAGAZINES

Within the print media, magazines and periodicals embrace the most flexibility in terms of format, subject matter, and advertising policy. The most successful (judged by circulation figures) are those that in proven evangelical fashion appeal to a very wide variety of readers, have little coverage of specific denominational matters, and utilize the most up-to-date technology in color, editing, photography, layout, and the like. These are, by the early 1990s, *Christianity Today, Charisma and Christian Life, Discipleship, Christian Herald,* and *Moody*.[44] A wide variety of other magazines equally committed to evangelicalism also are publishing but have chosen more specialized subject matter and less aggressive advertising, these being *The Other Side* and *Sojourners* and (defunct as of 1988) *Eternity*.[45]

How these magazines reach the popular religion audiences depends on several factors, an important one being the extent to which they address issues of personal interest in daily life rather than matters important to specific denominations and their journals. Print magazines, being responsible to changing interests and events, can move quickly to present materials in permanent form to which the reader can return again. Hence, it can present devotional materials, Bible studies, tips for teens, humor, book, film, video and other recording reviews, poetry, letters to the editors, question-answer features, news of the religious world at home and overseas, testimonials, and the like.[46]

A second reason for these successes is the extensive attention and research given to providing what the readers prefer to read. Rather than reflecting specific denominational bureaucratic policy, as do most denominational journals, these magazines focus on providing what they learn the readers choose to have available, a position close to evangelicalism's historic transdenominationalism.[47]

A third reason, although market research has not been made on this, is that this diversification means readers need subscribe to only one or two such journals rather than subscribe to several specialized publications. It is known that renewals for journals run low, suggesting that readers are shopping around, keeping editors trying to stay positioned a few months ahead of what trend or new interest may appear.[48]

Billy Graham's monthly *Decision* has a large circulation also but chooses to concentrate almost entirely on evangelizing instead of a smorgasbord format. To the surprise of many, an old, well-regarded journal, *Eternity*, went under financially in 1988. Some of its problems were financial; it was undercapitalized. It was also unpopular in some evangelical circles for its vigorous, not to say outspoken criticism of fellow believers on major social issues such as race relations, foreign policy, and domestic programs for the underprivileged.[49]

Beyond that, Tyndale House publishers (and after a 1991 buyout by *Christianity Today*) brings out a highly popular evangelical version of *The Reader's Digest*, this entitled *The Christian Digest*. In its bimonthly format of about one hundred pages per issue, it reprints a variety of short articles from both well-known and obscure writers; some articles come from sources other than the traditional evangelical ones (such as *Lutheran Woman Today* or the Roman Catholic *Salt*). Its major thrust is inspirational, personal testimony, and mildly conservative endorsements on national public issues.[50]

Today's high tech prowess with desktop publishing opens up new possibilities for evangelicals wanting to bring out their own journals. The cultural critic Kenneth Myers has a thoughtful journal, *Genesis*. In North Carolina *World* is now flourishing after a late-1980s startup year with a slowly growing readership. And in true evangelical "with-it" fashion, one can find a monthly called *Christian Computing*. The crusade that sparked the full Christian pop culture explosion, the Jesus movement, has continued to bring out a totally distinctive, multimedia publication while uncounted dozens of others have failed. Known as *Cornerstone*, it unabashedly addresses itself to teens and young adults. Its very ability to be able to survive, even to grow, and its distinctive eclecticism in centering on the arts in all their dimensions serves as a fitting conclusion to this discussion of print media.

## NOTES

1. See Will's column of June 6, 1991, *Minneapolis Star Tribune*, p. 18A.

2. Jack Sims, "Baby Boomers: Time to Pass the Torch," *Christian Life*, January 1986, pp. 21–25.

3. See Alister Fowler, "Genre," in Eric Barnouw, ed., *International Encyclopedia of Communications*, vol. 1 (New York: Oxford University Press, 1989), pp. 215–17; George Barna, *What Americans Believe* (Ventura, Calif.: Regal Books, 1991), pp. 139–43; William Griffin, "Decatrends," *Publishers Weekly*, February 10, 1992, pp. 25–29.

4. "The Best Sellers of the 70s," *Publishers Weekly*, March 14, 1987, pp. 82–83; news story, *Minneapolis Star Tribune*, February 3, 1991, p. 6E.

5. H. Edelman, "Publishing, Religious," in Daniel G. Reid, ed., *Dictionary of Christianity in America* (Downers Grove, Ill.: InterVarsity, 1990), pp. 960–63; Judith S. Duke, *Religious Publications and Communications* (White Plains, N.Y.: Knowledge Industry Publications), p. 79.

6. Edelman, "Publishing"; Duke, *Religious Publications*.

7. Wayne Elzey, "Popular Culture," in Charles H. Lippy and Peter W. Williams, eds., *Encyclopedia of the American Religious Experience*, vol. 3 (New York: Scribners, 1987), pp. 1729–34; Randall Balmer, "Bible Bazaar," in *Mine Eyes Have Seen the Glory: A Journey into the Evangelical Subculture of America* (New York: Oxford University Press, 1989), pp. 155–70.

8. Paul D. Daebler, quoted in William Griffin, "2000, An Extraordinary Year," *Publishers Weekly*, March 4, 1988, p. 41; mainline church publishing went much another way; see Barbara Wheeler, "Theological Publishing: In Need of a Mandate," *Christian Century*, November 23, 1988, pp. 1066–70.

9. Robert M. Price, "Evangelism as Entertainment," *Christian Century*, November 4, 1981, pp. 1122–24; see Carolyn Marvin, "Literary Canon," in Barnouw, *Communications*, vol. 2, pp. 441–43; John P. Ferre, "Searching for the Great Commission: Evangelical Book Publishing since the 1970s," in Quentin J. Schultze, ed., *American Evangelicals and the Mass Media* (Grand Rapids, Mich.: Zondervan, 1990), pp. 99–117.

10. Leslie H. Stobbe, "Reader, Beware!" *Moody Monthly*, November 1971, pp. 30–32: see "Books," an interview of Doug Ross, executive director of ECPA, printed in *Charisma and Christian Life*, April 1989, p. 36; Tony Wales, "Crossing Over," *Publishers Weekly*, March 7, 1986, p. 41; Walter A. Elwell, "Christian Publishing Is Caught Up," *Christianity Today*, July 17, 1981, pp. 973–74; the book ministry of Ligonier Ministries, Orlando, Florida, is aimed directly at this goal.

11. David Hazard, "Megatrends in Christian Publishing," *Charisma*, August 1985, p. 136.

12. Ibid., p. 136; Meg Cullar, "Promoting Religious Books," *Publishers Weekly*, March 3, 1989, pp. 31–33.

13. Lisa See, "Spreading the Word," *Publishers Weekly*, March 7, 1986, pp. 36–37; see also the use of fax to send orders; news story, *Publishers Weekly*, July 6, 1990, p. 24.

14. See Duke, *Religious Publications*, pp. 103–60, chs. 6, 7, 8, all on book publishing. Another comprehensive listing is Paul A. Soukup, *Communication and Theology: Introduction and Review of the Literature* (London: World Association for Christian Communication, 1983).

15. Elzey, "Popular Culture," p. 1734.

16. An excellent overall view is Giles Gunn, ed., *The Bible and American Arts and Letters* (Philadelphia: Fortress Press, 1983).

17. Jack Houston, "Behind Those Best Sellers," *Moody*, November 1971, pp. 28, 68–69.

18. News story, *Christian Retailing*, August 15, 1988, p. 25; Elzey, "Popular Culture," p. 1730.

19. David Kopp, "High Tech Heeds a Higher Calling," *Moody*, April 1990, pp. 77–84; see note 44 below; news story, *National Christian Reporter*, September 14, 1990, p. 1.

20. Elzey, "Popular Culture," pp. 1729–35; helpful statistics on evangelical reading habits are tabulated in Barna, *What Americans Believe*, pp. 286–94.

21. Balmer, *Mine Eyes*, pp. 155–70; see the annual issue on religious publishing in *Publishers Weekly*; for instance, on July 6, 1990, p. 116; news story, *Minneapolis Star Tribune*, July 4, 1989, p. 10E; news story, *Publishers Weekly*, September 2, 1988, pp. 54–58; "Money, Power, and Sex at the CBA," *Publishers Weekly*, August 30, 1985, pp. 44–48; *National Christian Reporter*, August 15, 1986, p. 1; "Bookselling and Marketing," *Publishers Weekly*, August 26, 1983, pp. 31–36.

22. See Richard I. Prevo, "Entertainment and Early Christian Literature," *Explor* [*sic*], 7 (Fall 1984): 29–30 (an annual journal published by Garrett Evangelical Theological Seminary).

23. For a different interpretation see Janice A. Radway, *Reading the Romance: Women, Patriarchy, and Popular Literature* (Chapel Hill: University of North Carolina Press, 1984).

24. Kay Mussell, "The Romance," in Barnouw, *Communications*, vol. 4, pp. 481–84; see also the essay "Romantic Fiction," in Thomas Inge, ed., *Handbook of American Popular Culture*, vol. 2 (Westport, Conn.: Greenwood Press, 1982), pp. 317–43.

25. Shirley Nelson, *The Last Year of the War* (New York: Harper and Row, 1978).

26. Phil Landrum, "Can Christian Fiction Survive?" *Moody Monthly*, February 1965, p. 39.

27. "Books," *USA Today Magazine*, December 1985, p. 11; Kenneth Woodward, "Inspirational Romances," *Newsweek*, February 20, 1984, p. 69.

28. William Griffin, "Fiction for the Faithful," *Publishers Weekly*, April 19, 1991, p. 27.

29. Ad in *Today's Christian Woman*, November/December 1990, p. 1; Dan O'Neil, "The Supernatural World of Frank Peretti," *Charisma and Christian Life*, May 1986, pp. 48–52; this article centers on Peretti's youth and first writings.

30. See Russell Chandler, *Understanding the New Age* (Waco, Tex.: Word Books,

1988); and Ted Peters, *The Cosmic Self: A Penetrating Look at Today's New Age Movements* (San Francisco: HarperSanFrancisco, 1991).

31. "Interview," *The Door*, 109, January/February 1990, pp. 6, 7.

32. Frank E. Peretti, *This Present Darkness* (Wheaton, Ill.: Crossway Books, 1986), p. 36; see Steven Starker, *Evil Influences: Crusades against the Mass Media* (New Brunswick, N.J.: Transaction Books, 1991).

33. O'Neil, "World," p. 50; see the list of interpretations of this subject, with brief evaluations, in "Books," *Christianity Today*, November 11, 1991, pp. 63–64.

34. Ibid.; O'Neil, "World," pp. 49, 52; Jeffrey Burton Russell, *The Devil in the Modern World* (Ithaca, N.Y.: Cornell University Press, 1986).

35. O'Neil, "World," p. 48; Robert A. Guelich, "Spiritual Warfare: Jesus, Paul, and Peretti," *Pneuma: The Journal of the Society for Pentecostal Studies*, 13, 1 (Spring 1991): 53, 57; review of Peretti by Steve Rabey in *Christianity Today*, December 9, 1986, p. 69; an excellent background study is Marguerite Shuster, *Power, Pathology, Paradox: The Dynamics of Good and Evil* (Grand Rapids, Mich.: Zondervan, 1987). Later, *Prophet: A Novel* (Westchester, Ill.: Crossway Books, 1992) became a runaway bestseller.

36. Guelich, "Warfare," p. 57.

37. "Interview," *The Door*, January/February 1990, pp. 6, 7.

38. See the brief biographical sketch by Steven R. Graham, "Hal Lindsey," in Charles H. Lippy, ed., *Twentieth-Century Shapers of American Popular Religion* (Westport, Conn.: Greenwood Press, 1989), pp. 247–55, which includes a bibliography.

39. Timothy P. Weber, "Premillennialism and the Branches of Evangelicalism," in Donald W. Dayton and Robert K. Johnston, eds., *The Variety of American Evangelicalism* (Knoxville: University of Tennessee Press, 1991), pp. 5–21.

40. See Graham, "Lindsey," pp. 247–51, esp. pp. 249–50.

41. See the "Interview" of Hal Lindsey in *Publishers Weekly*, March 24, 1977, pp. 30–32; the quote is on p. 31; Duke, *Religious Publications*, p. 155; Marlin Jeschke, "Pop Eschatology and Evangelical Theology," in C. Norman Kraus, ed., *Evangelicalism and Anabaptism* (Scottdale, Pa.: Herald Press, 1979), pp. 123–47; Rodney Clapp, "Overdosing on the Apocalypse," *Christianity Today*, October 28, 1991, pp. 26–29.

42. Nathan Hatch, "Evangelicalism as a Democratic Movement," in George Marsden, ed., *Evangelicalism and Modern America* (Grand Rapids, Mich.: Eerdmans, 1984), p. 79.

43. "News" column, *Christianity Today*, March 11, 1991, p. 60; news story, *New York Times*, February 2, 1991, pp. 1, 10; *Minneapolis Star Tribune*, February 3, 1991, p. 18A; Dave Hunt, *Global Peace and the Rise of the AntiChrist* (Eugene, Ore.: Harvest House, 1991); Texe Marrs, *Rush to Armageddon* (Wheaton, Ill.: Tyndale House, 1987).

43. "News," *Christianity Today*, March 11, 1991, p. 60; *New York Times*, February 3, 1991, pp. 1, 10; *Minneapolis Star Tribune*, February 3, 1991, p. 18A; Hunt, *Global Peace*; Marrs, *Rush to Armageddon*.

44. Steven Board, "Moving the World with Magazines: A Survey of Evangelical Periodicals," in Schultze, *American Evangelicals*, pp. 119–42; see also Soukup, *Communication*, and the annual list of religious periodicals in *The Yearbook of American and Canadian Christian Churches*, published by Abingdon Press. *Moody* is, of course, the new title for *Moody Monthly*. The name change occurred in 1980.

45. *Christian Herald* may have closed down by the time this book appears; *National and International Religion Report*, February 10, 1992, p. 6; Barna, "Are We Reading Christian Magazines?" *What Americans Believe*, pp. 136–43.

46. Board, "Moving the World," pp. 119–42; see the circulation statistics for each of these magazines in the annual publication by Gale Research Company, Detroit, Michigan.

47. Board, "Moving the World," pp. 121, 131–32.

48. Ibid., pp. 133–35.

49. News item, *National Christian Reporter*, December 22, 1988, p. 3; news story, "Magazine Scene," *Christian Retailing*, July 1, 1988, p. 58; James D. Fairbanks, "Politics and the Evangelical Press, 1960–1985," in Ted Jelen, ed., *Religion and Political Behavior* (New York: Praeger, 1989), pp. 243–57; see the information on *Christianity Today* and *Moody Monthly* in Charles H. Lippy, ed., *Religious Periodicals of the United States: Academic and Scholarly Journals* (Westport, Conn.: Greenwood Press, 1986), pp. 134–40, 368–71.

50. *The Christian Reader*, P.O. Box 1913, Marion, OH 43216-9604; circulation in 1991 was 215,000; *Genesis*, Berea Publications, Powhatan, VA 23239; *Christian Computing*, P.O. Box 438, Belton, MO 64142; *Cornerstone*, 920 W. Wilson, Chicago, IL 60640.

# 8

# Popular Religion and Evangelical Music: The Perfect Blend

Music is a mode of expression that has no parallel for scope or diversity in the life of faith. One evangelical observer writes, "In a faithless world filled with disappointments and fears where nothing seems to make sense, music can impart passion for living in the here and now."[1] Within Christendom it serves for many, as it has for centuries, as a principal mode of winning the world for Christ, rekindling one's own faith, and expressing the uniqueness of a defined religious faith community and also as a universal language reaching out to find common bonds with those of other persuasions.

Within our definition of evangelical popular religion, the importance of music can hardly be exaggerated. Music serves a multitude of basic purposes; some overlap and others stand at sharp odds with one another. Music, for instance, both reflects the wide diversity of ways to express the faith and seeks the primary goal to save the world for Christ, two goals that are not always in smooth harmony. Beyond that, music for many believers is a tool in the attempt to make America a Christian society, a unifying goal; yet at the same time it produces intense conflict and disagreement within its family boundaries. Hence a heavy dose of irony runs through its many forms and several usages. Further irony appears in its nature as both elusive and universal. Music is elusive because it is made from such intangibles as "melody and rhythm and tone," but it is universal because it is found in every culture, in endless forms of expression.[2]

Further, those who study music find incongruity everywhere through the consensus view that, even though the musical features differ widely, lyrics that faithfully express the evangelical faith somehow are pleasing to God in all their diversity. Testimony from many varying sources makes valid what otherwise seems to be a very discordant group of art forms, that is, Christian "rockers" music or "Christian Lite" music may be detested by enthusiasts for other forms; but as long as the witness is true, it all works out somehow in God's providential care.

The universal appeal of music shows up in its rank as third in popularity throughout American society among nonworktime activities, after watching television and reading a daily newspaper. Some 46 percent of all Americans listen to records or music tapes at home every day, and 27 percent more about once or twice a week.[3] Among evangelicals, specifically, it has the same kind of universal appeal, broadcast often through video or certain televised programs. It embraces what evangelicalism has done so well in its years of resurgence by drawing upon a variety of high technology media to appeal to both specialized and general audiences. It combines what to many evangelicals is the best and most effective of evangelistic genres, testimony lyrics set to the highly appealing sounds of general popular music.[4]

To spell out more precisely the transforming quality of this art form, evangelicals in recent years have come to believe music now, far more than before, consists of lyrics and melody belonging to and written for the rank and file of the faithful expressed outside of that music traditionally performed in "the Western concert tradition" or that with "strong non-Western, traditional and folk affiliations." Popular music embraces a very wide diversity of musical genres. It is this diversity that gives it such widespread appeal within the ranks where each major community asserts it has at least one major claim to understanding the truth of God's revelation.[5]

Further, music qualifies within our list of forces that lead to the creation of popular religious expression because it has so effectively drawn on the technological power of the silicon chip, integrated circuitry, and the compact cassette. It utilizes well the same appeal of supercelebrity preachers and athletes in its glorification of specific star performers; and its appeal almost always is transdenominational, reaching across the social divisions of denomination, doctrine, and social class. Finally, it like modern evangelicalism itself in several ways evolves from one form or genre to another, holding fast to some expressions and pressing on elsewhere to embrace the latest new fad. Robert A. Cook notes that "like everything else in life, music is constantly changing. Especially in religious and emotionally involved areas, one tends to defend most stoutly that to which one has become accustomed."[6]

To illustrate how strong evangelical preference for popular religion music is, in contrast to rank and file respect for their leaders' theological teachings, we look briefly here at what some of those leaders advocate. Within the many families of evangelicalism, considerable and often irreconcilable differences exist among leaders of the varied schools of expression of music. The more academic aestheticians such as Harold M. Best and Frank E. Gaebelein hold fast to the priority of music as a reflection of the grandeur, majesty, and richness of this art form; "whatever is true, whatever is just, whatever is pure, whatever is lovely, whatever is gracious." Best, for instance, rejects the popular culture fondness for repetition. To him the artist, including the musician, should consciously avoid "the temptation to clone or repeat," a quality indigenous to popular culture. Rather, Best insists, great art requires "the artist's own unique imagination" to avoid degrading that art "to nothing but repetition."[7] Great creative music, that which is truly imaginative, leads us to "applaud God, more than each other—God, the giver of 'every good and perfect gift.' " Great artists stretch unused muscles, disturb listeners, and even "raise our hackles."[8]

Gaebelein, meanwhile, starts from a more negative position (in which he is defended by other evangelicals) in saying they must reject music that is pretentious, vulgar, and reeking with sentimentality, merely ear-tickling adornment. Great music is simple and direct, yet it can be complex and sophisticated, honest and filled with integrity. Not all great music is explicitly religious but it is uplifting, pointing hearers to the greatness of God's inexhaustible creativity.[9]

However, these spokespersons are very limited in number and influence within evangelical arts. These two commentators, indeed, among a small handful represent only a minuscule number of established critics of the enormously popular and continually growing field of "Contemporary Christian Music" (CCM), to use the most widely used title for this phenomenon. With its tradition of transdenominationalism and populism plus its embrace of high technology, this broad style of music (CCM) demonstrates the power, appeal, and fascination of popular religion for evangelicals. This chapter focuses on that world of "performance music," while chapter 9 concentrates on music within the formal boundaries of church worship.

By the early 1990s the wide diversity of taste within evangelicalism regarding expressions of popular culture has become manifestly, even bewilderingly evident. The listening audience for CCM is "a mosaic of subgroups, some similar and others totally dissimilar in tastes, values, and even language." It includes all levels of stratification variables: in education, age, locale, race, ethnicity, income, gender, singleness, married couples, and parents.[10] To the aestheticians and others such eclecticism often is turned by money-making entrepreneurs into "cheap commercialism," too concerned with drawing on the models and the musicology of popular music to be truly religious.[11] It is, one editorial states, "so theologically shallow that it hurts." It has become the preferred style of music demanded by those under thirty wanting hymns written since 1970.[12]

Yet despite such critiques the CCM industry (as seen in chapter 1) has become a multimillion-dollar enterprise with enormous powers to attract, hold, and inspire millions of evangelicals. It thus also faithfully reflects much of the ongoing fragmentation or tribalization of American society in its conscious creation and promotion of several explicit, even formulaic types of evangelical music. Enough variations flourish among the basic classifications of religious music to give it an enormous holding power over its audience.

Although specialists disagree over definitions, it seems fair to identify these six forms: traditional, gospel quartet, country gospel, contemporary, Christian rock, and black gospel. Boundaries overlap, and the categories are anything but neat and tidy.[13] Traditional means music associated with the evangelical world over the last few centuries; gospel quartet is "old-style Southern gospel music" performed by a group; country gospel is essentially secular country music with religious lyrics; contemporary is a generic term covering more moderate, "lite" music closely parallel to folk tunes; Christian rock blends with the secular hard, heavy-metal music; and black gospel is "upbeat foot-stomping" in nature.[14]

Unfortunately, this is the most precise definition of CCM in musicology terms we have been able to achieve. No agreed-on set of definitions or structure dominates the various forms of CCM, probably because of the diversity of its audiences; its market-driven energy leads it to keep evolving and testing various expressions to keep up with the keen competition among evangelicals for listeners.[15] What might be "contemporary" in one short time span (say, two years), may soon become "lite," and so on.

The history of how this unfolded (because CCM has few traceable roots in the near past) is told in several places, among the most helpful being Donald Paul Ellsworth, *Contemporary Music in Contemporary Witness: Historical Antecedents and Contemporary Practice*.[16] In essence, CCM evolved informally but rapidly at the same tempo of change characteristic of the larger American society. It was served in part by the rapid increase in the number of amateur musicians, with guitars, mouth organs and/or tambourines who were searching for their own voice of testimony. It came from some innovative brass ensembles within the Salvation Army who started to extemporize on the traditional hymnology of that tradition. It was aided enormously by the high tech production of amplification at comparatively low costs to amateur or semiprofessional groups. It drew heavily, as did the larger counterculture hippie world, from older and newer music of a decidedly folk definition, usually rustic or rural in origin, played by a single person or small group with simple, sing-along kinds of tunes.

Another new form was "sacred pop music," hard to define but clearly recognizable to its friends. One tracker, Audrey T. Hingley, states that the soundtrack album of Billy Graham's 1966 movie, "For Pete's Sake," "marked the beginning of contemporary Christian music."[17] Close to older gospel hymn tunes, these numbers exuded an atmosphere of spontaneous praise. At the same time early forms of Christian "rock" appeared, especially around the records of Larry Norman, known in the 1960s as "the father of Jesus rock."[18] This led quickly in that decade to musicians, drawing on heavy metal and pulsating rhythm beat, performing within some evangelical circles. As suggested in chapter 1, much of this came together in a very loose but attractive form through the Jesus movement of CCM.

Among other features what stands out here is the growth of this genre outside the supervision or direction of the organized denominations. That trend along with the distaste many evangelicals felt for such forms of music contributed strongly to the rancor and divisiveness within their ranks over the appropriateness of such music. Pop Christian music advocates insisted from the outset they were not selling out to the larger world but were instead taking religious music outside the formal church buildings, away from the stultifying insistence on traditional music, and into the hands of those who might otherwise have remained aloof from such forms of witnessing.[19]

Underlying the arguments over appropriateness rested the age-old dilemma with any music and its audiences. As a symbolic language, its meaning has less precision and clarity than the language of words. Also, the need for innovation and change is rooted deeply in each society's own culture; hence what is appropriate for one group may be unsatisfactory for another. Finally, with their loyalty to the Bible as final authority, evangelicals find that book lacking in teachings on aesthetics and musicology. It lacks specificity when searchers look to it for proof texts to buttress their own positions.[20]

By about 1980 the popularity of CCM was such that traditionalist objections were virtually ignored. The larger popular culture that had created rock and pop music now had such popularity through technology and affordable audience equipment that its impact on popular religion music was irresistible. Its supporters pointed out that the classic hymns still sung today were once simple folk tunes; that music is to be used not only for worship and teaching but also for testifying and witness; that the decisions about what defines the essence of religious music should not be "constructed between the common man and the intellectual"; and finally, artistry is too personal and faith too internal a matter to be decided in an authoritarian manner by any one group.[21]

In sum, what had occurred was the identification of large numbers of evangelicals with the persona of Jesus of Nazareth being portrayed in much of the new music. They approved of his living nomadically and communally, financially dependent upon the generosity of others. He used everyday speech, rejected materialism, and showed deep concern over personal relationships rather than those involved with hierarchical institutions. As

Richard A. Hawley suggests, "Jesus is what every uncertain adolescent at one time fancies himself to be: the persecuted rebel. He always seems wiser than his elders, able to sidestep legalistic ethics and in general dramatizing their archetypal situation."[22]

In the 1980s CCM continued to expand its popularity, fragment its several styles of music, turn by several innovations more into a business than a witness, and in general continue to reflect the ongoing diversification of evangelical popular religion. Unabashedly, many composers and/or artists consciously modeled their music upon the music of popular secular artists. A close student, Paul Baker, presents extensive research findings demonstrating how "Christian artists"—among the better known being Debbie Boone, Andrae Crouch, Phil Driscoll, Amy Grant, Dallas Holm, Sandi Patti, and Steve Taylor (to name only a few among dozens of the famous)—identified their music with one or more of the hundreds of not religiously aligned musicians.[23]

The first evangelical superstar to make all the charts of top records, Amy Grant, saw her album "Age to Age" at the top for over two years, slipping only when her second album, "Straight Ahead," moved ahead.[24] Much of the spontaneous, often raw and unpolished Christian music of earlier years came in the 1980s under the direction of more skilled, professional technicians and promoters in Nashville and other large-scale, well-equipped studios. Some artists started to "overlap" or "cross over," presenting material that was less directly evangelistic and more appealing to consumers who might otherwise have been offended or bored by the more direct testimonial character of earlier CCM. At the same time the world of evangelical "praise" music found a rapidly growing audience and, as a result, several imitators within CCM circles.[25]

Some of the appeal in the 1980s harmonized well with the general evangelical aim of helping a large but immeasurable number of evangelicals who wanted to create a more Christian society in America. Much CCM music, especially gospel, was advertised and perceived by listeners as harmonious with the conservative sociopolitical agenda of President Ronald Reagan, the Moral Majority, and related groups.[26]

Yet "cross-over" stood as only one of the several forms of music clearly established by the early 1990s among its followers. Inspirational music, hymns both traditional and recent, southern gospel, black gospel, middle of the road, rock, and heavy metal rock continue to find strong responses as they evolve and overlap within the world of popular religious music.

So overwhelming has this movement been that it requires a more detailed account of the several elements that gave it such appeal. Among the most important within the realm of popular culture has been the sheer accessibility of contemporary Christian music. Like books, it has its own customer clubs offering a sampling of albums with inducements of bonuses, lower prices, and promotion gifts such as tote bags. Membership is extremely simple to complete, usually by sending in a pullout card from an evangelical magazine or by calling a toll-free telephone number. The many bookstore/religious supply stores across the country almost all carry at least some albums in compact disc or cassette form. Some of the giant publishers such as Word also carry a full line of musical items, which are accessible in the familiar outlets just mentioned. The concerts so popular with evangelical youth also give them the opportunity to purchase records and other memorabilia of the performing artists. In sum, this form of popular religion is accessible, almost always at prices within the reach of the customers.[27]

Accessibility also depends on the vast system of intertwining and networking of evangelical music groups. Easily the most influential of all magazines focusing on all aspects of the music is *Contemporary Christian Music*, first appearing in the late 1970s out of Laguna Hills, California. It is almost impossible for observers to exaggerate its impact on and power over CCM; the magazine serves many heartfelt needs for its readers. It has highly attractive, slick advertisements in various sizes for those aspiring to rise on the charts and carries smoothly crafted, stylized personality pictures of the superstars posing with brief mention of their new album. The magazine carries "feedback" comparable to "letters to the editors," a feature that adds grass-roots opinion, often critical of *CCM* editorials, on the subject and helps readers in more isolated areas identify in terminology of their own peer groups to what, as they say, "is going down." *CCM* presents profiles, evaluative essays, book reviews, insider kind of news about the superstars, top seller lists, itineraries of the famous superstars on tour, and extensive reviews of new albums and related items. Its success is due in large part to the format reflecting diversity, eclecticism, and up to date news, all written in language congenial to the readers. *CCM* thus becomes a national forum, capable of launching or slowing down aspiring artists and, by its tone and scope of subjects, the primary agency to define what is acceptable in this area of popular religion.[28]

Alongside *CCM* stand several smaller journals, more specialized and modest in scope, seeking to reach the huge market they know is there. These have more trouble staying afloat because of their small readership; one survivor has been *The Cutting Edge* of Orlando, Florida, with most of its emphasis on review of new items.[29] Another has been *Vortexx*, advertising itself as a journal covering "heavy metal, new wave, jazz and the 'avant-garde.' " It also has carried, compared to *CCM*, more information on "underground" artists, thus giving its personality more of an insider, out-of-the-mainstream tone, which appeals to some aficionados.[30] Among true admirers, journals on heavy metal find readers; these include *Heaven's*

*Metal, Gospel Metal, White Throne,* and *Notebored.* Another publication of this genre has been *The Revealer* out of Evansville, Indiana, which before it stopped publishing brought out up-to-date information on videos, festivals, album reviews, and evangelism through contemporary Christian music.[31]

Accessibility and networking flourish in a variety of other modes, thus making even remote towns and individuals aware of the latest trends. For instance, in Ashland, Oregon, *The Christian Music Directory* is published, revised frequently. The second edition, for instance, of 1987 listed over 4,000 companies involved in the recording, distribution, and promotion of Christian music. Its primary goal is to keep people and companies "up to date with the rapidly changing Christian music scene" by carrying information on publishers, record labels, producers, radio stations and religious video companies.[32] A comparable publication is the *Christian Booking and Program Directory* in Ojai, California, with similar information; by the late 1980s it was in its fifth edition.[33]

On the more regional and local level are the offerings of evangelical newspapers; for example, the *Twin City Christian* (Minnesota) offers a semiannual "Artist Directory," listing people with "performance-type ministry" for individuals, congregations, and similar groups to consider.[34] In Pittsburgh the religious television station serves as a meeting place for "young, active Christians" exchanging news about entertainment, youth activities, and opportunities to perform. *Cornerstone* offers similar listings of opportunities for performance ministry. It also served and continues to set a much-imitated format in the production of Christian rock videos meant to witness and to combat the preoccupation of youth audiences with secular video and television such as MTV.[35] Locally produced evangelicalist videos and audiocassettes have increased interest and attention at local congregations such as Elmbrook Church near Milwaukee, which broadcasts locally made videos of parts of its worship services over local cable systems. For retailers certain special interest groups such as "the Christian Music Retailers Group" organized in the late 1980s to promote common interests, especially to protect locally owned retail outlets against what they considered unfair retail practices by the giants such as Zondervan.[36]

Perhaps the most influential of all accessibility and networking opportunities is the annual "Christian Artists' Music Seminar in the Rockies," by 1990 in its fifteenth year. Basically it offers education through hands-on, how-to seminars and classes on a wide variety of evangelistic programs including worship and singles ministry. It centers around performance ministry in vocal, dance, songwriting, computers, synthesizers, gospel music, business opportunities, and related topics. Its central appeal is to music leaders in the continually expanding field of evangelistic arts. This includes choir directors, church music administrators, specialists on handbell music, and the technical phases of lighting, sound, and amplification in the arts ministries. It also presents a variety of both superstars and less well-known artists. Attendance had increased from a few at the outset to over a thousand annually by the late 1980s.[37]

All this activity continues to create extremely sharp debate and conflict within evangelical circles over a variety of issues inherent in this form of popular religion. The balance of this chapter explores these as evidence of how and where the tensions within popular religion have appeared and how in the name of the evangelical voice of faith they have been addressed.

One dispute that attracts little national attention but suggests the depth of feeling among some evangelicals is over the enormous emphasis evangelical magazines, record companies, and related media place on the "charts" or "polls" of what songs and albums are bestsellers and on the annual "Dove" and "Grammy" award competitions similar to the "Oscars" for movies. In its few years of existence *CCM* has decided on several categories for such competition, including "gospel vocal solo, female and male," "gospel performance by a duo, Group, Choir or Chorus," "best soul performance, male and female," and "Best Soul performance" by a duo or group, and best inspirational performance, best recording for children, and the like. These are specific categories within the Grammy awards, which also include awards for nonreligious music in the country-western genres. The Doves are given for explicitly evangelistic music with categories such as "song of the year," "songwriter of the year," "male and female vocalist of the year," "group of the year," "artist of the year," rock, contemporary, inspirational, and others.

Further, the leading charismatic/Pentecostal magazine, *Charisma and Christian Life*, annually runs its own polls using the same general categories. Winning one or more of these over the years obviously helps a performer increase sales enormously. The selections also serve as a helpful indication of the tastes and preferences in popular religious music of its consumers, largely evangelicals.[38] What a survey (such as this author has made) over the years of such polls suggests is that innovation among the superstars is very rare, that slight improvisation and updated high technology tend to keep listeners loyal to specific major celebrities.

But all this, obviously closely patterned after Oscars and related awards in the world of secular mass entertainment, raises some hard questions for certain evangelicals. Rather than rejoice as the millions of buyers do in the immense variety of productions available, from the famous to the unknown, these believers take another position. Readers writing to *Charisma* state such awards are "unscriptural. God's Word teaches us to be humble and abased, not to prefer one person above another and not to think too highly of ourselves. Let's forget the glitz and get back to doing things God's way."[39]

A second controversy, not at the forefront of evangelical discussion but suggestive of inner-family conflict, centers over a feature rarely discussed. Despite "the richness and diversity" that exists in CCM, the rank and file find another, less desirable change occurring: "Kids don't sing any more. I wonder if, because there are so many professional Christian musicians, many of the kids in my church feel intimidated. . . . I am beginning to wonder if the *cumulative* effect of professional Christian music isn't causing young people to feel that, when the music starts, they are supposed to sit and listen."[40] A well-known editor, Larry Tomczak, asked whether the lyrics of this music exalted God or man, whether listening to a recording or a concert dulls one's vision for ministry, whether the sound weakens one's sensitivity to the power of the Holy Spirit or might be a stumbling block to young believers, among other queries.[41]

In a similar vein, evangelical critic John Fisher asks whether after these several years of new Christian music—whereby audiences were told they would win the war against Satan, that Christ was coming back to punish the bad and reward the good—it has made any real difference. He asks, "But how many ways can we say these things? Might not the listeners be hard of hearing and bored with all this? Had they been told to care for their neighbors, those of lonely hearts, the sick, the outcasts, the undesirables of society? Had new Christian music sung of the snares of spiritual pride, sexism, racism and bigotry? Did it awaken concern for global issues?" Fisher suggests clearly that such music had failed in these areas. Others suggested such music was actually glorifying "unseen spiritual aspects . . . of Satanic influence."[42]

However, lively as these issues were, they paled in comparison to what became the major issue emerging in the 1980s, centering around the perceived transformation of the original spontaneous, soul-winning nature of Christian music to a highly profitable, commercially slick hucksterism hardly distinguishable from secular music aimed at youth. In a highly competitive world in which listener ratings help determine the financial charges the broadcasters can charge potential advertisers, the trend according to close observers is toward greater commercialization and less spontaneous testimony and witness. These observers acknowledge the "sloppy, amateurish and foolish way some Christians use the media."[43] Others reply that many Christian artists are much like Old Testament prophets speaking a critical biblical word to believers and others alike. They like earlier prophets are discovering they are being criticized by liberals and conservatives, Christians and non-Christians, "well-meaning fools and meaningless 'wise men.' "[44]

Finally, after presenting a carefully researched critique of the over-commercialization of CCM, two specialists, William D. Romanowski and Quentin J. Schultze, conclude, after attending the annual conference of the Gospel Music Association in Nashville that the gospel music world is "ministry" in terms of sales success ratings and bestsellers; it "is alive and well and appearing every April in Nashville—a city whose convention motto is 'Let Us Entertain You.' "[45]

From another direction comes the plea from a specialist on teens, Al Menconi, that this music, for all its commercialism, often serves a helpful purpose in improving parent-child relations. Today's music, he argues, can be seen as "a window to our child's soul," a clue parents can use in building better relations when they understand why their offspring are devoted to what seems so weird and distasteful a form of emotional expression. Because rock music obviously will not disappear soon and because parents' decisions to ban such music from their home by their own teenage children will only drive the latter to friends' houses, then parents and children must learn how to share directly and spontaneously their deep-felt emotions about this divisive force.[46]

A further complication in this highly charged scene is the acceptance by CCM fans of the "star" or "celebrity" system, a form of promotion indigenous to and essential for the secular world of entertainment in movies, television, and radio—the full range of media expression. The "star" system centers around the highly skillful means used by the producers and entrepreneurs of new Christian music to promote specific, clearly identified personalities as both exemplars of cherished evangelical values because of their testimony in music and representatives of specific styles of music such as country, gospel, or lite. Stars such as Amy Grant, Sandi Patti, Phil Driscoll, Steve Taylor, and others are promoted in the same manner as superstars Rod Taylor, Bruce Springsteen, and dozens more who have come through such promotion and performance to be heroes and even idols of their audiences. Promotional biographies and fan-magazine articles on Grant and Patti, for instance, tell of their early struggles, the convictions that inspire their testimony, and their current struggles to remain at the top.[47]

The fame of the superstars was enhanced further by the extensive and growing practice of having their albums turn up on videocassettes, available for purchase or rental at a wide variety of outlets. Other innovative forms of performance included the annual tour of a variation on the famed oratorio by G. F. Handel, the *Messiah*, now re-entitled "The Young Messiah Tour" on the Christmas season circuit, featuring Patti, Driscoll, Russ Taff, Sheila Walsh, Larnelle Harris, and other blockbuster celebrities.

Those stars who performed outside the familiar boundaries of known evangelical audiences (such as Bible colleges) risk the evaluation of non-evangelical critics. Largely, the latter point out that as long as these stars imitate the secular leaders such as Gloria Estefan, Paula Abdul, or Cher, their performances rank as only mildly effective. But, as one critic wrote, "Grant [Amy] eventually converted this non-believer when she began singing about Jesus. Suddenly, she focused and forgot the canned gestures and show-biz trappings. She sang a tune about doubt and declared that the answer was Jesus, which brought a huge cheer in midsong from the crowd of 12,000."[48]

Further, by the early 1990s the varieties and nuances within the full field of CCM continued to grow, as did the willingness of many performers to comment critically on the performances and motivations of others in the same general field. The superstar-celebrity system flourishes unabated, but so too does the ministry of dozens of slightly less well-known groups in all parts of the country playing to smaller audiences, in smaller towns, and selling fewer albums, often rarely known to the general public. Invariably, to judge by the heavy press coverage given them in the best-known evangelical journals, these groups find that their audiences respond the most strongly when the artists present their own testimonies of conversion and born-again experience, especially those who have come out of less savory life-styles. They have come to represent, as do the superstars, a whole new genre of heroes and roles models among American youth. Yes, teenagers have in turn, swooned over Frank Sinatra, fainted over Elvis Presley, and so on. That phenomenon is nothing new. But today, within evangelical popular religion, it has achieved a stature and rootedness that helps point the tracker to one of the most fundamental sources of that faith's strength, its involvement with contemporary Christian music.

## NOTES

1. Roy M. Anker, ed., "Risky Business: Youth and the Entertainment Business," *Dancing in the Dark: Youth, Popular Culture, and the Electronic Media* (Grand Rapids, Mich.: Eerdmans, 1991), p. 101, see also pp. 76–110.

2. Clyde Ryken, ed., *The Christian Imagination* (Grand Rapids, Mich.: Baker Book House, 1991), p. 399; on on "Christian America" see William Romanowski, "Contemporary Christian Music: The Business of Music Ministry," in Quentin J. Schultze, ed., *American Evangelicals and the Mass Media* (Grand Rapids, Mich.: Zondervan, 1990), pp. 143–44; Grant Wacker, "Searching for Norman Rockwell: Popular Evangelicalism in Contemporary America," in Leonard I. Sweet, ed., *The Evangelical Tradition in America* (Macon, Ga.: Mercer University Press, 1984), pp. 289–315; Don Cusic, *Sandi Patti: The Voice of Gospel* (New York: Dolphin Books, 1988), pp. 46–50, 82–87, 159–62; the subject matter ranges more widely than the title suggests; Don Cusic, *The Sound of Light: A History of Gospel Music* (Bowling Green, Ohio: Bowling Green State University Popular Press, 1992).

3. Dennis A. Gilbert, ed., *Compendium of American Public Opinion* (New York: Facts on File, 1988), p. 292.

4. Tony Jasper, *Jesus and the Christians in a Pop Culture* (London: Robert Royce, 1984); John Shepard, "Popular Music," in Eric Barnouw, ed., *International Encyclopedia of Communications*, vol. 3 (New York: Oxford University Press, 1989), pp. 98–99; Alan Wells, "Popular Music," *Journal of Popular Culture*, 24, 1 (Summer 1990): 105–17; Glenn Kaiser, "Can Music Truly Be Evangelistic?" *Religious Broadcasting*, April 1991, pp. 16–17; Robert Cook, "That New Religious Music," *Christian Herald*, December 1976, p. 4.

5. See the citations in note 4, especially Shepard, "Popular Music," p. 99; see also

William D. Romanowski's doctoral dissertation, "Rock 'N' Roll Religion: A Socio-Cultural Analysis of the Contemporary Christian Music Industry," Ph.D. dissertation, Bowling Green State University, 1990, pp. 13–50.

6. Cook, "New Music," p. 4; Romanowski, "Rock 'N' Roll," pp. 13–50; Kaiser, "Can Music," pp. 16–17; Erling Jorstad, *Holding Fast/Pressing On: Religion in America in the 1980s* (Westport, Conn.: Greenwood Press, 1990), pp. 121–24.

7. Harold Best, "Christian Responsibility in Music," in Ryken, *Christian Imagination*, pp. 402–5.

8. Ibid., p. 405.

9. Frank Gaebelein, "The Christian and Music," in Ryken, *Christian Imagination*, pp. 442–45.

10. Robert N. Niklaus, "Airing Our Views," editorial, *Religious Broadcasting*, May 1983, p. 3; a very comprehensive study is Barna Research Group, *Profile of the Christian Music Consumer* (Glendale, Calif.: Barna Research Group, 1990), passim.

11. James Lany, "Christian Record Publishers," *Christianity Today*, November 12, 1982, p. 81.

12. Editorial, *Christian Herald*, November 1983, p. 83.

13. Cook, "New Music," pp. 4–7; see Romanowski, "Contemporary Christian Music," pp. 149–52.

14. Ibid.; Judith S. Duke, *Religious Publications and Communications* (White Plains, N.Y.: Knowledge Industry Publications, 1981), pp. 195–96.

15. Letter by William Romanowski to me, January 10, 1991, on musicology; for a discussion of black soul music (which would be an excellent model to use for filling in the absence of evangelical musicology study), see George Lipsitz, *Time Passages: Collective Memory and American Popular Culture* (Minneapolis: University of Minnesota Press, 1989), pp. 109–10.

16. Ellsworth, *Christian Music in Contemporary Witness: Historical Antecedents and Contemporary Practice* (Grand Rapids, Mich.: Baker Book House, 1979), p. 79, and see his bibliography.

17. Audrey T. Hingley, quoting Lois Ferguson, *Christian Herald*, June 1985, p. 35.

18. Ibid.

19. Romanowski, "Contemporary Christian Music," pp. 145–49; Ellsworth, *Christian Music in Contemporary Witness*, pp. 121–54; for critics, see Harold Best, "Music: Offerings of Creativity," *Christianity Today*, May 6, 1977, pp. 12, 16.

20. Ellsworth, *Christian Music in Contemporary Witness*, p. 165.

21. Ibid., pp. 190–94; see also the summary, Tom Winfield, "Musical Trends in the 90s" [which is about trends in the 1980s], *Charisma and Christian Life*, February 1990, pp. 86–89.

22. Richard Hawley, "Some Thoughts on the Pop Jesus," *Anglican Theological Review*, 55, 3 (July 1973): 342–43.

23. Paul Baker, *Contemporary Christian Music*, rev. ed. (Westchester, Ill.: Crossway Books, 1985), pp. 242–57.

24. Romanowski, "Contemporary Christian Music," p. 157.

25. Ibid., p. 158; Cusic, *Patti*, pp. 117–18.

26. Cusic, *Patti*, pp. 46–50, 82–87, 159–62.

27. Winfield, "Musical Trends," pp. 92–93; Sandy Smith, "Gospel Artists in the Mainstream," *Religious Broadcasting*, April 1992, pp. 26–28.

28. 25231 Paseo de Alicia, Suite 201, Laguna Hills, CA 92653; or P.O. Box 6300, Laguna Hills, CA 92654.

29. 8303 Hilton Way, Orlando, FL 32810; Kaiser, "Can Music," p. 16.

30. *Cornerstone*, 15, 78 (n.d.), n.p.; see Barna, *Profile*, passim.

31. Ibid.; Kaiser, "Can Music," pp. 16–17; Ellsworth, *Christian Music in Contemporary Witness*, p. 127.

32. *The Christian Music Directory*, Box 3, Ashland, OR 97520; see again Barna, *Profile*.

33. Cornerstone, 15, 88 (n.d.), p. 86.

34. *Twin City Christian*, August 11, 1988, "Supplement," passim; ad, ibid., December 31, 1987, p. 15A.

35. News story, *Religious Broadcasting*, April 1989, p. 18; *Cornerstone*, 17, 89 (n.d.); news story, *Christianity Today*, September 20, 1985, p. 53; "People" Column, *World Wide Challenge*, May/June 1986, pp. 47–48.

36. News story, "Retailers Demand Improved Music Service," *Christian Retailing*, June 7, 1989, pp. 1, 14.

37. Brochure, "Christian Artists," P.O. Box 1984, Thousand Oaks, CA 91360.

38. Carol Ward, *The Christian Sourcebook*, rev. ed. (New York: Ballantine Books, 1989), pp. 280–81; column, "Media World," *Religious Broadcasting*, March 1986, p. 45; news story, *Charisma and Christian Life*, October 1990, p. 56; news story, *Christian Retailing*, May 15, 1989, p. 8.

39. Letter in *Charisma and Christian Life*, September 1989, p. 24; see this page for several similar letters.

40. Les Christie, "Whatever Happened to Singing?" *The Wittenburg Door*, August/September 1984, p. 123; Russell Baker, "Hear America Singing," *New York Times*, November 2, 1991, p. 11.

41. Larry Tomczak, "Today's Music," *People of Destiny*, May/June 1986, p. 12.

42. John Fisher, *Real Christians Don't Dance* (Minneapolis: Bethany House, 1988), pp. 138–39.

43. Chuck Fromm, "Who Is Converting Whom?" *Charisma*, July 1987, p. 46.

44. Gary J. Hineman, "Christian Artists: Today's Prophets?" *CCM*, August 1987, p. 9; anon., "All Wrapped Up" video, 1991, from Word Ministry, P.O. Box 2518, Waco, TX 76702-2518; Lloyd Billingsly, "Rock Video," *Christianity Today*, July 13, 1984, p. 70.

45. William D. Romanowski and Quentin J. Schultze, "Praising God in Opryland," *The Reformed Journal*, November 1989, p. 14; also an early statement of this position is Richard D. Dinwiddie, "Moneymakers in the Church: Making the Sounds of Music," *Christianity Today*, June 26, 1981, pp. 853–56.

46. Al Menconi, "Talking 'Bout the Way I Feel," *Christian Parenting*, April 1990, pp. 24–27, 50; and his book, *Today's Music: A Window to Your Child's Soul* (Elgin, Ill.: David C. Cook, 1990).

47. Cusic, *Patti*; Carol Legget, *Amy Grant* (New York: Pocket Books, 1987); Bob Millard, *Amy Grant: A Biography* (New York: Doubleday, 1986); interview, "Billy Rae Hearn Talks about Today's Christian Music," *Charisma*, July 1985, pp. 69–75; Paul Baker, "Must the Show Go On?" *Charisma*, February 1986, pp. 57–68; "Horizons," *U.S. News & World Report*, August 25, 1986, pp. 5–6.

48. Jon Bream, "A Review," *Minneapolis Star Tribune*, July 31, 1991, p. 2B.

# 9

# Popular Religion and Evangelical Church Music: The Heritage Lives

The centrality of music in popular religion touches the lives of all evangelicals. As the preceding chapter suggested, much of its appeal to youth and young adults comes from its intertwining with the larger pop music scene in America. Equally powerful as an expression of the faith is the domain of music more directly associated with organized church life and more formal worship services, the subject of this chapter.

The argument over whether Christianity can authentically be expressed in lite or rock form has for several decades had its parallel in a comparable argument over the purpose and the very nature of religious music within organized evangelical church life. The emergence of the latter in the United States largely created the revival meetings and the attendant foot-tapping, soul-stirring gospel hymns perhaps best exemplified by those of Ira Sankey (1840–1908), music director for the famed evangelist Dwight L. Moody. From the years when those two led revivals across the country (and in Europe) within the confines of organized religious life, evangelical church music has consciously created and nurtured a style and content in musicological terms of hymnody distinct from mainline liturgical bodies.

With the infusion of high technology, simple access to the mass media, and the exploding acceptance of popular religion themes, evangelical hymnody in the last thirty years exemplifies as clearly as any other theme discussed in this book the heart of popular religion. Because music touches such immensely deep human emotions as nostalgia, loyalty to one's heritage, expression of one's strongest emotions, and the desire to worship God in this form, it stands at the center of evangelical witness. Whatever its specific shape—fundamentalist, evangelical, charismatic, or Pentecostal—music is recognized as being at the very heart of both understanding and expressing personal and corporate faith.[1]

Within the ranks of evangelicalism's families, an ongoing contest goes on, revolving around the extent to which the local congregation and/or the denomination should hold fast to those great hymns and other musical forms of worship of the past, or as with so much else in evangelical life in recent decades, should embrace and extend the several new forms of music and worship in hymn and liturgy. Generally, the contest centers mostly between specialists who seek to preserve the best of the past, identifying often with the classical tradition in religious music of J. S. Bach, Ludwig van Beethoven, Johannes Brahms, and others, and those who find in their born-anew converted lives the openness to embrace some of the many new specific forms available, especially in what has become known as "praise" music.[2]

The former group, although minuscule in number, often hold key positions in evangelical colleges and Bible schools where they teach future parishioners and advocate their case for holding fast. The latter group includes a vast number of both professional and amateur music writers who seek to make so vital a part of the worship of the parish harmonize with the newness of a converted life in the new music. Some in both camps seek a mediating center position. What everyone involved agrees on is that music, such as hymnody and in liturgy, is explicitly commanded of believers by the authority of the Bible. They agree with the general evangelical norms that it must be used to win souls for Christ, to re-energize their own spiritual lives, and to witness for the faith to the world. One of the traditional camp, Robert Elmore, writes, "Music is the Christian art par excellence. From that awe-inspiring moment in the past when the morning stars sang together and the sons of God shouted for joy, to that wondrous time in the future when Christians will join in the song of the redeemed, the Bible is full of references to music."[3]

The dispute, often acrimonious and divisive, centers on how close to the classical tradition and the popular tradition of the evangelical tradition such expression should be.[4] Classicists state that much popular music is unnecessarily light, sugary, and sentimental, drawing its inspiration far too much from secular pop culture motifs. With other commentators, however, evangelism and dedication to moral rectitude is mandated as ranking above evangelical concern with the fine arts dimension of music.[5]

Aestheticians reply that music is essentially an offering to God, not primarily a means to get people into a certain receptive mood to "get them interested in Jesus." One writes, "It's wrong to use music to prepare people to feel a certain way or to lead them into feeling so as to confuse the presence of God with cultural ecstasy." Music becomes in this camp a sort of lubrication into the church—"the big evangelistic message." Knowing what the other side will say, they state that in a worship service they want the Holy Spirit, not the music, to shape the audience's receptivity.[6]

The popular music supporters insist on placing the sermon and moral exhortation at the center of the worship experience, avoiding distractions that take the focus away from converting souls. For some, anything richer than the simplest music distracts and dilutes the mandate to preach and convert.[7]

The tussle, which has been resolved in some previously factionalized congregations, attracts the concern of other leaders seeking a middle ground. Of such, perhaps, the most influential leader has been Don Hustad, formerly the director of music for the Billy Graham ministry and more recently a professor at the Southern Baptist Theological Seminary, Louisville, Kentucky. His many-sided career has taught him the importance of finding among the faithful acceptable answers that keep the faith alive while helping avoid fruitless controversy. His productive scholarship serves the whole religious scene well, especially a book used closely here, *Jubilate! Church Music in the Evangelical Tradition*, first appearing in 1981 and updated since.[8]

Recognizing the seriousness of the issues just outlined, Hustad calls for a recognition that what is wrong is a communications gap among the participants. The music (meaning here, the sound) *as such* has no intrinsic religious value. It is the cultural baggage that people bring along and use to identify and respond to the music that causes the gaps and the problems. Songs once considered secular have been turned into meaningful sacred hymns; worship practices considered "papist" (i.e., Roman Catholic) or "elitist" by some are understood by others as bringing the best they can offer to God.[9]

What Hustad proposes as a mediating course has two tracks: a recognition of mistakes, flaws, and biases by all concerned and, two, a workable set of standards for evangelical church music use. On the first track comes this confession; everyone concerned commits these (if not more) sins: (1) that of pride, believing one set of practices is superior to those of others; (2) that of hedonism, meaning that many evangelicals think the central meaning in church music is "pleasure," immediate emotional satisfaction; (3) that of spectatorism, in which evangelicals would rather listen than sing for themselves (to Hustad this practice leaves out a central feature of worship in song); and (4) the sin of sentimentalism, embracing largely those more contemporary hymns and songs that stay on one's "top 20" hit list, inspired largely by American popular culture and promoted heavily by certain evangelical publishing and recording houses—in a word, "formula" music.[10]

Soul-winning music and worship should avoid both holding on to the past for its own sake and embracing the latest fads simply because they are the latest. To provide constructive alternatives Hustad then moves to the second track, laying down specific standards, recognizing the validity of local priorities and levels of theological sophistication. First, music should have appropriate text and music that make clear to the audience the gospel message. Second, music should strive for excellence, offered "in love, humility, gratitude, and grace," and avoid invidious comparisons to other persons or cultures. Third, music needs to underline, in various forms, the unique strengths of each evangelical subculture, keeping balance among their respective priorities. Fourth, music should recognize the musical needs of each community, respecting its commitments to worship, outreach, and fellowship. Fifth, music needs to keep a clear balance among the emotions, intellect, and physical qualities of believers, shunning sentimentality; and sixth, it must avoid the trite and hackneyed as well as the abstruse and elitist features of hymns and worship.[11]

We explore Hustad's analysis here in detail because to this point it encapsulates vividly one of the central issues in popular religion: How can the Christian faith, standing for some 2,000 years with its rich traditions and expressions, survive in a world and society in which the new, the novel, the culture-bound forms of expression provide such strong meaning and attractiveness to the rank and file?

What seems to be happening in the world of evangelicalism is the gradual but pervasive overtaking of the more traditional forms by the contemporary school of music. Although measurable empirical evidence of this trend is not available, the appeal of the music that appeared at the time of the evangelical growth takeoff closely allied with the Jesus movement seems to be irresistible in its high technology/ever-present condition.

It is not that the traditionalists have not tried to hold fast. The leading nondenominational journals frequently carry articles on the richness of Bach's religious music or Handel's *Messiah* and related topics. At times the news reports that evangelicals (largely intellectuals) are embracing more liturgical church traditions, such as from the Eastern Orthodox and Roman Catholic traditions.[12]

But the contemporary mode continues to grow. Televangelist expert Quentin J. Schultze attributes this largely to the influence of religious television. To hold a wide audience, thus offending the fewest viewers and thereby enhancing the possibilities for wide financial support, the televised worship service comes to the public as entertainment, a "Hollywood production." The defenders of such programs identify their success as due to the "relaxed, informal," "interesting," and "relevant" qualities of their shows. Worship, Schultze argues, is subsumed by popular culture rather than being a part of the prophetic, not of this world, character of the church. The fallout from this is found on the local church level. Having seen the spectacular productions of a Jimmy Swaggart, Oral Roberts, D. James Kennedy, Charles

Stanley, or Kenneth Copeland, viewers come to expect the same from the services in their local parish, a change that for some has turned into a celebration of secular values.[13]

Although empirical evidence substantiating that conclusion is impossible to collect (it would mean doing a time study of the music patterns of evangelical churches over a considerable time period), we can trace, from considerable available data, three dimensions of this expression of popular religion. These are, first, the trend in hymns or hymnody; second, the full dimension of "praise" music; and third, the various controversies over formal liturgical worship within the evangelical family.

As suggested, evangelical tradition plays a great role in helping today's believers understand why they are singing the hymns they do, with the specific music and text each of them uses. Such congregational singing first appeared with the reforms made by Martin Luther (1483–1546) in an attempt to make clear to his parishioners the full meaning of the words of the Bible. The first hymnal appeared in 1524 and their numbers have increased by tens of thousands since then; their popularity comes from the ability of the rank and file to understand and state their faith through the wondrous dimension of text in melody. Later John Calvin (1509–1564) produced a hymnal, the *Genevan Psaltar*, with equally strong results. In short, hymns came to be essential to the Protestant faith, growing more diverse and expressive through the writings of such leaders as Isaac Watts (1674–1748) and Charles Wesley (1707–1788) and John Wesley (1703–1791), founders of Methodism. Just as Protestantism became more diverse, dividing along ethnic, theological, and geographical lines, so too hymnody came to reflect the specific needs of each participating group.[14]

From the American evangelical tradition came specifically the "gospel song" often created by amateurs in a spontaneous way, embracing simple, easily remembered melodies and words. By the later nineteenth century these had become a staple feature of many evangelical bodies, the best known, according to Hustad, being "Savior, Like a Shepherd Lead Us," "We Would See Jesus," "I Need Thee Every Hour," and "More Love to Thee, O Christ" among others. They were made an essential ingredient by Ira Sankey and Dwight L. Moody in their precedent-shaping revivals of the later part of that century.[15]

During the twentieth century hymns again took on more diversity and popularity among evangelicals, who carefully followed the growing number of radio preachers, evangelical programs such as "Youth for Christ," and the radio and television ministry of "Mr. Evangelical," Billy Graham.[16] With its egalitarian tradition, its penchant for transdenominational teaching, its receptivity to high technology and ready use of mass media, evangelicalism became the most fertile, if also contentious, source for promoting the use of gospel hymns in church services.

Unquestionably, these forces all reconverged during the Jesus movement and the following takeoff period of television and radio growth. This greatly helped create the movement toward adapting contemporary hymns in addition to, and in some cases in place of, traditional ones of the past.

Specifically, folk and rock musicals, as Robert Ellsworth points out, introduced the use of electronic equipment to religious (or sacred) music expression, "giving even the most amateur group a feeling of power." The appeals of beat and rhythm in rock music also contributed to the popularity of such hymns.[17] Further, within mass media outlets, publishers found a growing, steadily increasing demand by customers for the new pop, contemporary-style songs. So also did producers of albums, and the combined effort of these high tech entrepreneurs through the established evangelical channels of merchandising made the new music instantly available at prices within a reasonable range.[18] Here, proponents argued, was the new way to win souls for Christ; not by repeating the old and to many youth tiresome hymns of the past but in presenting upbeat, "more emotional, and less cerebral" music in harmony with the larger popular culture. The content centered around the secular cue's emphasis on positive thinking and somewhat humanistic theme of happiness, joy, inner discovery, and ecstasy.[19]

As the traditionalist critics made their indictment of such music, the replies came back that such music was fully in harmony with the widely popular style of popular preaching in the churches, on the radio, and on television. Those preachers were using everyday, down-to-earth experiences and stories to make their points; and so too should the musicians who were "into" the new pop music.[20]

Finally, the trend was enhanced immensely when nonevangelical composers and producers put on the popular stage two runaway money-making, youth-oriented, religious musicals during this decade, "Jesus Christ, Superstar" and "Godspell," thus helping fans legitimate their preferences by claiming that even Broadway was going their way. Acknowledging these productions were not "hymns" written to be sung in churches, their supporters nonetheless found them popular at youth and young adult services as well as on the campuses of evangelical colleges. They became the most widely known "hymns" for the general public.

The crunch time for all this would come, however, at the local congregational level: How would all this be accepted there? In general, introduced by the likes of Bill and Gloria Gaither, the new hymns in all their variety soon found their way onto the mimeographed handout sheets at Sunday services and then eventually into the new hymnals and spiral-bound praise songbooks. An additional major factor contributing to their popularity was the trend toward multiple versions or translations of the Bible. With evangelical loyalty to that book so firm, parishioners who had found novelty and understanding of long-standing teachings and theology were now finding these new translations appearing in the new pop hymns. Hustad explains why: "Modern songs express the same truth in contemporary styles." He added his own endorsement, "But *we all change*, and the comparison of any group's successive hymnbooks will prove this."[21]

Hustad put his finger directly on the key media ingredient involved, the many new hymnals and songbooks coming in huge numbers from the evangelical presses. As will be shown, they reflect a major transformation among evangelicals seeking to utilize their renewed popular religion in the spirit of change they exhibit in the other major phases of their faith. The strength of their popularity lay, according to informed observers, in their authentic lyrics, original melody, and harmony. "There is a sincere concern to reach people, an awareness that broad communication requires broad appeal, refreshing honesty about the spiritual life, an exciting enthusiasm, and an emphasis on true Christian love."[22]

Alongside these, notes Hustad, appeared a variation, the "diminutive hymn," mostly short refrains repeated with variations. These are interspersed throughout a church service, usually focusing on praise rather than personal experience, using phrases such as "Alleluia," "He's My Savior," "He Is Worthy," and "I Will Praise Him." All in all, Hustad summarizes, since about 1960, evangelicals "have seen the greatest explosion of popular hymnody in history," not the least of its contributions being that such "material may transcend denominational and theological boundaries."[23]

In the early 1990s this movement branched out into attempts by some evangelicals, admittedly small in number, to find a synthesis in worship, including music with mainline traditions. The leader, Professor Robert Webber, who himself converted to Roman Catholicism, produced an irenic study of how certain signs show that the several liturgical traditions are actually converging across the country. Obviously, the movement is in its infancy, but at least it is being noted and discussed.[24]

The rapid improvement in high technology printing and mass media distribution contributed strongly to this increased popularity. By the late 1980s a large number of hymnals, songbooks, and collections of new minihymns and other forms of the new music found their way into evangelical parishes. Some were elegantly bound in the traditional manner, others were spiral-bound and pocket sized; many contained only a folk-style text or simple melody line. The use of the guitar or similar chord-producing instruments showed up with symbols inserted above the rest. Among the former, those that have continued in wide use are, from Hope Publishing Company, *The Worshiping Church: A Hymnal*, 1982, revised in 1990;

Hustad's *Hymns for the Living Church*, 1987, and *The New Church Hymnal*, 1976.[25]

The implementation of the new hymnody on the local parish level has taken many different forms. *Eternity* magazine, for instance, recommended some twenty different ways in which this can be achieved. These include having a hymn of the month, information in the weekly bulletin about hymns, hymn-playing classes, hymn festivals, having members hold hymn sing-ins for shut-ins and the aging, and creating a congregational lending library of hymn recordings, adding hymn textbooks to the library, encouraging hymns for home devotions, dramatizing hymns, using filmstrips on hymns, and having congregational hymn rehearsals and hymn-writing contests, among other suggestions.[26] The list suggests the extent to which this form of religious expression ranks highly within the boundaries of popular religion.

## PRAISE MUSIC

Bill and Gloria Gaither have been mentioned as pioneers in this movement. Coming from the Church of God, in Anderson, Indiana, they pioneered in the form of music dominant in popular hymnody. Hustad explains that they listened to the anguishing problems of current secular music performers and then wrote out theological answers. Usually, they concentrated on a refrain and one simple phrase such as "Let's just praise the Lord." Their popularity helped encourage similar contributions by such evangelical musicians as Andrae Crouch, Ken Medena, and William J. Reynolds, among many others.[27]

Of equal significance has been the immense influence coming out of an original Jesus movement church, Calvary Chapel of Costa Mesa, California, known as "Maranatha! Music." Its practitioners use scriptural texts set to simple, repeatable phrases. Its first album appeared in 1972, and by the early 1990s it had become a multimillion-dollar enterprise continuing to follow its original ministry, adding high technology in CDs, mass-produced textbooks, spiral-bound songbooks, and related items. Another firm, Integrity Music, started a similar ministry with a variety of popular hymns under the label of "Hosanna! Music Products." Both enterprises quickly reached a huge audience by linking up to such giants in evangelical media as Word Books, through album-of-the-month clubs, steadily increasing numbers of reviews in the nondenominational journals, and winners of Grammy and Dove annual awards. So also "Sparrow Music," backed by the Domain Group, has made fresh contributions in the last few years.[28]

In sum, praise music had become, with no single center of direction or leadership, a proven genre of expression, clearly emerging from the rank and file rather than conservatories of music, appealing in a popular culture way because of its simplicity and repetition, eschewing a more denominational identification, and remaining readily accessible. It has proven to be an ideal vehicle for transmission of what the popular dimension in the larger movement represents.

As evidence that evangelical music, be it of the performance genre or hymnody, is in constant flux, in the late 1980s a new expression, "public praise," appeared in several cities across the nation. Evangelicals in numbers from a few dozen up to 5,000 believers gather and march through a city singing songs of praise, often accompanied by banners stating, for instance, "Jesus is Lord over St. Louis." Stating they are patterned after the Old Testament model of Joshua leading the Israelites in a parade around Jericho and the well-known marches of the Salvation Army in the last century, leaders point also to the newness of this movement, consisting of the praise songs and the variety of people involved. The rank and file participate for a variety of reasons: as a show of unity, as a demonstration of care for the larger community, as a fresh form of evangelism, and, for some, as part of "a battle plan for spiritual warfare."[29] With counterparts in cities in the British Isles, praise-song marchers' activities suggest an ongoing current of energy looking for new ways to find expression.

Such parades also suggest the existence of another central, widely varying form of evangelical popular expression, the act of worship at church services. Since its emergence in the early nineteenth century, evangelicalism has carefully avoided joining with the high liturgical churches—Roman Catholic, Episcopalian, Lutheran, Greek Orthodox—and has maintained a firm loyalty to more spontaneous, less-structured forms of congregational worship. That tradition has received strong reaffirmation during the surge of popular religion in recent decades. Perhaps the decline in membership of liturgical mainline churches in those years has not been due to its careful following of orderly worship. But surely the growth of evangelical congregations stems in some large degree from the popularity of its informal worship services.[30]

Once the impact of innovation inherent in the Jesus movement found its way into local congregations, a vast series of experiments and innovations caught up evangelicals in finding new ways to express their worship in a corporate manner. Some used (and a few still do) only hymns, scripture, the sermon, and the invitation or altar call. Others used mostly praise music, testimony, sharing with embraces, and spontaneous prayers. What stood out clearly was the preference in evangelical circles for allowing worship to develop as the rank and file chose it to unfold. This is attributed to the populist, nonelitist tradition of evangelicalism, of course, but also to another situation. Most evangelical seminaries and Bible schools have no required courses in worship as part of ministerial preparation, leaving that to be expressed in the familiar "free church" tradition.[31]

However, during the 1980s the earlier enthusiasm for "far-out" worship has, according to Hustad, declined, while in the Pentecostal world the trend has been somewhat similar.[32] The order of service is more carefully planned ahead of time; a wider variety of hymns, especially those of praise, seems dominant over the older standards; and in rapidly growing churches without their own auditorium greater informality in physical symbolism and greater functionality seem to be on the increase.[33]

Again, considerable disagreement among leaders and members comes into public view over what seems to be the direction of biblical teaching in corporate worship. In this era's loyalty to "doing your own thing," many opt to let each congregation work out for itself what seems most meaningful (and the least controversial).[34] The use of high tech, as discussed by "Eutychus," the regular humor columnist for *Christianity Today*, brought on the suggestion that instead of using hymnals, worshipers read the words from an overhead projector to the tunes of the contemporary period, such as "Bridge over Troubled Waters." In describing that service the columnist suggested, with something more than humor in mind, that "we asked the pastor just to print the salient points of his sermon on a transparency, aim it at the wall, then serve coffee and croissants while we interpret the meaning of the lesson in light of our varied backgrounds and experiences."[35]

In summary, hymnody, praise hymns, and worship as they have unfolded in the last thirty years faithfully reflect the many-sided extent of how incongruity and irony contribute to the manner in which evangelicals choose to express their convictions through the medium of music. Believers are saying, yes, there is the *mysterium tremendum* of Christian faith, but that should not require seekers to alter their long-standing commitment to the traditions they have known from their past, bringing some parts of them up to date but holding fast to the source of power and wisdom, the choices of the believers in the ranks.[36]

## NOTES

1. A brief history is by Paul Westermeyer, "Music, Christian," in Daniel Reid et al., eds., *Dictionary of Christianity in America* (Downers Grove, Ill.: InterVarsity, 1990), pp. 786–90; Mel R. Wilhoit, "Sing Me a Song: Ira D. Sankey and Congregational Singing," *The Hymn*, 42, 1 (January 1991): 13–19; Don Hustad, "Where Are We Going in Church Music?" *Moody Monthly*, March 1966, pp. 18–21; see the interpretive column by religion writer Clark Morphew, "Favorite Hymns Still Can Pack Amazing Grace," *St. Paul Pioneer Press*, August 18, 1990, p. 6B.

2. See later section on "praise" music; see the new magazine, *Worship Leader*, 1, 1 (February/March 1992), published by CCM Publications out of Nashville.

3. Robert Elmore, "The Place of Music in Christian Life," in Leland Ryken, ed., *The Christian Imagination* (Grand Rapids, Mich.: Baker Book House, 1981), pp. 429–32; Don

Hustad, *Jubilate! Church Music in the Evangelical Tradition* (Carol Stream, Ill.: Hope Publishing Co., 1981), pp. 1–13.

4. Elmore, "Place," p. 431; Hustad, *Jubilate!*, pp. viii–ix, 16–25, 29–31.

5. See Samuel S. Hill, "Religion," in Charles Reagan Wilson and William Ferris, eds., *Encyclopedia of Southern Culture* (Chapel Hill: University of North Carolina Press, 1989), p. 1272.

6. "Interview" with Harold Best, *Christianity Today*, May 6, 1977, pp. 860–63.

7. Elmore, "Place," p. 430; Hill, "Religion," p. 1272.

8. Hustad, *Jubilate!*, p. 11; advertisements over the years in the journal *The Hymn* provide information on several similar titles.

9. Hustad, *Jubilate!*, pp. 34–35.

10. Ibid., p. 37.

11. Ibid., pp. 38–39; the issue was discussed as early as 1978; see Paul Johnson and Lenny Seidel, "Music: Two Viewpoints," *Religious Broadcasting*, May 1978, pp. 311–32; Donald Paul Ellsworth, *Christian Music in Contemporary Witness: Historical Antecedents and Contemporary Practices* (Grand Rapids, Mich.: Baker Book House, 1979), pp. 189–201.

12. Bruce Vantine, "Art: Sanctity in Time and Tune," *UEA*, Summer 1982, pp. 16–17; news story, *Religion Watch*, April 1990, p. 1; ibid., December 1986, p. 1; Robert E. Webber, "The Impact of the Liturgical Movement on the Evangelical Church," *Reformed Liturgy and Music*, 21, 2 (Spring 1987): 111–14; Don Johnson, "Music," *Religious Broadcasting*, November 1984, pp. 26, 28; Ken Myers, "Whatever Happened to Classical Music," *Eternity*, November 1986, pp. 23–26; Ken Myers, *All God's Children and Blue Suede Shoes: Christians and Popular Culture* (Westchester, Ill.: Crossway Books, 1989), pp. 119–32; Deidra Duncan, "The Miracle of the Messiah," *Fundamentalist Journal*, December 1985, pp. 25–27; Tom Raabe, *The Ultimate Church* (Grand Rapids, Mich.: Zondervan, 1991), pp. 101, 148–49.

13. Quentin J. Schultze, *Televangelism and American Culture: The Business of Popular Religion* (Grand Rapids, Mich.: Baker Book House, 1991), pp. 211–12; see chapter 10 on the megachurches; the "Baby Boomer" penchant for informal worship is discussed in W. C. Roof, "Return of the Baby Boomers to Organized Religion," in Jacques Constant and Alice M. Jones, eds., *Yearbook of the American and Canadian Churches* (Nashville, Tenn.: Abingdon Press, 1990), pp. 284–91; Doug Murren, *The Baby Boomerang* (Ventura, Calif.: Regal Books, 1990).

14. E. Margaret Clarkson, "Christian Hymnody," in Ryken, *Imagination*, pp. 415–18.

15. Hustad, *Jubilate!*, pp. 248–49.

16. Ibid., pp. 137–39.

17. Ellsworth, *Christian Music in Contemporary Witness*, p. 175.

18. Ibid.

19. Ibid., pp. 177–78.

20. Ibid., p. 179.

21. Hustad, *Jubilate!*, p. 270; see the new album, "Silver Celebration: A Tribute to Bill and Gloria Gaither," *Moody*, February 1992, p. 46.

22. Richard D. Dinwiddie, "Music Is a Contemporary Citizen," *Christianity Today*, September 3, 1982, pp. 86–87; see also Tom Bisset, "The Rebirth of Hymns," *Religious Broadcasting*, September 1988, pp. 24, 43; Frank E. Gaebelein, "The Christian and Music," in Ryken, *Imagination*, pp. 443–44.

23. Don Hustad, "The Explosion of Popular Hymnody," *The Hymn*, 33, 3 (July 1982): 165, 167; Garth Bolinder, "Closer Harmony with Church Musicians," *Leadership*, Spring 1986, pp. 94–99.

24. Robert Webber, *Signs of Wonder: The Phenomenon of Convergence in Modern Liturgical and Charismatic Churches* (Nashville, Tenn.: Abbott Martyn, 1992), reviewed in *Worship Leader*, February/March 1992, pp. 26–27.

25. "An Interview with Ralph Carmichael," *Eternity*, March 1977, pp. 16–21; Bert Ghezzi, "New Worship Music," *Christian Retailing*, April 15, 1990, p. 30; Elizabeth Coden Newenhuysen, "The Hymnal Maze, Supplement to Church Supplies" in *Leadership*, Summer 1990, pp. 24–26; Carol R. Theissen's review of Don Hustad's *The Worshipping Church*, in *Christianity Today*, October 22, 1990, pp. 66–68.

26. James R. Snyder, "20 Ways to Stimulate Congregational Singing," *Eternity*, March 1982, pp. 222–26.

27. Hustad, *Jubilate!*, pp. 163–65; Stephen R. Graham, "Bill and Gloria Gaither," in Charles H. Lippy, ed., *Twentieth-Century Shapers of American Popular Religion* (Westport, Conn.: Greenwood Press, 1989), pp. 155–62; J. Gordon Melton, *Religious Leaders of America* (Detroit: Gale Research, 1991), p. 166.

28. News story, *Religious Broadcasting*, February 1992, p. 31; Integrity Music, P.O. Box 16833, Mobile, AL 36616-0832; news story in *Christianity Today*, November 22, 1985, pp. 53–55; news story, *Christianity Today*, April 29, 1991, pp. 44–47; interview in *Wittenburg Door*, October/November 1984, p. 24; Tom Winfield, "Musical Trends in the 90s," *Charisma and Christian Life*, February 1990, pp. 86–93; Maranatha, 25411 Cabot Road, Suite 203, Laguna Hills, CA 92653; see also the publications of The Fisherfolk, especially "Celebration," Box 309, Aliquippi Way, PA 15001-9900; for an illuminating parallel on similar matters within Roman Catholicism, see Thomas Day, *Why Catholics Can't Sing: The Culture of Catholicism and the Triumph of Bad Taste* (New York: Crossroad, 1990); Domain, P.O. Box 337, Wheaton, IL 60189; see also the programs of Sight and Sound Entertainment, calling itself "The World's Largest Christian Arts Centre," Route 896, P.O. Box 310, Strausburg, PA 17579.

29. News story on worship, "Praise in the Streets," *Christianity Today*, October 28, 1991, pp. 48–51; Randy Robison and John Archer, "Praise Him in the Streets," *Charisma and Christian Life*, May 1992, pp. 22–28.

30. See Hustad, *Jubilate!*, pp. 166–93, 332–40; James C. White, in Reid, *Dictionary*, pp. 649–65; James C. White, "The Missing Jewel of the Evangelical Church," *The Reformed Journal*, June 1986, pp. 11–16.

31. Hustad, *Jubilate!*, p. 167; a critical evangelical view is Henry Boonstra, "With Reservations," *Reformed Journal*, 20 (1991): 36–37.

32. Hustad, *Jubilate!*, p. 332.

33. Ibid., pp. 332–33.

34. See the excellent study by James C. White, *Protestant Worship: Traditions in Transition* (Louisville: Westminster/John Knox, 1990).

35. "Eutychus," *Christianity Today*, January 14, 1991, p. 6; Martin E. Marty, *Context*, May 1, 1991, p. 6.

36. "Worship Forum," *Leadership*, Spring 1986, theme issue, pp. 12–121.

# 10

# Popular Religion in the Churches: An Estimate

One major characteristic of evangelical popular religion is its capacity both to appeal strongly and to be sharply criticized and at times rejected by a variety of subcultures within the same community. Both harmony and dissonance flourish at the same time. Given the four families—Pentecostal, fundamentalist, evangelical, and charismatic—their members may well consume some or all or none of popular religion according to personal preference rather than by direction from a specific denomination. No precisely measurable correlation (that this writer has found) exists between, say, Pentecostal and fundamentalist or evangelical and charismatic preferences for any of the broad categories of popular religion sketched out so far in this book. Scholars well insist that it is primarily if not exclusively those sharp, even impenetrable theological doctrinal walls that keep the several evangelical families apart, away from being a coherent movement. Although those barriers certainly do exist, as we will attempt to show in this chapter, they are not as exclusive or as tidily defined as many academic and clerical spokespersons suggest. A remarkable unity of involvement in popular religion does indeed flourish even though it may not be so precisely measurable or demonstrable as some evangelical trackers espouse.

That homogeneity needs to be kept in mind as we attempt in this chapter to find where within the organizational groupings that observers use that popular religion has its broadest, its narrowest, and its various in-between levels of appeal. We must perforce keep this discussion and the boundaries very wide, acknowledging the existence of a recognized lack of precision among followers as to just why this or that organized group chooses or shuns this or that expression of popular religion.

Such a situation, of course, turns us back to remembering that irony and paradox flourish throughout, that incongruity abounds among the rank and file who freely consume such expressions in a manner that the pattern makers, the scholars who emphasize almost entirely the theological and doctrinal issues, cannot include in their much-needed pattern making. Unquestionably doctrine and specific denominational practices count greatly in keeping evangelicalism from becoming one large monolithic movement. Undoubtedly evangelical insistence on moral rectitude and committed discipleship both brings like-minded evangelicals together and keeps other seekers outside their fold.

Where the movement comes together, this writer suggests, is in seeing how pervasive and transdenominational the access to popular religion really has become. This is the case because, by contrast to something like thirty years ago, the popularity of parachurch ministries and the influence of the mass media created by high technology have put popular religion within the physical and financial reach of evangelicals everywhere.

To be sure, doctrinal conflict and denominational rivalry among evangelicals continue to abound and flourish as in pretelevision days; disputation over teaching, scriptural interpretation, and ministerial leadership also runs through the full evangelical world. The internal battle over holding fast to that which is true, honorable, just, pure, lovely, and gracious goes on as always. But, as this writer hopes he has indicated with the evidence cited this far, popular religion in often immeasurable but profound ways helps hold the movement together.[1]

Having said that, we can describe here before enumerating the specific participating bodies those factors helping to keep evangelicals away from the internecine battles endemic within the mainline. We may also be able to understand if not always to agree with what their like-minded cohorts are pursuing in their efforts to win the world for Christ. First, they understand that the final authority in any dispute is the Bible and zestfully argue over the specific meanings and applications of the teachings found there. That is a major starting point for our understanding, a commitment that is often not so widely pursued by other Christians in America (such as mainliners and Roman Catholics).

Second, they expect the seekers' religious commitment to be expressed in some demonstrable way to show that a turning around of supernatural origins has occurred in their lives, not simply a new response to religious "warm fuzzies." Third, while many in recent times give increasing attention to inner spirituality, still evangelicals stand in contrast to other religious bodies as those willing to testify and witness publicly. Fourth, with some notable exceptions evangelicals eschew loyalty to past traditions for its own sake and replace it with the confidence that God has yet much to show them about the future.

Fifth, as this book argues throughout, they enthusiastically find in everyday life, in the ordinariness of daily experience, very concrete and nurturing evidence of the ongoing presence of the almighty, all-powerful God. In these ways, it is suggested here, evangelicalism for all the diversity that we now will unpack, does cohere, because as John Weborg suggests, in using "evangelicalism" as a term describing coherence, it "is more connotative than denotative, more descriptive than definitional"; the ingredients just listed above "are at best a circumference of a circle." Whether or not popular religion provides a "center" for this circle is an issue over which the discussion continues.[2]

The complexity of substantiating this interpretation and of unearthing measurable data for such investigations is well illustrated by the fact that many we have called "evangelical" in this book remain by choice within mainline denominations. Within the United Methodist Church, the Episcopalian Church, the Evangelical Lutheran Church in America, the United Church of Christ, and the Presbyterian Church, USA, among other, are pockets of organized evangelicals who seek largely to maintain these bodies' emphasis on personal holiness and evangelism. Known generally as "renewal" groups, they embrace a variety of members, some caught up in charismatic renewal, in liturgical reform, in protesting social outreach, or in holding in check the perceived increase of bureaucratic power at the national level of governance.[3]

Among evangelicals, the problem of gathering dependable data is made more complex because many attend Sunday worship on a regular basis but do not actually become members whose presence can be counted as evidence of growth and thus new life. That is the case because, as Randall Balmer shows, many evangelicals require that baptism, "especially infant baptism, is not sufficient" as the basis for membership. These folk, in classic evangelical manner, require "some sort of public profession of faith" before being placed on the membership rolls. This keeps some regulars away from being counted. Further, a number of megachurches do not use membership rolls.[4] All this creates a situation where we cannot tell from such data as book purchases, the number of radio listeners or television watchers, and church membership precisely *who consumes* what forms of popular religion. As shown, we can try to approximate what seem to be common-sense interpretations of those data, which we have done here.

Given that, who since the days of the first evangelical surge seem to be the most clearly involved in popular religion? Obviously, we include by definition those associated with the National Association of Evangelicals, who have very close institutional, doctrinal, and popular levels of affiliation with evangelicalism as defined in this book. As suggested earlier, the NAE umbrella by definition cannot cover all evangelicals engaged in popular religion.

But what can be indicated, by way of general introduction to who is in and who is not, is the support given Billy Graham. Often, when the matter of a viable definition of evangelicalism arises, some observers reply, "It is the religious faith and ministry of Billy Graham." That comment, while obviously not fully inclusive, comes as close as any one-sentence definition to explain how the general public understands this movement. The subject of many biographies and dissertations and hundreds of articles in a variety of journals (from *The Journal for the Scientific Study of Religion* to the gossipy tabloid *Star*), Graham has become the most widely recognized personality within the Christian community in all of recorded history. No one has preached to more listeners, no other minister commands the ear of the Oval Office more readily, no one has stayed the course with more integrity in televangelism than has Graham.[5]

The explanations for this astounding record reflect the predilections of the interpreters and the ongoing appeal of evangelical popular religion. Seen overseas by some as a slick agent of American imperialism, even as a spy, and at home by some observers as the purveyor of very thin theology or the high priest of American civil religion, among other interpretations, Graham's teachings, use of the mass media, personal life-style, determination to turn America into a Christian society, and determination to win souls stems in large part from his sharply honed, carefully prepared utilization of popular religion; its theology, its hymnody, its aggressive use of high technology, its transdenominational character, and its populist, anti-elitist tendencies. Martin E. Marty states it well:

Put it down boldly: in the television era, Christianity and celebrity rarely mix well. The celebrity is only as good as her last act; her next one must be ever more sensational. One creates a persona to meet the fads and fashions of the moment. Graham, however, for all his fame, keeps being who he is and doing what he did, and remaining a self, a saved sinner, a wounded healer.[6]

Graham created no denomination, no cult of personality, no movement, no cathedral, no "gushing fountains," and no political bloc and has managed as witnessed by the huge crowds attending his rally in Central Park, New York, in 1991 to convince large numbers of nonwhites, nonevangelicals, and skeptics to take his message seriously.[7]

Given this blanket definition, in this chapter we focus on who the evangelicals are. We list names, programs, and organizations. We can profit at this point from learning what Graham considers "the most significant changes on the American church scene" in the last quarter-century. He lists the rise of evangelicalism as being the most important, followed by the surge of myriads of paracollege organizations, the vastly improved relations between Catholics and Protestants, the more direct involvement of evangelicals in organized politics, and the charismatic and new neo-Pentecostalist movements.[8]

The latter movements, along with the classical Pentecostalists, have witnessed rapid expansion in recent years for at least three reasons: the skillful use of high technology and mass media in finding consensual themes on which conservatives of all families can agree (such as family, Americanism, popular hymnody, and the like); second, on the determination as with all evangelicals to continue unabatedly their desire to win the world for Christ; and third, early but convincing signs these several groupings here all placed under the "evangelicalist" umbrella are showing signs of increasingly deeper understandings of each other. Given the existence of many exceptions (such as fundamentalist Rev. Jerry Falwell expelling three Pentecostalist students for witnessing publicly to their faith from his Liberty University in 1991), observers such as Professors Randall Balmer and George M. Marsden and others find clear signs of increased goodwill among the four major families considered in my estimate all to qualify as evangelicals.[9]

There exist at least four general trends to demonstrate this new direction. Each in its own way is expressing new forms of faith, shaped largely by involvement with popular religion. First, overall with but few exceptions, those involved with popular religion are seeking to mute or downplay the rough edges and polemical fireworks formerly directed toward others outside their specific folds; they have acknowledged publicly that other evangelical types are expanding by means they heretofore have not endorsed. Second, a large number of fundamentalist churches have adapted several of the worship patterns of Pentecostals by using drama, more contemporary hymns, even the uplifting of arms as indicative of openness to God. Third, an increasing number of Pentecostalist seminarians are showing more interest in formal theology (a hallmark of fundamentalism) and accordingly less direct involvement in Holy Spirit–informed affective experience. Fourth, the speaking in tongues (glossolalia) so central to Pentecostal worship "has now disappeared especially from larger, suburban churches" during worship services. In the last twenty years, over half of the ten most watched weekly televangelism programs centered around Pentecostal preachers: Oral Roberts, Pat Robertson, Jimmy Swaggart, Jim Bakker, Kenneth Copeland, and Rex Humbard. Their messages, except for that of Swaggart, attempted to avoid the polemical features inherent in older Pentecostalism. Further, the three largest evangelical cable systems, TBN, PTL (now The Inspiration Network), and CBN, were directed by irenically minded Pentecostalists.[10]

This all means, even in such embryonic form, that evangelicalism shows increasing signs of being a more cohesive movement than in earlier years, even though some vast differences among the four groups still exist. That movement in turn reflects the greater respect each group has developed for the others, showing a greater acceptance of the geographical mobility of millions of Americans who in ever-increasing numbers move often around the country and attend several different churches, demonstrating the consensus outreach, seeking unity among the best-known, nationally based preachers on television and radio, and making use of the greater accessibility of low-priced, popular forms of evangelistic media to all evangelicals.

This, to repeat, is not to suggest that such signs are irrefutable evidence that all nonmainline conservatives will eventually end up in one large body. The fervent loyalty to historic traditions, the lack of information each group has about those outside their fold, the rapid rise and fall of media celebrity leaders, among other reasons all suggest that patterns of popular religion consumption exhibited in the 1990s will be more conciliatory but still alive and flourishing as regards specific loyalties to primary organized families of faith.

## PENTECOSTALISM

In looking briefly at who within each of the four traditions seems most responsive to the forces that are the subjects of this book, we turn first to the classic Pentecostalists. Claiming legitimation from the time of the outpouring of the Holy Spirit at Pentecost, fifty days after Jesus rose from a grave, these seekers since the early twentieth century have insisted that for those who receive the "second" or "Holy Spirit" baptism, alongside the initial believer's baptism, will manifest at least one if not more of the spiritual gifts defined by the apostle Paul, most clearly defined by him in 1 Corinthians 12:4–11 and centering there heavily on speaking in and interpreting tongues. From its inception in the early twentieth century until among some believers even today this experience in Pentecostal understanding requires the recipient (with but few exceptions) to leave any fellowship that is not "full Gospel," that is, does not espouse these gifts, and join a body that does full credence to these practices. Other gifts, even more controversial to some observers, are those given at the second baptism for physical and spiritual healing, discernment of spirits, foretelling the future, and exorcism of or deliverance from unclean, demonic spirits.[11]

Such emphasis, primarily new within Christendom when it started to find organizational form (in contrast to Roman Catholicism and mainline

Protestantism), focused very heavily on the ministry of the Holy Spirit, meaning necessarily less focus on the ministry of Jesus, and thus contained within it the seeds for developing a very wide variety and number of different Pentecostal bodies. Rather than assent to the liturgical/sacramental character of the mainline churches, Pentecostals over the years have joined, moved, created, taken down, and reshaped literally thousands of loosely organized bodies.[12]

The best known and most influential within classical (or original) Pentecostalism and most closely aligned with the larger evangelical movement have been and are the Assemblies of God, the International Church of the Four Square Gospel Movement, the Pentecostal Holiness Church, a variety of African-American Pentecostal bodies, and the United Pentecostal Church. They exist in all parts of the country, demonstrating special fervor in Appalachia and the largest metropolitan centers, embracing a wide variety of incomes, formal educational achievement, and employment patterns.

Today, the flourishing megachurch movement owes much of its expansion to the fervent, bursting energy of the classic Pentecostalists. The whole thrust has attracted considerable scholarly attention from the likes of trackers such as Edith L. Blumhofer, David Edwin Harrell, Jr., and Margaret Poloma, among others.[13] It has formed its own scholarly society, to help codify its theology and to refute the charge by some outsiders that Pentecostalism is only emotional experience–oriented without much emphasis on formal doctrine. Since the 1970s the Society for Pentecostal Studies has sought to understand and explain its unique place within American Christendom.

Yet, it must be said, classic Pentecostalism's scope, sense of mission, strong identification with locale, dependence on the charisma of the local leader, insider vocabulary, and widely flexible understanding of the varying personal transforming power available to seekers all add to a situation such that making broader, nationally applicable interpretations is rather shaky and complicated for trackers. Unquestionably, however, Pentecostalism's growth (and internal conflicts, which abound) are directly tied to the kind of movement detected by Dean Kelley and others and traced in its various popular forms throughout this book thus far.[14]

## CHARISMATIC RENEWAL

The growing inclusiveness of classical Pentecostalism has led in recent decades to several unexpected new developments. Some searchers looking for any existing larger patterns of interrelatedness see it and the attendant charismatic renewal (CR) as a part of the rapidly expanding trend within Christendom of what can be called "privatization." As defined by John F. Wilson, this form of self-examination reaches past the older pietistic dedication to searching soul and heart to center on maximizing "self-realization and personal growth and reward primary relationships. Divine commandments are transformed into instrumental strategies for achieving personal satisfaction."[15] Mary Jo Neitz suggests that Pentecostalists and charismatics focus "overwhelmingly" on personal problems, the protection of one's self and one's family. As do those persons involved in more secular personal-growth movements, these seekers find in the pursuit of the spiritual gifts a greater sense of self-understanding, direct contact with a higher reality, and a sense of personal spiritual growth.[16] The implied conclusion points to the movement's popularity, as is true with so much evangelical popular religion, as flowing alongside, even intermingling at times with a very popular secular movement.

Another vastly important dimension to the entire Pentecostal experience came in the 1950s with the founding of the Full Gospel Business Men's Fellowship International (FGBMFI) by a Pentecostal lay leader, Demos Shakarian. The organization brought together, usually at prayer breakfasts or lunches, those mostly outside the Pentecostal churches seeking nurture and fellowship free from the formal confines of the organized Pentecostal churches, which they saw as having limited vision and autocratic leadership. In some ways its rapid growth was tied to the secular culture, in that meetings of local chapters were held in commercial hotel dining rooms, attracting a broader and more diverse audience. By the 1980s the organization had been successful in directing several thousands of middle-class Americans to charismatic religion.[17] It closely paralleled the well-known business and professional associations of that socioeconomic class such as Lions, Kiwanis, or Rotary. In the late 1980s, after weathering some stormy battles over internal governance, FGBMFI seemed to hold fast to its long-established place on the continuum between organized Pentecostalism and the larger secular world of the professions and business, thus qualifying fittingly for the classification of "neo-Pentecostal."[18]

That same term came to characterize, at first, one of the most remarkable and, to many observers, unexpected turns within mainline Protestantism, closely allied to classic Protestantism, "charismatic renewal." One authority, Margaret Poloma, defines it as follows:

A charismatic is then defined as a born-again Christian who accepts the Bible as the inspired Word of God and who emphasizes a part of Christian tenet that is often down-played by other Bible believers, namely the power, the baptism, and the gifts of the Holy Spirit. Not only glossolalia, but prophecy healing, miracles, and an acceptance of other biblical paranormal phenomena are accepted as valid contemporary religious experiences.[19]

To this definition, as events unfolded throughout the 1960s, must be added one more key ingredient; those experiencing this second baptism while members of a mainline denomination would remain as members of their parent church, not coming out to join a specific Pentecostal, full-Gospel church as those in the classic tradition required.

Beginning with the experience of Episcopalian Reverend Dennis Bennett in Van Nuys, California, who on Whitsunday in 1960 announced his second baptism, the charismatic renewal in essence was born. Bennett's disclosure created an uproar within the congregation and the denomination. Bennett insisted he was still an Episcopalian, a claim supported by his bishop who transferred him to another Episcopalian parish, a tiny church in Seattle. Much the same experience befell the first Lutheran to make the same announcement, Reverend Larry Christenson of Trinity Lutheran Church, San Pedro, California. The key element in both cases was the insistence by the leaders that they still considered themselves faithful to their ordination vows and the creeds of their respective denominations. In both cases the bishops involved acknowledged that affirmation.[20]

So much has been written about charismatic renewal that it is necessary here only to show where and why it made connections and fit into the pattern of evangelical popular religious expression. The movement in those denominations, and soon in other major Protestant bodies, grew rapidly during its early years and well into the 1980s, when it reached a plateau in its expansion.

During the growth years in the 1960s, converts zealously attempted to introduce within mainline bodies specific classical Pentecostal expressions and teachings, as in hymnody, liturgy, small-group house prayer meetings, faith healing, and related themes. Each major denomination and some smaller ones formed "renewal" groups, dedicated to advancing the ministry of Holy Spirit renewal but within parent church boundaries.[21]

Many evangelical and almost all fundamentalist bodies remained critical of the movement in these early years of growth. To classical Pentecostalists it seemed just plain wrong and unbiblical that those touched by the second baptism did not come out and join one of their bodies. Much of the Roman Catholic hierarchy and laity saw it as very divisive, adding rancor and confusion in a time when the Roman Catholic faith had more than its share of internal difficulties. Evangelicals, traditionally suspicious of Roman Catholicism, wondered whether anything Roman could embrace authentic elements of Holy Spirit faith.[22] Fundamentalists often deplored the charismatic muting of formal, propositional doctrine, as the latter instead chose more emotional expression.

In turn Roman Catholic leaders, especially in the American Southwest, started leveling charges that Mormons, Seventh-Day Adventists, and other unnamed evangelicalists were using "unfair and coercive practices" to attract both older and newer Latinos in those areas away from their Roman Catholic loyalties.[23]

Later in the 1980s, a significant number of African Americans started to introduce charismatic and Pentecostal practices within their own churches. This constituted according to observers a major breakthrough in charismatic renewal, which had through the 1960s and 1970s remained largely white. One such body, the Church of God in Christ, after absorbing charismatic features, moved in membership from 425,000 in 1964 to over 3.7 million by 1982. Much of the growth was attributed to younger leaders no longer willing to maintain older African-American traditions but who promoted the emphasis on Holy Spirit baptism and its attendant spiritual gifts.[24]

Within the white mainline bodies embracing energetic charismatic input, a movement generally called "Restorationism" started to emerge in the mid-1980s. It claimed "God is telling many to. . .be willing to lovingly release those you've been witnessing to and disengage from confronting the denominational church with a message they've now had up to 25 years to obey. This will free you up to get about kingdom business."[25]

This potential for major change directly affected evangelical popular religion because those charismatics who were calling for severance from the parent church were also prepared to create their own independent, trans-denominational bodies. The obviously greater freedom for local autonomy, freed from national denominational authority, has great appeal for the restorationists, who like some evangelicals have been claiming they were "restoring" the purity of the original church in a day when they found apostasy and error running unchecked throughout the mainline. Thus, the appeal of popular religion with its informal liturgy, its openness to fresh expressions of doctrinal orthodoxy, its loyalty to moral rectitude, and its committed discipleship all made inroads, via this evangelist model, on the potential separationists.[26]

In that sense, the popular religion discussed in this book has had a direct influence on discontented, in this case, Holy Spirit–baptized mainliners. It is impossible to measure in numerical terms how widespread the movement has become by the early 1990s, largely because record keeping is at best sporadic, and some seekers move around frequently, leaving no traceable records of changing membership or altered religious behavior.

Within the large family of evangelicalism, however, the impact of charis-matic renewal (as opposed in general terms here to classic Pentecostalism), has been greatest by making the features of popular religion attractive. A leading scholar, Peter Hocken, suggests the points of intersection: fervent witnessing and praise to Jesus, pronounced emphasis through hymns and prayer on praise, renewed loyalty to the study of the Bible, the recognition that God speaks directly to individuals today about contemporary problems, a strengthening to win the world for Christ, a sharper awareness of the presence and power of Satan, a full expectation that the Last Days are near, and ready accessibility to spiritual power for daily living. Where evangelicals and charismatics differ mostly is over the matter of speaking in tongues and its interpretation, discernment of hostile spirits, and faith healing.[27]

In similar forms, both groups have active publishing houses, witness-forum journals and magazines, frequent regional and national rallies featuring celebrity preachers, and favorite television and radio personalities. Overlap in the world of media is impossible to measure because no quantifiable way exists to determine whether books by, say, James Dobson or Charles Swindoll are being read widely by charismatics.[28]

What clearly has emerged by the early 1990s is a wider acceptance if not outright endorsement by evangelical spokespersons of the charismatic and Pentecostal priorities. While some smaller groups, such as the Protestant Reformed Church of South Island, Illinois (to cite one example), maintain a strict Calvinist adherence to traditional doctrines, most evangelicals seem to be willing to coexist with the Holy Spirit–baptized rank and file.[29] Whereas in the 1970s some very sharp theological and doctrinal comment was aimed by the evangelicals at these groups, by 1989 a major spokesperson for the entire movement, Professor J. I. Packer, could write that this renewal movement was "in the mainstream of historic evangelical orthodoxy on the Trinity, the Incarnation, the objectivity of Christ's atonement and the historicity of his resurrection, the need of regeneration by the Holy Spirit, personal fellowship with the Father and the Son as central to the life of faith, and the divine truth of the Bible."[30]

Undoubtedly Packer speaks for many others in noting that the renewal movement on the other hand, reflected too much antitraditionalism, anti-intellectualism, romantic emotionalism, a search for "thrills and emotional highs," and a narcissistic absorption with healing, among other unpleasant qualities.[31] Yet, the movement toward greater acceptance of each other, noted at the beginning of this chapter, seems at this point (with the acknowledged exceptions) to characterize the center at least of the continuum of evangelical acceptance of this renewal. Popular religion, in turn, has shown its resilience and adaptability by being able to appeal to so wide and devoted a community of faith.

## THIRD WAVE

During the years of volatile change in the 1980s a variation on the Pentecostal/charismatic movement emerged first on the West Coast and then spread across the country. Given several names, it is best entitled as the

"Third Wave of Pentecostalism," somewhat like the first two waves but decidedly distinctive and decidedly involved in the use of popular religion to carry out its mission. Led by a number of pastors, especially Professor C. Peter Wagner and John Wimber, by the late 1980s it showed a combining of at least five elements that in their unity created this "third wave" of Holy Spirit power to renew those who sought what became known in the movement as "signs and wonders," with a heavy accent on "deliverance" ministry.[32]

Wagner suggests that the defining characteristics of the Third Wave have been: (1) the leadership and authority of the senior pastor; (2) in worship the expectation of full participation by every member but in ways far less structured than among earlier Pentecostalists; (3) an expectation that every adult member or family would give at least 10 percent of their income to the church; (4) in communication the expectation that every event within the body be fully known and publicized to prevent misunderstanding; and (5) a confidence that a new time of miracles, signs of God's ongoing power, was breaking out across the world. Wagner and others call this last item a "manifestation of what I am calling the Third Wave."[33]

Especially important is the conviction that seekers' lives are being transformed, healed, and delivered both physically and spiritually by this fresh sense of power energizing the Third Wave bodies, expressed through fervent prayer, casting out demons, deliverance ministry, and receiving prophecies. An example of prophecy was the prediction by a Third Wave pastor, Paul Cain, while visiting with Wimber (living in Anaheim, California) on December 3, 1990, that an earthquake would occur on that date and on the date of Cain's departure. Such an earthquake did occur in nearby Pasadena on December 3, and another occurred in Armenia on December 7, the date of Cain's return home.[34]

Beyond that, Third Wave teaching moves away from the first two waves in advocating that the second baptism occurs at conversion, rather than as a separate event. They also hold to a lesser emphasis on speaking in tongues, considered by Third Wave largely as a prayer language rather than proof of the second baptism. They are also more open to ways in which the power of the Holy Spirit expresses its vision for each believer. Further, Third Wave advocates believe in "avoidance of divisiveness at almost any cost. Compromise in areas such as raising of hands, in worship, public tongues, methods of prayer for the sick, and others is cordially accepted in order to maintain harmony with those not in the third wave."[35]

The Wave has created considerable controversy largely because of its emphasis on casting out demons, known as "deliverance." Objections also are made to its self-conscious variations on certain familiar Pentecostal themes and attractiveness to potential members who have for any number of reasons lost their enthusiasm for the first two forms.[36]

# HEALING

In a related area, popular religion has made deep inroads into the whole field of spiritually related healing. Long a strong force within Christianity, including Pentecostalists and charismatics, its renewed appearance in the 1970s and continuance to the present suggest its appeal owes at least some of its impact to certain parts of popular religion. Television especially helped bring the enormously powerful impact of full gospel healing into the living rooms of many who had never before witnessed such activity. No one knew this better than Oral Roberts, who became a celebrity with his professionally produced ministry for television, which set the standards for those to come.[37]

Since then a wide variety of evangelical leaders and laity have found in the healing ministry the most evident manifestation of God's power among people. Clearly, the power of popular religion has been at work in the rapidly growing ministries of Kenneth E. Hagin, Kenneth Copeland, Fred Price, Jerry Savelle, Charles Capps, Norvel Hayes, Robert Tilton, Lester Summral, Marilyn Hickey, Benny Hinn, and R. W. Schambach, to name only a few. Its appeal undoubtedly rests on its claims to be able to tap into the miraculous (read "nonhuman scientific") power of the Almighty to work miracles the secular world rejects.

Faith healing rests on a form of folk wisdom or frame of mind that, as seen in other areas, accepts incongruity in its unfolding. It stands apart from or alongside the healing of organized medicine, trusting as evangelicalism does in the wisdom of the born again. It serves to demonstrate to unbelievers the power of Christ available to them, a tool available to help convert the world. Healing helps the practitioner rejuvenate her or his own faith by believing that when such healings occur, it is further validation of their faith-inspired conviction that such miracles can happen.[38]

Within the full family of evangelicalism, considerable and often bitter disputation over healing between its critics and its proponents continues. Critics worry that some ailing persons' hopes are unnecessarily, even unbiblically raised; that the healing ministry of Jesus was for biblical times, not for today; and that those afflicted will not avail themselves of proven organized medical help. Proponents insist that Christian healing power is as much alive today as it has always been, that proven miracles can be established by accepted medical evidence, and that to believe God cannot perform astounding miracles is to show the seeker lacks faith in the omnipotence of God.[39]

# DENOMINATIONS

Popular religion also finds acceptance in more traditionally organized forms of faith, especially in two of the most rapidly growing denominations, the Southern Baptist Convention and the Assemblies of God. In many conscious ways, the two groups have continued to pursue their own agendas in theology, worship, social outreach, and other related ministries. Yet both also pursue many of the means of expression available in popular religion, including both print and electronic media. By tradition both allow individual congregations a good deal of latitude concerning worship, community involvement, education, and leisure-time pursuits—the full agenda of matters in which popular religion has made its contribution. Both also find themselves caught up often in extremely acrimonious internal debate. For instance, the Southern Baptist Convention by early 1992 had redefined itself by eliminating those whose theology and polity had failed to meet the standards of its conservative hierarchy.[40]

So too with the Assemblies of God; it has vast resources, a vital program of evangelization, and a tradition rooted in classic Pentecostalism and today streamlined in many places under the influence of popular religion. It has great difficulty in maintaining its traditional heritage of faithfulness to strict doctrine and moral rectitude in a world where popular religion makes its inroads, which leads at least some seekers to greater acceptance of popular religious expression.[41]

## CHURCH GROWTH MOVEMENT

Much of the controversy as well as much of the energy for the growth running throughout most of evangelicalism resides in a loosely joined but deeply felt set of principles, organization, and techniques known as the Church Growth Movement (CGM). This was created on the foreign mission field by Donald McGavran, while studying why some districts flourished and others languished. He travelled throughout the world learning about what he came to call "church growth," which he and others deemed a more appropriate term for soul-winning than "evangelism," for which CGM really stood.

In 1965 McGavran and a few others started a program in World Missions at the evangelically oriented Fuller Theological Seminary in Pasadena, California. By 1971 a member of that faculty, C. Peter Wagner, adapted much of the McGavran program for the American scene to his ministry. This led to the founding of the Institute of American Church Growth and a determination by many evangelicals to focus vigorously on the principles and techniques of CGM to win the world.

Over the years the movement has become a catalyst, a lightning rod for criticism, and a source of renewal and controversy among evangelicals, much of it over its unique use of popular religion.[42] Varying from group to group, and country to country, CGM, however, attracted the attention it did largely for two reasons. The first, in McGavran's words, was that "the congregation formed grows best if it is of one people." That is, there would be Hispanics in their church, Caucasians in theirs, and so on, where the comfortableness factor would make the task of conversion easier.[43] Second, it came to utilize some of the most sophisticated statistical and analytic jargon, concepts, and methodology of the behavioral sciences, often seeing church growth in terms of mathematical ratios, proportions, and related secular wisdom. In sum, it did not energize those wanting the church to expand numerically (its principal criterion of success) by a simple invocation of the power of the Holy Spirit. Rather, it produced seminars, classes, books, workshops, and a host of advocates who used the tools of the social sciences as tools for spreading the kingdom.

At Fuller and at regional conferences, attendees receive training in a wide variety of analytic tools on methodology, statistical analysis, motivation, strategies, user computers, time management tips, and related matters.[44] Aware that such emphasis has created considerable criticism, Wagner and others carefully reply by spelling out their goals. These include (1) "Biblical triumphalism" as opposed to the "theology of the Cross," which has lower expectations than these evangelicals over the possibility of growth in holiness during one's life on this earth; (2) direct help for the poor and oppressed (the movement started among these groups overseas); (3) a variety of ways for achieving ordination of ministers rather than holding to the mainline and some evangelical insistence on considerable academic, formal education; (4) in a related matter, giving the local church "high autonomy"; and (5) maintaining the familiar emphases on small-group Bible study, high-profile preaching, and an openness to Pentecostal leading.[45]

Some critics remain less than impressed, however, finding the widespread use of numerical ratios and behavioral science techniques aimed at one thing, the numerical growth used by Wagner as the bottom-line test for whether a local church is active and healthy.[46] All of this pertains directly to popular religion because the Church Growth Movement itself started to flourish at the same time popular religion began to make its influence known in evangelical circles. Those interpreters favorable to CGM influence pointed out that its power coincided with the forces outlined by Dean Kelley in *Why Conservative Churches Are Growing*. That is, church growth coincided with the triad of forces—doctrine, ethics, discipleship—championed by Kelley.[47] Thus the CGM merely codified and simplified what was underway, making it easier and keeping its priorities on soul winning for those caught up in the evangelical boom. Supporters could ask: What could be wrong with using statistics, ethnically homogeneous churches, and behavioral science techniques if they brought people, otherwise outsiders, inside church walls?

Critics again were less than impressed. To some it smacked too much of adapting secular marketing techniques, utilizing whatever worked rather than remaining faithful to strict biblical admonitions about recruitment. Quentin J. Schultze finds too much salesmanship at work, a use of "a hyperbolic rhetoric of salvation to create awareness" to sell products and services, "what the churches believe the solutions to humankind's problems are. Religious faith becomes one more product to sell as a consumer item."[48]

A California pastor, Wayne Jacobson, found little if any value in touting numerical success as evidence of spiritual growth. He presented several reasons: (1) The original gospel message shied away from "large-scale acclaim." (2) Speaking of CGM and popular religion, Jacobson stated they were "shaping our ministry to shape the masses, thus neglecting the nature of this evil age"; he thereby repudiated what he found to be the clever language, humor, and noncontroversial phrases that popular religion and CGM use as substitutes for the hard truths of the Bible. (3) Jacobson wrote that reaching large numbers often falls short of "successful pastoral ministry"; time for each parishioner is what is most significant. (4) The fruits of fast growth may be immediate but could also be only external, defined by the standards of success in the secular world.[49] In a long, searching critique, Richard John Neuhaus finds in the worship and theology of church growth congregations too much entertainment and thin theology.[50]

## MEGACHURCHES

Yet signs in recent times suggest that at least some of the excesses of the CGM have begun to wane. A major opinion shaper, the journal *Christianity Today*, in a cover article by editor Ken Sidey cited evidence showing that CGM leaders were accepting slow or no growth as not necessarily meaning declining vitality or showing endorsement by some mainline leaders of certain CGM principles. He concluded that someone must be doing something right in the late 1980s and the early 1990s because of the growth of a new phenomenon, the so-called megachurches, those with memberships expanding in the few years since their founding well into the thousands; usually 10,000 members is the criterion to qualify as what participants, leaders, and analysts call megachurches.[51]

Although the megas may turn out to be one more fad, fading as quickly as Fourth of July fireworks, it seems at this juncture that they thrive largely because of their adaptation of many phases of popular religion. For all of their differences in tradition, membership, and local priorities, the megachurches mark the fruition of the evangelical absorption of popular religion. They are for the most part transdenominational, feature high-voltage preaching, make full use of the most sophisticated high technology and mass media, and clearly believe that their own many-faceted programs of ministry reflect the evangelical conviction that religious faith is exhibited in every aspect of life.[52]

In March 1988, the trade journal *Religious Broadcasting* published the chart shown in Table 10.1 as evidence of the trend toward megachurch growth.[53]

Schultze explains the popularity of the megachurches as centering around six ingredients: high-powered celebrity preachers; TV-style worship; reliance on drama, popular music, and secular music instrumentation; an image of "anonymity that mirrors mass society" because some seekers feel uncomfortable in small-group settings; a wide variety of ministries, especially in mass media items; and a willingness to "change rapidly with the shifting whims of the marketplace," quickly dropping or adding programs according to congregational interests.[54]

Douglas Alan Walrath also finds their appeal resting in the wide range of services they provide: day care, counseling, bookstores, indoor recreation facilities, and the comforting impression that those who attend are mingling with like-minded believers rather than having to cope with the outside world. Here all aspects of life seem intertwined in an atmosphere conducive to congenial, relaxed pleasantness.[55] Famous megas besides those just listed include those of W. A. Criswell in Dallas, Bill Hybels in Chicago, and a few dozen more, depending on how one defines "mega" in megachurch.[56]

During the 1980s the superstar celebrity preachers were recognized as Pat Robertson, Jerry Falwell, Jimmy Swaggart, and Jim Bakker. Only Robertson now has a consistent national ministry in place. In their place have emerged the pastors already cited, plus a vast number of leaders who practice evangelical popular religion. With this community many of the best-known preachers lead traveling evangelistic ministries rather than a specific congregation. They find strong support and widespread recognition by conducting a typical evangelistic style of worship, the regional or national rally. These faithfully reflect both the wide diversity and the specific elements of unity within the community.

For example, African-American Pentecostal "Zoe Ministries" holds a month-long prophetic conference during Black History month, concentrating on worship, personal ministry, preaching, and teaching. In Dallas in 1987 under the sponsorship of Robert Tilton Ministries, those in attendance heard R. W. Schambach, Norvel Hayes, Tilton, and others as well as experiencing healing. Oral Roberts University offers a variety of such opportunities, with well-known preachers appearing alongside Roberts himself. Something of an all-star cast appeared in June 1989, with Roberts, Paul Yonggi Cho of Korea, Kenneth Copeland, Marilyn Hickey, Benny Hinn, Morris Cerullo, Larry Lea, Francis MacNutt, Earl Paulk, Vinson Synan, and others.[57]

Through television, print media, and personal appearances other evangelical

**Table 10.1**
**Leading Megachurches**

| TV | Radio | Church | Affiliation | Location | Pastor | 1985 | 1986 | Gain |
|---|---|---|---|---|---|---|---|---|
| * | * | Second Baptist | SBC | Houston | Ed Young | 4,146 | 6,988 | 2,842 |
| * |  | North Phoenix Baptist | SBC | Phoenix | Richard Jackson | 7,000 | 9,000 | 2,000 |
|  |  | Vineyard Christian Fellowship | IND | Anaheim | J. Wimber | 3,100 | 5,100 | 2,000 |
|  |  | Willow Creek Community Church | IND | S. Barrington, Ill. | B. Hybles | 5,000 | 7,000 | 2,000 |
| * | * | Family Worship Center | AG | Baton Rouge, La. | J. Swaggart & J. Rent | 2,675 | 4,328 | 1,707 |
| * |  | Orlando Christian Center | IND | Orlando, Fla. | B. Hinn | 2,800 | 4,500 | 1,700 |
| * | * | Calvary Temple | IND | Ft. Wayne, Ind. | P. Paino | 3,700 | 5,000 | 1,300 |
| * | * | Faith Tabernacle Assembly | AG | Oklahoma City | C. Barker | 1,800 | 3,000 | 1,200 |

Affiliation abbreviations: SBC, Southern Baptist Convention; IND, Independent; AG, Assemblies of God.

preachers bring popular religion to all parts of the country in a variety of formats. Well known is Jack Hayford, senior pastor of Church on the Way, Van Nuys, California. So also in Atlanta is Bishop Earl Paulk, with a flourishing ministry at Chapel Hill Harvester Church. Hickey broke new ground by creating near her church in Denver a Christian shopping mall. Well known to their followers are the ministries of W. V. Grant, Robert Tilton, Larry Lea, and Morris Cerullo.[58]

Controversy abounds among some of these and their close followers. Others, especially television viewers, see them more as saying the same thing in different forms, with different personal styles.[59] Two parts of the general Full Gospel movement have recently brought out their own study Bibles; Jack Hayford edited the *Full Life Study Bible*, and Kenneth Hagin edited *The Word*, being advertised as "The 1st [*sic*] Charismatic Bible."[60] The deep theological differences among the contributors shows through in a comparison reading of these Bibles.

Beneath all the publicity and emphasis on mass evangelism, of course, rests the small, local, independent evangelical congregation sometimes loosely affiliated with other like-minded bodies. Often of the storefront variety, these appear or fade too fast for the historian to make note of their contribution.

In sum, popular religion serves as at least one major portion of the concrete forces that hold together today's evangelical movement, as demonstrated by its continuing usage by those mentioned in this chapter. That it has such diversity is testimony to the diversity of human nature and to the idea suggested earlier that one reason evangelicalism holds together is that each of its voices claims to have part of the total truth of religious faith as indigenous to its full, true character. Thus a hundred, even a thousand roses can flourish in this garden, because it continues to champion diversity while also attempting to hold to that which is good, true, beautiful, honest, of good report.

## NOTES

1. This is particularly a response to the conclusions of Donald A. Dayton, who states that the term "evangelicalism" no longer has any viable meaning; "Some Doubts about the Usefulness of the Category 'Evangelical,'" in Donald A. Dayton and Robert K. Johnston, eds., *The Variety of American Evangelicalism* (Knoxville: University of Tennessee Press, 1991), pp. 245–51.

2. John Weborg, "Pietism: Theology in Service of Living toward God," in Dayton and Johnston, ibid., p. 175.

3. Randy L. Frame, "They'd Rather Fight Than Switch," *Christianity Today*, March 5, 1990, pp. 25–28.

4. Drawn from the regular columns for Religious News Service by Randall Balmer,

this one is entitled "Church Membership Data: Meaning May Lie in Baptism," *National Christian Reporter*, November 25, 1991, p. 1; see also Paul B. Tinlin and Edith L. Blumhofer, "Decade of Decline or Harvest?" *Christian Century*, July 10–17, 1991, pp. 684–87.

5. William Martin, *A Prophet with Honor: The Billy Graham Story* (New York: William Morrow and Company, 1991), pp. 559–73; *The Star*, February 5, 1991, p. 1.

6. Martin E. Marty, "Reflections on Graham by a Former Grump," *Christianity Today*, November 18, 1988, p. 25.

7. Ibid., p. 25; news story, *Christianity Today*, October 28, 1991, pp. 32–35.

8. Interview by the editors of *Christianity Today* with Graham, "Candid Conversation with the Evangelist," July 17, 1981, pp. 18–19; David Brying, "Keeper of the Faith," *Minneapolis Star Tribune*, September 15, 1991, pp. 19A, 26A.

9. Randall Balmer, *Mine Eyes Have Seen the Glory: A Journey into the Evangelical Subculture in America* (New York: Oxford University Press, 1991), pp. 227–35; George M. Marsden, *Religion and American Culture* (New York: Harcourt, Brace, Jovanovich, 1990), pp. 257–62; Chuck Smith, Jr., "Where Are They Taking Us?" *Christian Life*, January 1986, pp. 16–32; editorial, Steven Strang, "Building Bridges," *Charisma and Christian Life*, June 1991, p. 8; see the exhaustive listing, with addresses, of some 400 various Pentecostal bodies in America in J. Gordon Melton, ed., *The Encyclopedia of American Religions* (Detroit: Gale, 1989), pp. 351–420.

10. Randall Balmer, regular column for Religious News Service, in *National Christian Reporter*, July 5, 1991, p. 4; David Edwin Harrell, Jr., "Foreword," in Harold B. Smith, ed., *Pentecostals from the Inside Out* (Wheaton, Ill.: Victor Books, 1990), pp. 10–11.

11. See the several entries in Stanley M. Burgess and Gary B. McGee, *Dictionary of Pentecostal and Charismatic Movements* (Grand Rapids, Mich.: Zondervan, 1988) such as "Catholic Charismatic Renewal," pp. 110–26; "Charismatic Movement," pp. 130–60; "Church Growth," pp. 180–95; "Church, Theology of," pp. 211–18; "Classical Pentecostalism," pp. 219–22; "Discernment of Spirits," pp. 244–46; "Exorcism," pp. 290–94.

12. Many sources are available here, the latest being Burgess and McGee, *Dictionary*, passim; Charles Edwin Jones, *A Guide to the Study of the Pentecostal Movement*, 2 vols. (Atlanta: American Theological Society, Scarecrow Press, 1983); Norris A. Magnuson and William G. Travis, eds., *American Evangelicalism: An Annotated Bibliography* (West Cornwall, Conn.: Locust Hill Press, 1990), pp. 359–401.

13. Edith L. Blumhofer, *The Assemblies of God*, vol. 2 (Springfield, Mo.: Gospel Publishing House, 1989); Margaret M. Poloma, *The Assemblies of God at the Crossroads: Charisma and Institutional Dilemmas* (Knoxville: University of Tennessee Press, 1989); David Edwin Harrell, Jr., *Oral Roberts: An American Life* (Bloomington: Indiana University Press, 1985); see also Steven A. Gutzamacher et al., "Psychological Characteristics of Pentecostalists: A Literature Review and Psychodynamic Synthesis," *Journal of Psychology and Theology*, 16, 3 (1988): 234–45; J. W. Sheppard, "Sociology of Pentecostalism," in Burgess and McGee, *Dictionary*, pp. 794–99.

14. Elaine J. Lawless, *God's Peculiar People: Women's Voices and Folk Tradition in the Pentecostal Church* (Lexington: University of Kentucky Press, 1988); Lawless, *Handmaidens of the Lord: Pentecostal Women Preachers and Traditional Religion* (Philadelphia: University of Pennsylvania Press, 1988); see also the discussion by L. Grant McClun, "New Cultures, New Challenges, New Church," in Smith, *Pentecostals*, pp. 105–9; Russel Spittler, "Maintaining Distinctives: The Future of Pentecostalism," in Smith, *Pentecostals*, pp. 121–34.

15. Wilson, as defined in "The Sociology of Religion," in Charles H. Lippy and Peter W. Williams, eds., *Encyclopedia of the American Religious Experience*, vol. 1 (New York: Scribners, 1988), p. 27.

16. Mary Jo Neitz, *Charisma and Community: A Study of Religious Communities within the Charismatic Renewal* (New Brunswick, N.J.: Transaction Books, 1987), pp. 232–38; A. A. Lovekin, "Charismatic Experience," in Rodney Hunter, ed., *Dictionary of Pastoral Care and Counseling* (Nashville, Tenn.: Abingdon, 1991), pp. 139–41.

17. J. R. Zeigler, "Full Gospel Business Men's Fellowship," in Burgess and McGee, *Dictionary*, pp. 321–33; J. R. Zeigler, "Shakarian, Demos," ibid., pp. 781–82; Donald W. Dayton, "Pentecostal/Charismatic Renewal and Social Change," *Transformation*, 5, 4 (1988): 11.

18. News story, *Charisma and Christian Life*, October 1988, p. 30.

19. Margaret Poloma, "Pentecostals and Politics in North and Central America," in Jeffrey K. Hadden and Anson Shupe, eds., *Prophetic Religions and Politics: Religion and the Political Order* (New York: Paragon House, 1986), p. 330.

20. Michael Harper, *As at the Beginning: The Pentecostal Revival* (New York: Hadden and Stoughton, 1985); Erling Jorstad, *Bold in the Spirit: Lutheran Charismatic Renewal in America* (Minneapolis: Augsburg, 1974).

21. Harrell, *Roberts*, pp. 287–311.

22. A series of articles in a theme issue, "How Evangelical Is the Catholic Church?" *Christian Herald*, December 1985, pp. 48–53.

23. News story, *Los Angeles Times*, March 3, 1990, p. F15; news story, *New York Times*, October 14, 1991, p. A3; Samuel Solivan, "Storefront Churches' Roles among Hispanics," *USA Today*, March 1992, pp. 92–93.

24. Paul Thigpen, "The New Black Charismatics," *Charisma and Christian Life*, November 1990, pp. 58–67.

25. Jim Anderson, "Pressing On," *Lutheran Renewal Outreach*, 6, 3 (July 1988): 1–2; news story, *Religion Watch*, September 1988, p. 1; news story, *Christian Century*, December 7, 1988, p. 1117.

26. Cecil David Bradford, *New Pentecostalism: A Sociological Account* (Lanham, Md.: University Press of America, 1979); P. D. Hocken, "Charismatic Movement," in Burgess and McGee, *Dictionary*, pp. 136–40.

27. Hocken, "Movement," pp. 145–56; Hocken, *One Lord, One Spirit, One Body* (Gaithersburg, Md.: The Word among Us Press, 1987), passim.

28. Howard Earl, "The Charismatic Book Boom," *Charisma*, September 1985, pp. 72–80; Nick Cavnor, "Charismatic Books: Who's Buying What?" *Christian Retailing*, April 15, 1988, pp. 14–15; Jess Moody, "A Baptist Pastor Looks at the Charismatics," *Christian Retailing*, April 15, 1988, pp. 18–19.

29. See the materials of the Protestant Reformed Church, 6511 South Park Avenue, South Holland, IL 60473.

30. J. I. Packer, "Piety on Fire," *Christianity Today*, May 12, 1989, p. 20.

31. Ibid.; Spittler, "Maintaining Distinctives," in Smith, *Pentecostals*, pp. 124–25.

32. Smith, "Where Are They Taking Us?" pp. 26–29.

33. C. Peter Wagner, "Third Wave," in Burgess and McGee, *Dictionary*, pp. 843–44; see also the somewhat satiric, somewhat serious study made by Tom Raabe, *The Ultimate Church* (Grand Rapids, Mich.: Zondervan, 1991).

34. Vinson Synan, "Prophecy in the Pentecostal and Charismatic Movements," *Faith and Renewal*, July/August 1991, pp. 11–12; Raabe, *Ultimate Church*, p. 60.

35. Wagner, "Third Wave," p. 844; David B. Barrett, "The Twentieth Century Pentecostal/Charismatic Renewal in the Holy Spirit with Its Goal of World Evangelizing," *International Bulletin of Missionary Research*, July 11, 1991, pp. 119–29; Raabe, *Ultimate Church*, pp. 47–61.

36. News story, *Los Angeles Times*, February 17, 1990, p. I6; see the forum of evangelical

ministers, "The Power and the Presence," *Leadership*, Fall 1991, pp. 14–23; Jeff Dun, compiler, "Miracles: Six Amazing Testimonies," *Charisma and Christian Life*, November 1991, pp. 32–49; Colin Brown, "Should We Expect Miracles Today?" in David Neff, ed., *Tough Questions Christians Ask* (Wheaton, Ill.: Victor Books, 1989), pp. 61–75.

37. Harrell, *Roberts*, pp. 485–95.

38. See E. E. Thornton and H. N. Maloney, "Faith Healing," in Hunter, *Pastoral Care*, pp. 401–5; R. F. Martin, "Healing, Gift of," in Burgess and McGee, *Dictionary*, p. 350; P. G. Chappell, "Healing Movements," in Hunter, *Pastoral Care*, p. 384; Margaret Shuster, *Power, Pathology, Paradox: The Dynamics of Evil and Good* (Grand Rapids, Mich.: Zondervan, 1988); column, "Spring Religious," story on Benny Hinn, *Christianity Today*, October 28, 1991, pp. 44–45.

39. D. R. McConnell, *A Different Gospel: A Historical and Biblical Analysis of the Modern Faith Movement* (Peabody, Mass.: Hendrickson Press, 1988); Kenneth Hagin has some one hundred books in print; news analysis column, "Faith Healing: Moving toward the Mainstream," *Christianity Today*, July 10, 1987, pp. 50–51.

40. Nancy Tatom Ammerman, *Baptist Battles: Social Change and Religious Conflict in the Southern Baptist Convention* (New Brunswick, N.J.: Rutgers University Press, 1990); Joe E. Barnhart, *The Southern Baptist Holy War* (Austin: Texas Monthly Press, 1986); Bill Leonard, *God's Last and Only Hope: The Fragmentation of the Southern Baptist Convention* (Grand Rapids, Mich.: Eerdmans, 1990); see the many references to the current and possibly future developments in this denomination in Harold Bloom, *The American Religion: The Emergence of the Post-Christian Nation* (New York: Simon and Schuster, 1992).

41. See the two works cited in note 13, above, ch. 10, by Edith L. Blumhofer and by Margaret Poloma; see also Paul B. Tinian and Edith L. Blumhofer, "Decade of Decline," *Christian Century*, July 10–17, 1991, pp. 684–87; Austin Mills, *Setting the Captives Free: Victims of the Church Tell Their Stories* (Buffalo, N.Y.: Prometheus, 1990).

42. See the bibliography of the writings of McGavran and Wagner in Robin Dale Perrin, "Signs and Wonders: The Growth of the Vineyard Christian Fellowship," Ph.D. dissertation, Washington State University, University Microfilm Services, Order No. 9007804, pp. 232–40; see P. G. Chappell, "Healing," in Walter A. Elwell, ed., *Evangelical Dictionary of Theology* (Grand Rapids, Mich.: Baker Book House, 1984), pp. 497–98; Alan Schreck, "Church Growth Movement," in Daniel G. Reid et al., eds., *Dictionary of Christianity in America* (Downers Grove, Ill.: InterVarsity, 1990), p. 271.

43. Chappell, "Healing," pp. 497–98; Raabe, *Ultimate Church*, pp. 68, 113, 131.

44. Schreck, "Church Growth," p. 271; an excellent full-length study is the D.Min. dissertation by Thomas S. Rainer, "An Assessment of C. Peter Wagner's Contributions to the Theology of Church Growth," Southern Baptist Theological Seminary, University Microfilm Services, Order No. 8901500 (1988).

45. This summary is by Wagner in Burgess and McGee, *Dictionary*, pp. 193–94.

46. Rainer, "Wagner's Contributions," pp. 146, 185; James D. Berkeley, "Church Growth Comes of Age," *Leadership*, Fall 1991, pp. 108–15; Kent R. Hunter, "Measuring Integrity: The Body of Christ with a Backbone," in C. Peter Wagner, ed., *Church Growth: The State of the Art* (Wheaton, Ill.: Tyndale House, 1986), pp. 96–98.

47. C. Peter Wagner, "Aiming at Church Growth in the 80s," *Christianity Today*, November 21, 1980, pp. 141–45.

48. Quentin J. Schultze, *Televangelism and American Culture* (Grand Rapids, Mich.: Baker Book House, 1991), pp. 161–62.

49. Wayne Jacobson, "The Numbers Game: A Threat to Churches Large and Small," *Leadership*, Winter 1983, pp. 49–51.

50. Richard John Neuhaus, "The Lutheran Difference," *Lutheran Forum*, Reformation Issue, 1990, pp. 18–24.

51. Ken Sidey, "Church Growth Fine Tunes Its Formulas," *Christianity Today*, June 24, 1991, pp. 44–49; Kenneth Woodward, "A Time to Seek," *Newsweek*, December 17, 1990, pp. 52–53; see the several issues of the journal *Church Growth Today*, Megachurch Research Press, 1202 E. Austin, Bolivar, MO 65613 for up-to-the-minute data on megachurches.

52. See the Barna Research Group Report, *Successful Churches: What They Have* (Glendale, Calif.: Barna Research, 1990); George Barna, *How to Find Your Church* (Glendale, Calif.: Barna Research, 1989).

53. News story, *Religious Broadcasting*, March 1988, p. 22.

54. Schultze, *Televangelism*, pp. 220–21.

55. Douglas Alan Walrath, *Frameworks: Patterns of Living and Believing Today* (New York: Pilgrim Press, 1987), pp. 10–20; see also E. S. Caldwell, "Trend toward Megachurches," *Charisma*, August 1985, pp. 31–36; he has additional statistical tables.

56. Lyle Schaller, "Megachurch!" *Christianity Today*, March 5, 1990, pp. 20–23; he also has a table of memberships; see also Deidre Sullivan, "Targeting American Souls," *American Demographics*, October 1991, pp. 42–47; futurist projections are well summarized in Barna Research Group, *America 2000: What the Trends Mean for Christianity* (Glendale, Calif.: Barna Research, 1989), and Russell Chandler, *Racing Toward 2001: The Forces Shaping America's Religious Future* (Grand Rapids, Mich.: Zondervan, 1992).

57. Ad, *Charisma and Christian Life*, November 1991, n.p.

58. See, for example, the news story in *Charisma and Christian Life*, July 1988, p. 26.

59. Schultze, *Televangelism*, pp. 220–21.

60. Jack Hayford, *Full Life Study Bible* (Grand Rapids, Mich.: Zondervan, 1991); Kenneth Hagin, *The Word* (Tulsa, Okla.: Harrison House, 1992).

# Appendix: Membership, National Association of Evangelicals, January 1991

The year indicates when the body joined the association.

Advent Christian General Conference (1986)
Assemblies of God (1943)
Baptist General Conference (1966)
Brethren Church, The (Ashland, Ohio) (1968)
Brethren in Christ Church (1949)
Christian & Missionary Alliance (1966)
Christian Catholic Church (Evangelical Protestant) (1975)
Christian Church of North America (1953)
Christian Reformed Church in North America (1943–1951; 1988)
Christian Union (1954)
Churches of Christ in Christian Union (1945)
Church of God (Cleveland, Tennessee) (1944)
Church of God of the Mountain Assembly, Inc. (1981)
Church of the Nazarene, The (1984)
Church of the United Brethren in Christ (1953)
Congregational Holiness Church (1990)
Conservative Baptist Association (1990)
Conservative Congregational Christian Conference (1951)
Elim Fellowship (1947)

Evangelical Christian Church (1988)

Evangelical Church of North America (1969)

Evangelical Congregational Church (1962)

Evangelical Free Church of America (1942)

Evangelical Friends International of North America (1944)

Evangelical Mennonite Church (1944)

Evangelical Methodist Church (1952)

Evangelical Missionary Fellowship (1982)

Evangelical Presbyterian Church (1982)

Fellowship of Evangelical Bible Churches (1948)

Fire Baptized Holiness Church of God of the Americas (1978)

Free Methodist Church of North America (1944)

General Association of General Baptists (1988)

International Church of the Foursquare Gospel (1952)

International Pentecostal Church of Christ (1946)

International Pentecostal Holiness Church (1943)

Mennonite Brethren Churches, USA (1946)

Midwest Congregational Christian Fellowship (1964)

Missionary Church, Inc. (1944)

Oklahoma State Association of Free Will Baptists (1973)

Open Bible Standard Churches (1943)

Pentecostal Church of God (1954)

Pentecostal Free Will Baptist Church, Inc. (1988)

Presbyterian Church in America (1986)

Primitive Methodist Church, USA (1946)

Reformed Church in America, Classis Cascades (1986)

Reformed Church in America, Particular Synod of Mid-America (1989)

Reformed Episcopal Church (1990)

Reformed Presbyterian Church of North America (1949)

Salvation Army, The (1990)

Wesleyan Church, The (1948)

World Confessional Lutheran Association (1984)

Some 120 state and local associations, 125 schools, 100 organizations, and large numbers of individuals hold membership (National Association of Evangelicals pamphlet, 1991).

# Selected Bibliography

## REFERENCE WORKS

Among the many excellent sources, two annotated guides stand out especially, that of Blumhofer and Carpenter and that of Magnuson and Travis. These are the starting points to the entire literature.

Barnouw, Eric, ed. *International Encyclopedia of Communications*. 4 vols. New York: Oxford University Press, 1989.

Benner, David G., ed. *Baker Encyclopedia of Psychology*. Grand Rapids, Mich.: Baker Book House, 1985.

Blumhofer, Edith L., and Joel A. Carpenter, eds. *Twentieth-Century Evangelicalism: A Guide to the Sources*. New York: Garland, 1990.

Burgess, Stanley M., and Gary B. McGee, eds. *Dictionary of Pentecostal and Charismatic Movements*. Grand Rapids, Mich.: Zondervan, 1988.

Chase, Elise, comp. *Healing Faith: An Annotated Bibliography of Christian Self-Help Books*. Westport, Conn.: Greenwood Press, 1985.

Eliade, Mircea, ed. *The Encyclopedia of Religion*. 16 vols. New York: Macmillan, 1987.

Gilbert, Dennis A., ed. *Compendium of American Public Opinion*. New York: Facts on File, 1988.

Hill, Samuel S., ed. *Encyclopedia of Religion in the South*. Macon, Ga.: Mercer University Press, 1984.

Hunter, Rodney J., ed. *Dictionary of Pastoral Care and Counseling*. Nashville, Tenn.: Abingdon Press, 1990.

Jacquet, Constant H., and Sarah Jones, eds. *Yearbook of American and Canadian Churches*. Nashville, Tenn.: Abingdon Press, annual.

Lippy, Charles H., ed. *Religious Periodicals of the United States: Academic and Scholarly Journals*. Westport, Conn.: Greenwood Press, 1986.

———. *Twentieth-Century Shapers of American Popular Religion*. Westport, Conn.: Greenwood Press, 1989.

Lippy, Charles H., and Peter W. Williams, eds. *Encyclopedia of the American Religious Experience: Studies of Traditions and Movements.* 3 vols. New York: Scribners, 1988.

Magnuson, Norris A., and William G. Travis, eds. *American Evangelicalism: An Annotated Bibliography.* West Cornwall, Conn.: Locust Hill Press, 1990.

Melton, J. Gordon, ed. *A Bibliographical Guide to the Founders and Leaders of Religious Bodies, Churches, and Spiritual Groups in North America.* Detroit: Gale Research, 1991.

——. *The Encyclopedia of American Religion.* 3d ed. Detroit: Gale Research, 1989.

Proctor, William, ed. *The Born Again Christian Catalog: A Complete Sourcebook for Evangelicals.* Old Tappan, N.J.: Revell, 1979.

Reid, Daniel, ed. *Dictionary of Christianity in America.* Downers Grove, Ill.: InterVarsity, 1990.

Soukup, Paul A. *Communication and Theology: Introduction and Review of the Literature.* London: World Association for Christian Communication, 1983.

Wilson, Charles Reagan, and William Ferris, eds. *Encyclopedia of Southern Culture.* Chapel Hill: University of North Carolina Press, 1989.

## NEWSPAPERS

*National and International Religion Report*, Roanoke, Virginia.
*National Christian Reporter*, Dallas, Texas.
*Religion Watch*, North Bellmore, New York.

## SCHOLARLY JOURNALS

*American Quarterly*
*International Bulletin for Missionary Research*
*Journal for the Scientific Study of Religion*
*Journal of American Culture*
*Journal of Christianity and Psychology*
*Journal of Popular Culture*
*Journal of the American Academy of Religion*
*Religion and American Culture*
*Religious Research Review*
*Religious Studies Review*
*S/A. Sociological Analysis*

## GENERAL JOURNALS

*CCM* (Contemporary Christian Music)
*Charisma and Christian Life* (separate publications before Fall 1987)
*Christian Century*
*Christianity Today*
*Cornerstone*
*The Door* (formerly *The Wittenburg Door*)
*Eternity* (ceased publication in 1988)

*Fundamentalist Journal* (ceased publication in 1989)
*Leadership*
*Moody Monthly*
*The Other Side*
*The Reformed Journal*
*Sojourners*
*Today's Christian Woman*
*Virtue*

## SECONDARY WORKS

Ableman, Robert, and Stewart M. Hoover, eds. *Religious Television: Controversies and Conclusions.* Norwood, N.J.: Ablex, 1990.

Ammerman, Nancy Tatom. *Bible Believers: Fundamentalists in the Modern World.* New Brunswick, N.J.: Rutgers University Press, 1987.

Antoun, Richard T., and Mary Elaine Hegland, eds. *Religious Resurgence: Contemporary Cases in Islam, Christianity, and Judaism.* Syracuse, N.Y.: Syracuse University Press, 1987.

Balmer, Randall. *Mine Eyes Have Seen the Glory: A Journey into the Evangelical Subculture in America.* New York: Oxford University Press, 1989.

Barna, George. *What Americans Believe.* Ventura, Calif.: Regal, 1991.

Beckford, James, ed. *New Religious Movements and Rapid Social Change.* Beverly Hills: Sage, 1986.

Blackwell, Lois S. *The Wings of the Dove: The Story of Gospel Music in America.* Norfolk, Va.: Dunning, 1978.

Bradbury, M. L., and James Gilbert, eds. *Transforming Faith: The Sacred and Secular in Modern American History.* Westport, Conn.: Greenwood Press, 1989.

Bruce, Steve. *A House Divided: Protestantism, Schism, and Secularization.* New York: Routledge, 1990.

———. *Pray TV: Televangelism in America.* New York: Routledge, 1990.

Burkett, Larry. *Business by the Book: The Complete Guide of Religious Principles for Business Men and Women.* Nashville, Tenn.: Thomas Nelson, 1990.

Capps, Walter H. *The New Religious Right: Piety, Patriotism, and Politics.* Columbia: University of South Carolina Press, 1990.

Chalfant, Paul H. *Religion in Contemporary Society.* 2d ed. Sherman Oaks, Calif.: Alfred Publishers, 1987.

Cohen, Norman J., ed. *The Fundamentalist Phenomenon: A View from Within: A Response from Without.* Grand Rapids, Mich.: Eerdmans, 1990.

Collier, James Lincoln. *The Rise of Selfishness in America.* New York: Oxford University Press, 1991.

Collins, Gary. *Calm Down.* Chappaqua, N.Y.: Christian Herald, 1981.

Dayton, Donald W., and Robert K. Johnston, eds. *The Variety of American Evangelicalism.* Knoxville: University of Tennessee Press, 1991.

Dudley, Carl. *Where Have All Our People Gone? New Choices for Old Churches.* New York: Pilgrim Press, 1979.

Duke, Judith S. *Religious Publishing and Communications.* White Plains, N.Y.: Knowledge Industry Publications, 1981.

Fishwick, Marshall W., and Ray B. Browne, eds. *The God Pumpers: Religion in the Electronic Age.* Bowling Green, Ohio: Popular Press, 1987.

Flake, Carol. *Redemptorama: Culture, Politics, and the New Evangelicalism.* Garden City, N.Y.: Doubleday, 1984.

Frankl, Razelle. *Televangelism: The Marketing of Popular Religion.* Carbondale: Southern Illinois University Press, 1987.

Gaebelein, Frank E. *The Christian, the Arts, and Truth: Regaining the Vision of Greatness.* Portland, Ore.: Multnomah, 1985.

Gallup, George, Jr., and Jim Castelli. *The People's Religion: American Faith in the 90s.* New York: Macmillan, 1989.

Gay, Craig M. *With Liberty and Justice for Whom? The Recent Evangelical Debate over Capitalism.* Grand Rapids, Mich.: Eerdmans, 1991.

Goethels, Gregory T. *The Electronic Golden Calf: Images, Religion, and the Making of Meaning.* Cambridge, Mass.: Cowley, 1990.

Greeley, Andrew M. *God in Popular Culture.* Chicago: Thomas More, 1988.

————. *Religious Change in America.* Cambridge: Harvard University Press, 1989.

Gunn, Giles, ed. *The Bible and American Arts and Letters.* Philadelphia: Fortress, 1983.

Hadden, Jeffrey K., and Charles F. Longino. *Gideon's Gang: A Case Study of the Church in Action.* Philadelphia: Fortress, 1974.

Harrell, David Edwin, Jr. *All Things Are Possible: The Healing and Charismatic Revivals in Modern America.* Bloomington: Indiana University Press, 1975.

————. *Oral Roberts: An American Life.* Bloomington: Indiana University Press, 1985.

————. *Varieties of Southern Evangelicalism.* Macon, Ga.: Mercer University Press, 1981.

Hatch, Nathan O. *The Democratization of American Christianity.* New Haven: Yale University Press, 1989.

Hoge, Dean R., and David A. Roozen, eds. *Understanding Church Growth and Decline, 1950–1979.* New York: Pilgrim Press, 1979.

Hoover, Stewart M. *Mass Media Religion: The Sources of the Electronic Church.* Newbury Park, Calif.: Sage, 1988.

Horsefield, Peter G. *Religious Television: The American Experience.* New York: Longman, 1984.

Horton, Michael Scott. *Made in America: The Shaping of Modern American Evangelicalism.* Grand Rapids, Mich.: Baker Book House, 1991.

Hunter, James Davison. *American Evangelicalism: Conservative Religion and the Quandary of Modernity.* New Brunswick, N.J.: Rutgers University Press, 1983.

————. *Culture Wars: The Struggle to Define America.* New York: Basic Books, 1991.

————. *Evangelicalism: The Coming Generation.* Chicago: University of Chicago Press, 1987.

Hustad, Don. *Jubilate! Church Music in the Evangelical Tradition.* Carol Stream, Ill.: Hope Publishing, 1981.

Jasper, Tony. *Jesus and the Christian in a Pop Culture.* London: Robert Royce, 1984.

Jones, Stanton L., ed. *Psychology and the Christian Faith.* Grand Rapids, Mich.: Baker Book House, 1982.

Kelley, Dean M. *Why Conservative Churches Are Growing.* Rev. ed. New York: Harper and Row, 1977.

Kubey, Robert, and Mihaly Csikszentmihalyi, eds. *Television and the Quality of Life: How Viewing Shapes Everyday Experience.* Hillsdale, N.J.: Lawrence Erlbaum, 1990.

Lawhead, Steven. *Turn Back the Night.* Westchester, Ill.: Crossway Books, 1985.

Lawless, Elaine J. *God's Peculiar People: Women's Voices and Folk Tradition in a Pentecostal Church.* Lexington: University of Kentucky Press, 1988.

Levitan, Sar A., ed. *What's Happening to the American Family? Tensions, Hopes, Realities.* Rev. ed. Baltimore: Johns Hopkins University Press, 1988.

Lipsitz, George. *Time Passages: Collective Memory and American Popular Culture*. Minneapolis: University of Minnesota Press, 1989.

McConnell, D. R. *A Different Gospel: A Historical and Biblical Analysis of the Modern Faith Movement*. Peabody, Mass.: Hendrickson Publishers, 1988.

McGavran, Donald A. *Understanding Church Growth*. Grand Rapids, Mich.: Eerdmans, 1980.

McGuire, Meredith B. *Ritual Healing in Suburban America*. New Brunswick, N.J.: Rutgers University Press, 1988.

Marsden, George M. *Understanding Fundamentalism and Evangelicalism*. Grand Rapids, Mich.: Eerdmans, 1991.

Martin, William. *A Prophet with Honor: The Billy Graham Story*. New York: William Morrow, 1991.

Miles, Austin. *Setting the Captives Free: Victims of the Church Tell Their Stories*. Buffalo, N.Y.: Prometheus Books, 1990.

Miller, J. Keith. *Sin: Overcoming the Ultimate Deadly Addiction*. San Francisco: Harper and Row, 1987 (later retitled *Hope in the Fast Lane*).

Myers, David G., and Malcolm A. Jeeves, eds. *Psychology through the Eyes of Faith*. San Francisco: Harper and Row, 1987.

Nash, Ronald H. *Evangelicals in America: Who They Are, What They Believe*. Nashville, Tenn.: Abingdon, 1987.

Nelson, John Wiley. *Your God Is Alive and Well and Appearing in Popular Culture*. Philadelphia: Westminster, 1976.

Neuhaus, Richard John, ed. *The Bible, Politics, and Democracy*. Grand Rapids, Mich.: Eerdmans, 1987.

Numbers, Ronald L., and Darrell W. Amundsen, eds. *Caring and Curing: Health and Medicine in the Western Religious Traditions*. New York: Macmillan, 1987.

Parsons, Paul F. *Inside America's Christian Schools*. Macon, Ga.: Mercer University Press, 1988.

Passantino, Robert, and Gretchen Passantino. *Witch Hunt*. Nashville, Tenn.: Thomas Nelson, 1990.

Patterson, James, and Peter Kim. *The Day America Told the Truth: What People Really Believe about Everything That Really Matters*. Englewood Cliffs, N.J.: Prentice-Hall, 1991.

Phy, Allene Stuart, ed. *The Bible and Popular Culture in America*. Philadelphia: Fortress, 1985.

Poloma, Margaret. *The Assemblies of God at the Crossroads*. Knoxville: University of Tennessee Press, 1989.

———. *The Charismatic Movement: Is There a New Pentecost?* Boston: Twayne Publishers, 1982.

Postman, Neil. *Amusing Ourselves to Death*. New York: Viking Penguin Books, 1985.

———. *The Disappearance of Childhood*. New York: Delacorte Press, 1982.

Provenzo, Eugene F., Jr. *Religious Fundamentalism and American Education: The Battle for the Public Schools*. Albany: State University of New York Press, 1990.

Quebedeaux, Richard. *By What Authority: The Rise of Personality Cults in American Christianity*. San Francisco: Harper and Row, 1982.

Raabe, Tom. *The Ultimate Church: An Irreverent Look at Church Growth, Megachurches, and Ecclesiastical "Show-Biz."* Grand Rapids, Mich.: Zondervan, 1991.

Reisser, Paul C. et al. *The Holistic Healers: A Christian Perspective on New-Age Health Care*. Downers Grove, Ill.: InterVarsity, 1983.

Roof, Wade Clark, and William McKinney. *American Mainline Religion: Its Changing Shape and Future*. New Brunswick, N.J.: Rutgers University Press, 1987.

Ruegsegger, Ronald W., ed. *Reflections on Francis Schaeffer*. Grand Rapids, Mich.: Zondervan, 1986.

Ryken, Leland, ed. *Work and Leisure in Christian Perspective*. Portland, Ore.: Multnomah, 1987.

————. *The Christian Imagination: Essays on Literature and the Arts*. Grand Rapids, Mich.: Baker Book House, 1981.

Scherer, Ross P. *American Denominational Organization: A Sociological View*. Pasadena, Calif.: William Carey Library, 1980.

Schultze, Quentin J. *Televangelism and American Culture: The Business of Popular Religion*. Grand Rapids, Mich.: Baker Book House, 1991.

————, ed. *American Evangelicals and the Mass Media: Perspectives on the Relationships between American Evangelicals and the Mass Media*. Grand Rapids, Mich.: Zondervan, 1990.

Schultze, Quentin J. et al., eds. *Dancing in the Dark: Youth, Popular Culture, and the Electronic Media*. Grand Rapids, Mich.: Eerdmans, 1991.

Seary, Davin. *Stairway to Heaven: The Spiritual Roots of Rock and Roll: From the King and Little Richard to Prince and Amy Grant*. New York: Ballantine/Epiphany, 1986.

Shelley, Bruce. *The Gospel and the American Dream*. Portland, Ore.: Multnomah, 1989.

Shepard, Charles E. *Forgiven: The Rise and Fall of Jim Bakker and the PTL Ministry*. New York: Atlantic Monthly Press, 1989.

Sims, Patsy. *Can Somebody Shout Amen! Inside the Tents and Tabernacles of American Revivalists*. New York: St. Martin's, 1988.

Smith, Harold B., ed. *Pentecostals from the Inside Out*. Wheaton, Ill.: Victor Books, 1990.

Spilka, Bernard. *The Psychology of Religion*. Englewood Cliffs, N.J.: Prentice-Hall, 1985.

Sweet, Leonard I., ed. *The Evangelical Tradition in America*. Macon, Ga.: Mercer University Press, 1984.

Wagner, C. Peter. *Spiritual Power and Church Growth*. Altamonte Springs, Fla.: Strang Communications, 1986.

————. *The Third Wave of the Holy Spirit*. Ann Arbor, Mich.: Servant Books, 1988.

Wagner, C. Peter, and Douglas Pennoyer, eds. *Wrestling with Dark Angels: Toward a Deeper Understanding of the Supernatural Forces in Spiritual Warfare*. Ventura, Calif.: Regal, 1990.

Walrath, Douglas Alan. *Frameworks: Patterns of Living and Believing Today*. New York: Pilgrim Press, 1987.

White, James F. *Protestant Worship: Traditions in Transition*. Louisville: Westminster/John Knox, 1989.

White, Jerry. *The Church and the Parachurch: An Uneasy Alliance*. Portland, Ore.: Multnomah, 1983.

White, John. *When the Spirit Comes with Power: Signs and Wonders Among God's People*. Downers Grove, Ill.: InterVarsity, 1988.

Wilcox, Clyde. *God's Warriors: The Christian Right in Twentieth-Century America*. Baltimore: Johns Hopkins University Press, 1992.

Williams, Don. *Signs, Wonders, and the Kingdom of God: A Biblical Guide for the Reluctant Skeptic*. Ann Arbor, Mich.: Servant Books, 1988.

Williams, Peter W. *Popular Religion in America: Symbolic Change and the Modernization Process in Historical Perspective*. Urbana: University of Illinois Press, Illini Books Edition, 1990.

Wuthnow, Robert. *The Restructuring of American Religion: Society and Faith since World War II*. Princeton: Princeton University Press, 1988.

——. *The Struggle for America's Soul: Evangelicals, Liberals, and Secularism*. Grand Rapids, Mich.: Eerdmans, 1989.

Yancey, Phillip. *I Was Just Wondering*. Grand Rapids, Mich.: Eerdmans, 1989.

——. *Open Windows*. Westchester, Ill.: Crossway Books, 1982.

Zolberg, Vera. *Constructing a Sociology of the Arts*. Cambridge: Cambridge University Press, 1990.

# Index

Wilson, John F., on privatization, 70
Wimber, John, 190
Word, Inc., 118
Work ethic and evangelicalism, 56
World Wide Pictures, 119
Worship, church music, 168–76
Wuthnow, Robert, cited, 7–8

Yancey, Phillip, 55
Young Life, 33, 59
Youth for Christ, 6, 23, 33, 59

Zoe Ministries, 195

## ABOUT THE AUTHOR

ERLING JORSTAD is Professor of History and American Studies at St. Olaf College. Among his many publications are *That New-Time Religion: The Jesus Revival in America* (1973), *Bold in Spirit: Lutheran Charismatic Renewal in America* (1974), *Being Religious in America: The Deepening Crises over Public Faith* (1986), and *Holding Fast/Pressing On: Religion in America in the 1980s* (Greenwood Press, 1990).